THE MASNAVI

RUMI, known in Iran and Central Asia as Mowlana Jalaloddin Balkhi, was born in 1207 in the province of Balkh, now the border region between Afghanistan and Tajikistan. His family emigrated when he was still a child, shortly before Genghis Khan and his Mongol army arrived in Balkh. They settled permanently in Konya, central Anatolia, which was formerly part of the Eastern Roman Empire (Rum). Rumi was probably introduced to Sufism originally through his father, Baha Valad, a popular preacher who also taught Sufi piety to a group of disciples. However, the turning-point in Rumi's life came in 1244, when he met in Konya a mysterious wandering Sufi called Shamsoddin of Tabriz. Shams, as he is most often referred to by Rumi, taught him the profoundest levels of Sufism, transforming him from a pious religious scholar to an ecstatic mystic. Rumi expressed his new vision of reality in volumes of mystical poetry. His enormous collection of lyrical poetry is considered one of the best that has ever been produced, while his poem in rhyming couplets, the *Masnavi*, is so revered as the most consummate expression of Sufi mysticism that it is commonly referred to as 'the Qur'an in Persian'.

When Rumi died, on 17 December 1273, shortly after having completed his work on the *Masnavi*, his passing was deeply mourned by the citizens of Konya, including the Christian and Jewish communities. His disciples formed the Mevlevi Sufi order, which was named after Rumi, whom they referred to as 'Our Lord' (Turkish 'Mevlana', Persian 'Mowlana'). They are better known in Europe and North America as the Whirling Dervishes, because of the distinctive dance that they now perform as one of their central rituals. Rumi's death is commemorated annually in Konya, attracting pilgrims from all corners of the globe and every religion. The popularity of his poetry has risen so much in recent decades that the *Christian Science Monitor* identified Rumi as the most published poet in America in 1997.

JAWID MOJADDEDI, a native of Afghanistan, is currently Associate Professor and Director of Graduate Studies at the Department of Religion, Rutgers University. Dr Mojaddedi's translation *The Masnavi: Book One* (Oxford, 2004) was awarded the Lois Roth Prize by the American Institute of Iranian Studies. His previous books include *Beyond Dogma: Rumi's Teachings on Friendship with God and Early Sufi Theories* (Oxford, 2012) and *The Biographical Tradition in Sufism* (Richmond, 2001).

T0026281

OXFORD WORLD'S CLASSICS

*For over 100 years Oxford World's Classics have brought
readers closer to the world's great literature. Now with over 700
titles—from the 4,000-year-old myths of Mesopotamia to the
twentieth century's greatest novels—the series makes available
lesser-known as well as celebrated writing.*

*The pocket-sized hardbacks of the early years contained
introductions by Virginia Woolf, T. S. Eliot, Graham Greene,
and other literary figures which enriched the experience of reading.
Today the series is recognized for its fine scholarship and
reliability in texts that span world literature, drama and poetry,
religion, philosophy, and politics. Each edition includes perceptive
commentary and essential background information to meet the
changing needs of readers.*

OXFORD WORLD'S CLASSICS

═══

JALAL AL-DIN RUMI

The Masnavi

BOOK THREE

═══

Translated with an Introduction and Notes by
JAWID MOJADDEDI

OXFORD
UNIVERSITY PRESS

OXFORD

UNIVERSITY PRESS

Great Clarendon Street, Oxford OX2 6DP
United Kingdom

Oxford University Press is a department of the University of Oxford.
It furthers the University's objective of excellence in research, scholarship,
and education by publishing worldwide. Oxford is a registered trade mark of
Oxford University Press in the UK and in certain other countries

© Jawid Mojaddedi 2013

The moral rights of the author have been asserted

First published as an Oxford World's Classics paperback 2013

All rights reserved. No part of this publication may be reproduced, stored in
a retrieval system, or transmitted, in any form or by any means, without the
prior permission in writing of Oxford University Press, or as expressly permitted
by law, by licence or under terms agreed with the appropriate reprographics
rights organization. Enquiries concerning reproduction outside the scope of the
above should be sent to the Rights Department, Oxford University Press, at the
address above

You must not circulate this work in any other form
and you must impose this same condition on any acquirer

Published in the United States of America by Oxford University Press
198 Madison Avenue, New York, NY 10016, United States of America

British Library Cataloguing in Publication Data

Data available

Library of Congress Control Number: 2013938935

ISBN 978-0-19-965203-7

Printed in Great Britain by
Clays Ltd, Elcograf S.p.A.

Links to third party websites are provided by Oxford in good faith and
for information only. Oxford disclaims any responsibility for the materials
contained in any third party website referenced in this work.

For Janajan

ACKNOWLEDGEMENTS

I SHOULD like to express my gratitude to my immediate family, my friends, and all the teachers I have studied under. Time spent with Dr Alireza Nurbakhsh and Paul Weber has served as an instructive reminder of the living reality of what Rumi points to in his thirteenth-century poem. Gregory Angus's comments about mystical knowledge at a meeting in Washington DC in 2012 helped shape the introduction to Book Three presented here. Once again, I have been very fortunate to work with an editor as supportive and cooperative as Judith Luna. I am also grateful for the comments and criticisms offered by readers of initial drafts of this translation, especially Dick Davis, and for the encouragement I have received from readers to continue this project. I alone am responsible for any flaws.

CONTENTS

THE MASNAVI

BOOK THREE

x   *Contents*

INTRODUCTION

Book Three of the Masnavi

RUMI'S *Masnavi* is probably the longest mystical poem ever written by a single author from any religious tradition. It consists of about 26,000 verses, divided into six books. The current volume is a translation of the third book of the *Masnavi*, and follows Book One and Book Two, also published in Oxford World's Classics.[1]

Much has been written on Rumi and his *Masnavi*. However, one point which has not been explored extensively is its organizational framework. Would Rumi have had an overall framework in mind when he compiled this long and complex poem? The richness of the *Masnavi* makes it very hard to draw any definitive conclusions. On the one hand, that Rumi divided his poem into six books of roughly equal length, each with its own distinct introduction, may suggest an overall framework of some kind. On the other, Rumi's many digressions, as well as his emphasis on the divine origin of his poetry, can give the impression that he did not feel constrained by any particular framework, or perhaps did not want the reader to be distracted by it from the immediate focus.

A comparison of the first three books of the *Masnavi* reveals first of all that they are very similar in form. The poetry is divided into numerous sections by means of section headings. These headings range from a single word to several lines, which occasionally incorporate an interpretation of the poetry that follows. Each book can also be roughly divided into about a dozen major stories.[2] These major stories differ from the more numerous shorter stories because they are usually made up of many sections, which represent not only the consecutive parts of the narrative, but often also commentaries

---

[1] Rumi, *The Masnavi: Book One*, tr. J. Mojaddedi (Oxford, 2004); *The Masnavi: Book Two*, tr. J. Mojaddedi (Oxford, 2007). Further background on Rumi and his times can be found in the Introductions to these two volumes.

[2] Concerning the importance of the story for performance of the *Masnavi*, see M. Mills, 'Folk Tradition in the *Masnavi* and the *Masnavi* in Folk Tradition', in A. Banani, R. Hovannisian, and G. Sabagh, eds., *Poetry and Mysticism in Islam: The Heritage of Rumi* (Cambridge, 1994), 136–77.

and elaborations (sometimes in the form of further shorter stories), which break up the main narrative.[3] If one were to consider the dozen or so major stories of this kind in each book to be Rumi's main building-blocks, then, by analysing their functions, one may be able to decipher the rationale behind Rumi's division of the poem into books, and the order of the major stories in each one.

While there is substantial overlap between the three books—at times almost identical verses are used—each book can be seen to focus on a specific aspect of Sufism. Like many previous works of the Persian mystical *masnavi* genre, the order of presentation of the major stories of the first book sketches the progress of the mystic on the Sufi path. Book One begins with the well-known 'Song of the Reed' (I, vv. 1–18), which describes the longing of a reed to return to the reed-bed from which it has been cut, and this is usually interpreted by commentators as representing the birth of the human being into this world and his longing to return to his original spiritual nature in God's presence. The final major story in Book One depicts the Prophet Mohammad's disciple Ali as a mystic who has reached the end of the path. He throws away his sword when an enemy soldier, whom he is about to slay, spits in his face (I, vv. 3735–4004). This action is explained as a sign that he has returned to subsistence in God after self-annihilation, since his every action is now determined by God and not by his own will.

Although the content of each book of the *Masnavi* is too rich and diverse to be neatly categorized, one can none the less observe a logic to the selection and order of the major stories. For instance, those of Book One seem to be presented in the order of progression on the Sufi path as far as the climax represented by the aforementioned final story about Ali.

As one might expect of any writing designed to instruct Sufi disciples, Book Two also describes aspects of the Sufi path, especially the struggle against the self. However, this is not its main focus. Instead, the major stories in Book Two are primarily concerned with the challenge of discerning the true nature of people behind appearances, in order to identify with whom one should associate so as to

---

[3] The use of indentation in the Contents pages is a simplified representation of this multilayered structure.

progress on the mystical path. The extensive exordium introduces these specific issues to the reader from the outset (II, vv. 19–41).

The major preoccupation of Book Three is no mystery either, as it is pointed out at the very start of the Prose Introduction with which it begins. Rumi comments: 'Pieces of wisdom are the armies of God by which He strengthens the spirits of seekers, and keeps their knowledge away from the tarnish of ignorance, their justice from the tarnish of tyranny, their generosity from the tarnish of self-display, and their intelligence from the tarnish of stupidity' (p. 3). The subsequent exordium develops this theme with an emphasis on the contrast between nourishment of the body through food and spiritual nourishment received from God. Book Three as a whole presents Rumi's epistemology by classifying different levels of knowledge, from the limited amount possessed by fools who are controlled by their lusts and the rational knowledge of the well-educated to the all-consuming mystical knowledge of the Sufi adept, or 'Friend of God' (*wali*). Moreover, consistent with his description here of knowledge as a source of strength for one's inner being, in Book Three Rumi frequently presents his teachings in the form of stories that involve food.

The first major stories highlight the limitations of rational knowledge which sees things only at immediate face value. For instance, hungry travellers ignore sage advice against satisfying their hunger by eating a baby elephant and then pay with their lives (III, vv. 69–171), while a townsman is disappointed when a bumpkin whom he has treated well fails to reciprocate or even acknowledge him after having invited him to his village with generous promises (III, vv. 236–720). With a more directly spiritual emphasis, the People of Sheba are irritated by the Prophets for disturbing their comfortable and pleasing current state of ignorance, unappreciative of their foreknowledge of impending doom (III, vv. 282–411), while Pharaoh tries in vain to prevent the birth of Moses through the logical methods of separating Jewish men from their wives at the time of conception and then eliminating all babies born at the time when his birth was foretold, overlooking in the process that his own Jewish treasurer, Emran, could father the expected Prophet (III, vv. 840–995). Rumi's subsequent major story about Moses' miracle of transforming his rod into a snake builds on this theme (III, vv. 1067–1259). All these major stories in the first quarter of Book Three recount the failures of a purely rational approach to knowledge, by highlighting the fact that it can be influenced by the self's desires, and that it cannot perceive anything of the future in contrast to the all-encompassing mystical knowledge of Prophets.

Possibly the most dramatic of twists comes in the major story about the man who prayed for a livelihood without having to work (III, vv. 1451–2571). This man is convinced that his prayer is being answered when a cow charges into his house, so he slays it. Reading this story rationally, the reader sympathizes with the owner of the cow who wants compensation, and yet, through divine communication, Prophet David discovers that the killing of the cow was perfectly correct. His prophetic communication from God informs him of the history of the present owner of the cow and the ancestors of the man who killed it, which shows that the former did not possess it legitimately and had in fact murdered the original owner. This story not only highlights the superiority of the divine communication received by Prophets over rational knowledge, but in this case there is a protagonist who appears at first to be foolish with his prayer to God for livelihood without the need to work, and yet his conviction that the cow's arrival at his house is an answer to this prayer is finally vindicated. The implication here is that such a conviction in divine communication is superior to rationalizing, a teaching that is also expressed explicitly elsewhere in Book Three.

While the arrival of the cow was a boon that was understood correctly to be divinely sent, the punishment faced by the ascetic who breaks his vows in the subsequent embedded story (III, vv. 1616–1722) highlights that it is the conviction in such divine communication that counts rather than the nature of the consequences, whether pleasant or painful. The ascetic in this story accepts the amputation of a hand even though he is innocent of the crime for which this punishment is dealt, because he recognizes this as a divinely ordained consequence of his breaking a vow earlier. In this case, any observer would be astonished at the seeming injustice he suffers, but the ascetic accepts it through his divinely communicated knowledge.

The visionary nature that divinely communicated knowledge can take is illustrated in the story about the extraordinary visions experienced by a character identified only by the name Daquqi of seven transforming candles–trees–holy men (III, vv. 1926–2307), which is at the heart of Book Three. This is a mystical vision that others cannot perceive. The seven men eventually disappear from Daquqi's vision too when he intercedes for distressed passengers on board a sinking ship. The seven are critical that he noticed the ship while leading the group in prayer and was moved to try to change God's ordinance. Daquqi is urged to keep on seeking individuals like these seven men who are so detached from the human realm, despite their disapproval of his becoming distracted during prayer. By implication, his visionary experiences are attainable by those still pursuing the Sufi path in the quest for complete mystical knowledge.

The potentially negative consequences of having extraordinary knowledge are highlighted in the story about the man who asks Moses to teach him the language of animals (III, vv. 3268–3400). The little that Moses is willing to teach him itself proves too much for this person, who does not have the capacity to receive it, because he soon learns about his own impending death from a clairvoyant cockerel's conversations with a dog.

The qualification for receiving divinely communicated knowledge is lack of consciousness of self, which makes one ready to accept what is disadvantageous to one as well as what is advantageous. This is memorably illustrated in the story of the Vakil (administrator) of the ruler of Bukhara, as he returns to his master in that city, whom he had previously fled, even though all rational advisers urge him to keep away. The logical consequence of his return appears to them to be his execution (III, vv. 3688–4751), and yet the Vakil is prepared to make that return, driven by his love for the ruler from whom he can no longer bear to be separated.

The Vakil represents the Sufi mystic who is drawn through the power of love for the Divine, against all logic and prudently self-preserving advice, then receives mystical knowledge and eternal life as a consequence of losing all consciousness of self. A similar gambling away of one's own self-interest and security is illustrated in the story embedded here about the man who stays overnight in the haunted mosque against all advice (III, vv. 3924–4379).

For Rumi, both Prophets and Sufi Friends of God are privileged to receive knowledge directly from God, and he emphatically denies any distinction between the kinds of divinely communicated knowledge that comes to them.[4] As a Sufi Friend of God who was also a prolific poet and teacher, divine communication was predictably a subject of special interest to him. It is well known that the *Masnavi* is often called 'the Qur'an in Persian', and Rumi himself made the first comparison between the two works, towards the end of Book Three (vv. 4230–94). Although he begins by comparing the reception these two books have had from fools who are dismissive of them, Rumi proceeds by developing an argument for the Friend of God's ability to receive the same kind of divine communication as Prophets, and for the *Masnavi* to be considered as representing the Qur'an because it is of the same divine origin.[5]

The final story of Book Three continues at the start of Book Four, a deliberate strategy referred to in the final verse of this book. Since this unique instance is at the exact centre of the six books of the *Masnavi* it provides promising support for the theory of Seyed Safavi and Simon Weightman that there is a ring structure to the whole work, in which the first three books mirror the last three books.[6] However, the actual story which forms the overlap, 'The Union of the lover who was not true', does not have the significance that one would expect in this position. This can easily be seen by comparing it with the immediately preceding story about the self-annihilating love of the Vakil for the ruler of Bukhara. Like other possible indications of a ring structure, Rumi uses such an organizational framework only loosely, unwilling to restrict himself or draw attention to it. He is more concerned that the reader should focus on what is immediately at hand rather than try to intellectualize the relationship of a part to the overall framework.

Rumi and Sufism

Rumi has long been recognized within the Sufi tradition as one of the most important Sufis in history. He not only produced the finest Sufi poetry in Persian, but was the master of disciples who later, under the

[4] See my *Beyond Dogma: Rumi's Teachings on Friendship with God and Early Sufi Theories* (Oxford, 2012), 64–7.

[5] Ibid. 67–72.

[6] See S. Safavi and S. Weightman, *Rumi's Mystical Design: Reading the Mathnawi, Book One* (Albany, NY, 2009).

direction of his son and eventual successor Soltan Valad, named their order after him. Moreover, by virtue of the intense devotion he expressed towards his own master, Shams-e Tabriz, Rumi has become the archetypal Sufi disciple. From that perspective, the unprecedented level of interest in Rumi's poetry over recent decades in North America and Europe does not come as a total surprise. Once his poetry finally began to be rendered into English in an attractive form, which coincided with an increased interest in mysticism among readers, this Sufi saint who expressed his mystical teachings in a more memorable and universally accessible form than any other began to become a household name.

Rumi lived some 300 years after the first writings of Muslim mystics were produced. A distinct mystical path called 'Sufism' became clearly identifiable in the ninth century and began to be systematized from the late tenth and early eleventh centuries with the compilation of the manuals and collections of biographies of past Sufi saints. The authors of these works, who were mostly from north-eastern Persia, traced the origins of the Sufi tradition back to the Prophet Mohammad, while at the same time acknowledging the existence of comparable forms of mysticism before his mission. They mapped out a mystical path, by which the Sufi ascends towards the ultimate goal of union with God and knowledge of reality. More than two centuries before the time of the eminent Sufi theosopher Ebn 'Arabi (d. 1240), Sufis began to describe their experience of annihilation in God and the realization that only God truly exists. The illusion of one's own independent existence had begun to be regarded as the main obstacle to achieving this realization, so that early Sufis like Abu Yazid Bestami (d. 874) are frequently quoted as dismissing the value of the asceticism of some of their contemporaries on the grounds that it merely increased attention to themselves. In this way, most Sufis began to regard love of God as the means of overcoming the root problem of one's own self, rather than piety and asceticism.[7]

The Sufi practice most widely discussed in the early manuals of Sufism is that of listening to music, commonly referred to as 'musical audition' (*sama'*). Listening to poetry being sung to music, while immersed in the remembrance of God and unaware of oneself,

---

[7] Translations of representative samples of the key texts of early Sufism are available in M. Sells, *Early Islamic Mysticism* (Mahwah, NJ, 1996).

induced ecstasy in worshippers. The discussions in Sufi manuals of spontaneous movements by Sufis in ecstasy while listening to music, and the efforts made to distinguish this from ordinary dance, suggest that this practice had already begun to cause a great deal of controversy. Most of the Sufi orders that were later formed developed the practice of surrendering to spontaneous movements while listening to music, but the whirling ceremony of the followers of Rumi, the Mevlevi order, is a unique phenomenon.[8] Although it is traditionally traced back to Rumi's own propensity for spinning around in ecstasy, the elaborate ceremony in the form in which it has become famous today was established only in the sixteenth century.[9]

The characteristics of the Sufi mystic who has completed the path to enlightenment is one of the most recurrent topics in Sufi writings of the tenth and eleventh centuries, but students of Sufism at the time would tend to associate with several such individuals rather than form an exclusive bond with one master. By the twelfth century, however, the master–disciple relationship became increasingly emphasized, as the first Sufi orders began to be formed. It was also during this century that the relationship between love of God and His manifestation in creation became a focus of interest, especially among Sufis of Persian origin, such as Ahmad Ghazali (d. 1126) and Ruzbehan Baqli (d. 1209).[10] The former's more famous brother Abu Hamid was responsible for integrating Sufism with mainstream Sunni Islam, as a practical form of Muslim piety that can provide irrefutable knowledge of religious truths through direct mystical experience.[11]

In this way, by the thirteenth century diverse forms of Sufism had developed and become increasingly popular. Rumi was introduced to Sufism by his father, Baha Valad, who followed a more conservative tradition of Muslim piety, but his life was transformed when he encountered the mystic Shams-e Tabriz. Although many of

---

[8] Concerning the contrast between the Mevlevi *sama'* and other forms of Sufi *sama'*, see J. During, 'What is Sufi Music?', in L. Lewisohn, ed., *The Legacy of Medieval Persian Sufism* (London, 1992), 277–87.

[9] See further C. W. Ernst, *The Shambhala Guide to Sufism* (Boston, 1997), 191–4.

[10] See further C. W. Ernst, tr., *Teachings of Sufism* (Boston, 1999), 82–94, and A. Ghazali, *Sawanih: Inspirations from the World of Pure Spirits*, tr. N. Pourjavady (London, 1986).

[11] The chapter of Mohammad Ghazali's autobiography that describes his experience on the Sufi path is available in translation in N. Calder, J. Mojaddedi, and A. Rippin, eds. and trs., *Classical Islam: A Sourcebook of Religious Literature* (London, 2003), 228–32.

the followers of the tradition of his father considered Shams to be unworthy of Rumi's time and attention, he considered him to be the most complete manifestation of God. Rumi expressed his love and utter devotion for his master Shams, with whom he spent only about two years in total, through thousands of ecstatic lyrical poems. Towards the end of his life he presented the fruit of his experience of Sufism in the form of the *Masnavi*, which has been judged by many commentators, both within the Sufi tradition and outside it, to be the greatest mystical poem ever written.

The Masnavi *form*

Rumi chose a plain, descriptive name for his poem, 'masnavi' being the name of the rhyming couplet verse form. Each half-line, or hemistich, of a *masnavi* poem follows the same metre, in common with other forms of classical Persian poetry. The metre of Rumi's *Masnavi* is the *ramal* metre in apocopated form (‒ ˘ ‒ ‒ / ‒ ˘ ‒ ‒ / ‒ ˘ ‒), a highly popular metre which was also used by Faridoddin ʿAttar (d. 1220) for his *Conference of the Birds.* What distinguishes the *masnavi* form from other Persian verse forms is the rhyme, which changes in successive couplets according to the pattern *aa bb cc dd* etc. Thus, in contrast to the other verse forms, which require a restrictive monorhyme, the *masnavi* form enables poets to compose long works consisting of thousands of verses.

The *masnavi* form satisfied the need felt by Persians to compose narrative and didactic poems, of which there was already before the Islamic period a long and rich tradition. By Rumi's time a number of Sufis had already made use of the *masnavi* form to compose mystical poems, the most celebrated among which are Sanaʾi's (d. 1138) *Hadiqatoʾl-haqiqat*, or *Garden of Truth*, and ʿAttar's *Manteqoʾt-tayr*, or *Conference of the Birds.*[12] According to tradition, it was the popularity of these works among Rumi's disciples that prompted Hosamoddin, Rumi's deputy, to ask him to compose his own mystical *masnavi* for their benefit.

Hosamoddin served as Rumi's scribe in a process of text production that is traditionally described as being similar to the way in which

---

[12] See e.g. F. Attar, *The Conference of the Birds*, ed. and tr. A. Darbandi and D. Davis (Harmondsworth, 1983).

the Qur'an was produced. However, while the Sufi poet Rumi recited the *Masnavi* orally when he felt inspired to do so, with Hosamoddin always ready to record those recitations in writing for him as well as to assist him in revising and editing the final poem, the illiterate Prophet Mohammad is said to have recited aloud divine revelation in piecemeal fashion, in exactly the form that God's words were revealed to him through the Archangel Gabriel. Those companions of the Prophet who were present on such occasions would write down the revelations and memorize them, and these written and mental records eventually formed the basis of the compilation of the Qur'an many years after the Prophet's death.

The process of producing the *Masnavi* was probably started about 1262, although tradition relates that Rumi had already composed the first eighteen couplets by the time Hosamoddin made his request; we are told that he responded by pulling a sheet of paper out of his turban with the first part of the prologue of Book One, 'The Song of the Reed', already written on it. References to their system of production can be found in the text of the *Masnavi* itself (e.g. I, v. 2947). They seem to have worked on the *Masnavi* during the evenings in particular, and in one instance Rumi begs forgiveness for having kept Hosamoddin up for an entire night with it (I, v. 1817). After Hosamoddin had written down Rumi's recitations, they were read back to him to be checked and corrected. The crucial role played by Hosamoddin as Rumi's assistant in this process is highlighted by the fact that Rumi refers to the *Masnavi* on several occasions as 'the Hosam book'.

Rumi's *Masnavi* belongs to the group of works written in this verse form that do not have a frame narrative. In this way, it contrasts with the more cohesively structured *Conference of the Birds*, which is already well known in translation. It is also much longer; the *Conference* is roughly the same length as just one of the six component books of the *Masnavi*. Each of the six books consists of about 4,000 verses and has its own prose introduction and prologue. There are no epilogues.

The component narratives, homilies, commentaries on citations, prayers, and lyrical flights which make up the body of the *Masnavi* are often demarcated by their own headings. The text of longer narratives tends to be broken up into sections by further such headings, as we have seen. Occasionally the section headings are positioned inappropriately, such as in the middle of continuous speech, which might be interpreted as a sign that they may have been inserted only after the text had been prepared. Occasionally they are actually longer than the passage that they represent, and serve to explain and contextualize what follows. It is as if, on rereading the text, further explanation was felt necessary in the form of an expanded heading. According to Safavi and Weightman, however, these inconsistent section headings are of crucial importance, in that they represent the original plan of the *Masnavi* and were therefore probably organized before any of the poetry had itself been composed.[13]

The frequency of breaks in the flow of narratives, which is a distinctive characteristic of the *Masnavi*, reveals that Rumi has earned a reputation as an excellent story-teller despite being primarily concerned with conveying his teachings as effectively as possible to his Sufi disciples. The *Masnavi* leaves the impression that he was brimming with ideas and symbolic images which would overflow when prompted by the subtlest of associations. In this way, free from the constraints of a frame narrative, Rumi has been able to produce a work that is far richer in content than any other example of the mystical *masnavi* genre. That this has been achieved often at the expense of preserving continuity in the narratives seems to corroborate Rumi's opinion on the relative importance of the teachings in his poetry over its aesthetic value, as reported in his discourses.[14] If it were not for the fact that his digressive 'overflowings' are expressed in simple language and with imagery that was immediately accessible to his contemporary readers, they would have constituted an undesirable impediment to understanding the poem. Where this leads Rumi to interweave narratives and to alternate between different speakers and his own commentaries, the text can still be difficult to follow, and, for

[13] S. Safavi and S. Weightman, *Rumi's Mystical Design*.

[14] In a famous passage among Rumi's discourses, he is reported to have compared writing poetry with serving to a guest something that one finds unpleasant like tripe, because that is what the guest wants (Rumi, *Signs of the Unseen: The Discourses of Jalaluddin Rumi*, tr. W. M. Thackston, Jr (Boston, 1994), 77–8). The main theme of the sixteenth discourse (pp. 74–80), in which this passage is found, is the relationship between form and content, and it includes Rumi's response to the charge that he is 'all talk and no action' (p. 78). The statement should therefore be understood in its proper context, rather than as evidence that Rumi disliked the art of writing poetry.

most contemporary readers, the relevance of citations and allusions to the Qur'an and the traditions of the Prophet will not be immediately obvious without reference to the explanatory notes that have been provided in this edition. Nonetheless, it should be evident, not least from the lengthy sequences of metaphors that Rumi often provides to reinforce a single point, that he has striven to communicate his message as effectively as possible rather than to write obscurely and force the reader to struggle to understand him.

Rumi made painstaking efforts to convey his teachings as clearly and effectively as possible, using simple language, the *masnavi* verse form, entertaining stories, and the most vivid and accessible imagery possible. The aim of this translation is to render Rumi's *Masnavi* into a relatively simple and attractive form which, with the benefit of metre and rhyme, may enable as many readers as possible to read the whole book with pleasure and to find it rewarding.

NOTE ON THE TRANSLATION

RUMI put his teachings into the *masnavi* verse form in order that, with the benefit of metre and rhyme, his disciples might enjoy reading them. I have therefore decided to translate Rumi's *Masnavi* into verse, in accordance with the aim of the original work. I have chosen to use rhyming iambic pentameters, since this is the closest corresponding form of English verse to the Persian *masnavi* form of rhyming couplets. These are numbered and referred to as verses in the Explanatory Notes and Introduction.

Book Three of the *Masnavi* consists of over 4,800 couplets, the continuity of which is broken up only by section headings. For the sake of clarity, in this translation further breaks have been added to those created by the section headings. In order for the Contents pages to fulfil their function effectively, alternative headings have been employed there, albeit at corresponding points to the major section headings in the text, which refer in many instances to merely the first few subsequent verses rather than representing the section as a whole.

Although the *Masnavi* is a Persian poem, it contains a substantial amount of Arabic text. This invariably takes the form of citations from Arabic sources and common religious formulae, but the sources for some of these passages are either unknown or oral. Italics have been used to indicate Arabic text, except in the section headings, which are fully italicized. Many Arabic terms and religious formulae have become part of the Persian language, and have therefore not been highlighted in this way. Capitalization has been used when reference is made to God. This includes, in addition to the pronouns and titles commonly used in English, the ninety-nine names of God of the Islamic tradition, as well as certain philosophical terms.

Most of the sources of the *Masnavi* are not widely available in English, if at all, and so references have been provided in the notes only for citations of the Qur'an. Verse numbering varies in the most widely available translations of the Qur'an, some of which do not in fact number individual verses, but since this variation is very slight (a maximum of a few verses) the reader should still be able to find the relevant passages without difficulty. The notes also identify those

passages in the translation which represent the sayings and deeds
of the Prophet Mohammad (*hadith*) when this is not already self-
evident in the text (e.g. by 'the Prophet said'). It should be pointed
out that citations in the original *Masnavi* are very often variants of
the original sources, including the Qur'an, rather than exact render-
ings, owing to the constraints of the metre that is used. The same
applies in this verse translation.

This translation corresponds exactly to the text of the third volume
of the edition prepared by Mohammad Estelami (six volumes and
index, 2nd edition, Tehran, 1990). This is by far the best critical
edition that has been prepared, since it offers a complete apparatus
criticus, indicating the variant readings in all the early manuscripts
more comprehensively and transparently than any other edition.
Although R. A. Nicholson's edition of the Persian text is more widely
available owing to the fact that it is published in Europe, its short-
comings for today are widely recognized and outweigh the advantage
of having his exactly corresponding prose translation and commen-
tary to refer to.

As far as possible, the English equivalents of technical terms have
been provided, in preference to giving the original in transliteration
and relying on explanatory notes. Where it is provided, the translit-
eration of names and terms has been simplified to such a degree that
no diacritics are used. It is designed simply to help the reader use
Persian pronunciation, especially where this would affect the metre
and rhyme.

SELECT BIBLIOGRAPHY

General Background

J. T. P. De Bruijn, *Persian Sufi Poetry: An Introduction to the Mystical Use of Classical Poems* (Richmond, 1997).

C. W. Ernst, *The Shambhala Guide to Sufism* (Boston, 1997).

L. Lewisohn, ed., *Classical Persian Sufism: From its Origins to Rumi* (London, 1993).

J. W. Morris, 'Situating Islamic Mysticism: Between Written Traditions and Popular Spirituality', in R. Herrera, ed., *Mystics of the Book: Themes, Topics and Typologies* (New York, 1993), 293–334.

J. Nurbakhsh, *The Path: Sufi Practices* (London; 2nd rev. edn, New York, 2006).

O. Safi, 'On the Path of Love towards the Divine: A Journey with Muslim Mystics', *Sufi*, 78 (2009–10), 24–7.

Reference

Encyclopaedia Iranica, ed. E. Yarshater (New York, 1985–); <http://www.iranica.com>.

Encyclopaedia of Islam, ed. H. A. R. Gibb et al., 12 vols. (Leiden, 1960–2003).

J. Nurbakhsh, *Sufi Symbolism*, 16 vols. (London, 1980–2003).

On Rumi

W. C. Chittick, ed., *The Sufi Path of Love: The Spiritual Teachings of Rumi* (Albany, NY, 1983).

F. Keshavarz, *Reading Mystical Lyric: The Case of Jalal al-Din Rumi* (Columbia, SC, 1998).

F. D. Lewis, *Rumi, Past and Present, East and West: The Life, Teachings and Poetry of Jalal al-Din Rumi* (Oxford, 2000).

J. Mojaddedi, *Beyond Dogma: Rumi's Teachings on Friendship with God and Early Sufi Theories* (Oxford, 2012).

Rumi, *Mystical Poems of Rumi 1 and 2*, tr. A. J. Arberry (New York, 1979).

Rumi, *Signs of the Unseen: The Discourses of Jalaluddin Rumi*, tr. W. M. Thackston, Jr (Boston, 1994).

N. Virani, ' "I am the nightingale of the Merciful": Rumi's use of the Qur'an and Hadith', *Comparative Studies of South Asia, Africa and the Middle East*, 22/2 (2002), 100–11.

Editions of the Masnavi

Masnavi, ed. M. Estelami, 2nd edn, 7 vols. (Tehran, 1990). Vols. i–vi each contain the editor's commentary in the form of endnotes; vol. vii is the Index.

Masnavi, ed. T. Sobhani (Tehran, 1994).

Masnavi-ye ma'navi, ed. A.-K. Sorush, 2 vols. (Tehran, 1996).

The Mathnawi of Jalalu'ddin Rumi, ed. and tr. R. A. Nicholson, E. J. W. Gibb Memorial, NS, 8 vols. (London, 1925–40). Vols. i–iii contain the Persian text; vols. iv–vi contain a full translation in prose; vols. vii–viii contain a commentary on Books One to Six.

Interpretation of the Masnavi

W. C. Chittick, 'Rumi and *wahdat al-wujud*', in A. Banani, R. Hovannisian, and G. Sabagh, eds., *Poetry and Mysticism in Islam: The Heritage of Rumi* (Cambridge, 1994), 70–111.

H. Dabashi, 'Rumi and the Problems of Theodicy: Moral Imagination and Narrative Discourse in a Story of the *Masnavi*', in A. Banani, R. Hovannisian, and G. Sabagh, eds., *Poetry and Mysticism in Islam: The Heritage of Rumi* (Cambridge, 1994), 112–35.

R. Davis, 'Narrative and Doctrine in the First Story of Rumi's *Mathnawi*', in G. R. Hawting, J. A. Mojaddedi, and A. Samely, eds., *Studies in Islamic and Middle Eastern Texts and Traditions in Memory of Norman Calder* (Oxford, 2000), 93–104.

A. Karamustafa, 'Speaker, Voice and Audience in the Koran and the *Mathnawi*', *Sufi*, 79 (2010), 36–45.

M. Mills, 'Folk Tradition in the *Masnavi* and the *Masnavi* in Folk Tradition', in A. Banani, R. Hovannisian, and G. Sabagh, eds., *Poetry and Mysticism in Islam: The Heritage of Rumi* (Cambridge, 1994), 136–77.

J. Mojaddedi, 'Rumi', in A. Rippin, ed., *The Blackwell Companion to the Qur'an* (Oxford, 2006), 362–72.

J. R. Perry, '*Monty Python* and the *Mathnavi*: The Parrot in Indian, Persian and English Humor', *Iranian Studies*, 36/1 (2003), 63–73.

J. Renard, *All the King's Falcons: Rumi on Prophets and Revelation* (Albany, NY, 1994).

S. Safavi and S. Weightman, *Rumi's Mystical Design: Reading the Mathnawi, Book One* (Albany, NY, 2009).

O. Safi, 'Did the Two Oceans Meet? Historical Connections and Disconnections between Ibn 'Arabi and Rumi', *Journal of Muhyiddin Ibn 'Arabi Society*, 26 (1999), 55–88.

Further Reading in Oxford World's Classics

The Masnavi, Book One, tr. and ed. Jawid Mojaddedi.
The Masnavi, Book Two, tr. and ed. Jawid Mojaddedi.
The Qur'an, tr. M. A. S. Abdel Haleem.

A CHRONOLOGY OF RUMI

1207   Rumi's birth in Balkh, north-eastern Persia

c. 1216   Rumi's family emigrate from Persia to Anatolia

1219   Alaoddin Kay Qobad ascends Seljuk throne in Anatolia

1220   Death of Faridoddin 'Attar

1221   The Mongol army conquers Balkh

c. 1222   Rumi's family settle temporarily in Karaman, Anatolia

1224   Rumi marries Gowhar Khatun

1226   Birth of Soltan Valad, Rumi's son and eventual successor

c. 1229   Rumi's family relocate to Konya, Anatolia

1231   Death of Baha Valad, Rumi's father

1232   Borhanoddin Termezi arrives in Konya

c. 1233   Rumi begins his studies in Syria

1235   Death of ebn al-Farez in Egypt

1237   Rumi returns to Konya as leader of Baha Valad's school
        Ghiyasoddin Kay Khosrow II ascends Seljuk throne in Anatolia

1240   Death of ebn 'Arabi in Damascus

1243   The Mongols extend their empire to Anatolia

1244   Rumi meets Shams-e Tabriz in Konya for the first time

1246   Shams leaves Konya

1247   Shams returns to Konya

c. 1247   Shams disappears
        Salahoddin the Goldsmith begins tenure as Rumi's deputy

1258   Death of Salahoddin
        Hosamoddin Chalabi begins tenure as Rumi's deputy
        The Mongols conquer Baghdad, the Abbasid capital

1260   The Mongols are defeated in Syria by the Mamluks

c. 1262   The *Masnavi* is started

c. 1264   The *Masnavi* is resumed after a pause on account of the death of
        Hosamoddin's wife

1273   (17 December) Death of Rumi in Konya

THE MASNAVI

BOOK THREE

Prose Introduction

Pieces of wisdom are the armies of God by which He strengthens the spirits of seekers, and keeps their knowledge away from the tarnish of ignorance, their justice from the tarnish of tyranny, their generosity from the tarnish of self-display, and their intelligence from the tarnish of stupidity. He makes accessible to them the understanding of the afterlife that had been too challenging for them, while also making easy for them the acts of obedience and self-exertion that had proven too hard before. This wisdom is also part of the evidences and proofs of the Prophets, informing about God's secrets and His sovereignty specially for mystics, and how He causes the luminous pearl-like heavens of His compassion to revolve above the vaporous global sphere, the same way that the intellect controls earthly forms and their external and internal senses. The revolving of those spiritual heavens controls the vaporous heavens, the radiant meteors, the illumined lamps, the nurturing winds, the expanses of land, and the constantly flowing waters. May God benefit His servants with them and increase their understanding.

Each reader can understand only according to the capacity of his mind, the pietist can only perform devotions according to the strength of his self-exertion, the mufti can give rulings only according to his ability to reason them out, the alms-giver can give alms only according to the limit of his means, the donor can give only from what he possesses, and the recipient of his generosity can only acquire what he can know about. However, he who seeks water in the desert will not be prevented from seeking it by his knowledge of what is contained in the seas, and he will be determined in his search for this Water of Life, so as not to be cut off from it by pre-occupation with daily life, nor to be hindered by illness, need, or the interference of desires between him and the goal to which he is hurrying. Knowledge will not be attained by the one who prefers lust, nor the one who relies on gentle treatment, nor the one who turns back from his search, nor the one who fears for himself, nor the one who is anxious about his own welfare, unless he takes refuge with God and prioritizes his spiritual affairs over his worldly ones, then takes from the treasure of wisdom such magnificent wealth that neither depreciates nor becomes inherited like worldly inheritance, and also acquires the glorious lights, the noble jewels,

and the precious domains, giving thanks for His grace, magnifying His
power, and glorifying His strength; and unless he seeks refuge in God
from the baseness of affluence and the ignorance of overvaluing the little
that he sees in himself while undervaluing the great amount he obtains
from others, causing him to become proud of things that God has not even
permitted for him. Rather, the seeker who possesses knowledge must learn
what he does not know and teach others what he has learnt, be compas-
sionate to those of weak intelligence, avoid becoming proud due to the folly
of the stupid, or becoming harsh towards the dull-witted: 'You used to be
that way before yourself, but then God was generous to you.'*

God is exalted far above the sayings of the blasphemers, the worship
of associate gods by polytheists, the accusation of defect by those who are
themselves deficient, the human comparisons of the anthropomorphists,
the evil suppositions of the intellectuals, and the estimations of those who
follow illusions. Praise belongs to Him and glory for the composition of
the divine and holy Masnavi. He is the One who enables success, the
Sender of Grace, and to Him belongs Power and Bestowal to His mystic
servants especially, despite a group who 'desire to extinguish the Light of
God with their mouths—God will make His light complete its course even
if the infidels hate it.'* 'We have sent down the reminder and We are its
guards.'* 'Whoever alters it after he has heard it will bear the guilt for
this. God is Hearing, Knowing.'* Praise be to God, the Lord of the worlds,
and blessings on our chief Mohammad, his family, and his pure and good
companions altogether, through Your Grace, O Most Gracious One!

Exordium

O Light of Truth, Hosamoddin, bring please
   Book Three—the Prophet would do things in threes.*
Open the box of secrets it contains;
   For more excuses no time now remains.
Your power arrives from God's power, its true source,
   Not from mere veins which pulse with lust's full force;
This lamp, the sun, itself burns radiantly—
   A cotton wick and oil aren't necessary;
And heaven's vault has stayed up for so long
   Without ropes or tall pillars which stand strong;   5

And Gabriel's power came not from food, but seeing
    The Master and Creator of all being—
The power of God's Abdals, His true elite,
    Derives from Him, not from the food they eat.
Even their bodies have been made with light,
    So they surpass the angels in God's sight.
You've gained God's attributes, so you're prepared—
    Walk through the flames like Abraham once dared!
Fire will become *'coolness and comfort too'**—   10
    Such elements will serve as slaves to you.
The natural elements are in each creature,
    But still your constitution is superior:
Your constitution's from beyond this sphere—
    It came to manifest His oneness here.
People's capacity to understand
    Is limited and it will not expand.
O Light of Truth, your piercing sight alone
    Can give the power to understand to stone;
Mount Sinai through that great epiphany   15
    Drank much more than its own capacity:
The mountain split apart due to one glance;
    Just like a camel it began to dance!*

Many kind men would give you meat tomorrow
    But only God gives throats with which to swallow;
One for your neck, one for your spirit too:
    He gives a throat to every part of you.
He'll give when you reflect His majesty,
    Once empty of deceit and vanity;
You then won't tell to every passer-by   20
    His secrets, thus leave sugar for a fly.
God's secrets only reach those who possess
    A hundred tongues but stay mute nonetheless.
God's grace bestows a throat to earth's soil, so
    It swallows water and help plants to grow;
And He gives creatures lips and throats, so they
    Consume plants and develop in this way.

Each animal that eats plants grows in size
   And serves as food for humans when it dies.
Once it returns to earth, it will consume   25
   The human corpse that's left beneath its tomb.
I've seen mere atoms open-mouthed, my friend;
   Describing their food takes too long to end.
Provisions are first nourished by His grace,
   And He feeds nourishers in the first place.
The Lord provides our sustenance below—
   Without their own food how could wheat fields grow?
The whole of this can never be expressed;
   This sample represents for you the rest.

Most things eat then are eaten by another;   30
   Eternal ones are fortunate, my brother.
This world is transient, as are those inside;
   The other world and its souls will abide.
Lovers of this world have become divided,
   Lovers of that world permanently united.
Noble ones for themselves desire to pour
   Water of Life which lasts for ever more.
The good deeds which endure come from these few
   Because they're flawless and they lack fear too;
Though they be thousands, they're just one inside,   35
   Unlike mere fancies, which get multiplied.
Throats are with swallowers and what they've eaten,
   As brains are with the conquerors and the beaten.
He gave a throat to Truth's rod, it's well known—
   It swallowed all the other rods then thrown;*
But it did not increase in size at all,
   Since it did not eat like an animal.
He also gave a throat to certitude,
   So it could make doubts vanish just like food.
Spiritual things have throats too, which seems odd,   40
   But the provider of such throats is God;
There's nothing in creation that's without
   A throat through which to feed, so have no doubt!

But when the soul's throat disregards its body,
    Its sustenance then comes straight from God's glory.
To change one's nature is the sole condition;
    An evil constitution brings perdition.
When a man starts to eat mud, he'll become
    Sickly and pale, miserable and glum;
But should his ugly nature change one night,   45
    His face would, like a candle, shine so bright.
The baby needs a wet-nurse who can treat
    Its mouth with kindness, making it taste sweet;
If she should block the way now to her breast,
    She'll open up to him the path that's best,
For nipples veil the child from what's in store—
    Bountiful feasts with food for ever more.
On weaning, therefore, human life depends—
    So keep on striving! Here this discourse ends.

A foetus feeds on blood, which is unclean*—   50
    Believers can still draw from that what's clean;
The infant moves from blood to milk instead,
    With solid food the final goal ahead.
Solid food makes him a Loqman, the aim:
    A skilful hunter of all hidden game.
If you had told that foetus in the womb:
    'Outside there is a realm with lots of room,
A pleasant, verdant realm that is so spacious
    With lots of food that you will find delicious,
With oceans, plains, and mountains waiting too,   55
    And farms and orchards growing fruit for you,
A lofty sky that shines the brightest light
    Through sunshine, moonbeams, and the stars at night,
And, due to winds from north, south, east, and west,
    Those orchards bloom with fragrance that is blest—
Such wonders that can't be described in full,
    So why stay in the dark so miserable?
Why stay here to drink blood in this cramped cell,
    Which is unclean and has an awful smell?'

The foetus would have just denied all day 60
    All of the things which you'd tried to relay,
Saying: 'Impossible, delusory!'—
    Blind minds can't picture what they cannot see:
Since they have never seen things of this sort,
    Their doubting ears will not hear your report.
That's like when mystics holding a high station
    Speak to men from the general population,
Saying: 'This world's a dark and narrow pit;
    There is a better world outside of it.'
These true words are not heeded; such instruction 65
    Is blocked from ears by lust, that huge obstruction;
Lust stops ears hearing, while base coveting
    Prevents their eyes from seeing anything.
The foetus also has this attitude
    For blood, which in the womb is its sole food:
Blood's all it knows while it stays tightly curled;
    Lust for blood stops it hearing of this world.

Story about those who ate a baby elephant, shunning the advice of a counsellor

This story set in India all should know:
    A sage saw a small gang once long ago,
All naked, empty-handed, looking hungry 70
    And like they'd been on an extended journey.
A deep compassion filled him instantly;
    He greeted them and blossomed like a tree:
'I know your hunger and lack of possessions
    Bring suffering just like Kerbala's transgressions.
For God's sake, glorious group, if you should hunt,
    Don't try to catch a baby elephant!
An elephant's in the vicinity—
    Don't hunt its babies! Listen now to me:
You'll see them as you travel on your way 75
    And they can tempt you easily to stray,

For they are gentle, very weak, and fat—
    Their mother, though, is watching out for that.
To find her children she'd search far and wide,
    And groan and sigh as anguish burns inside.
Her trunk emits huge flames and poisonous smoke,
    So don't dare harm her children—it's no joke!'

Saints are God's children, son, you must beware—
    In presence and in absence act with care!
Don't deem their absence a deficiency,   80
    Since God takes vengeance for them wrathfully:
He said, 'These saints are children of my own
    In exile, but all glory's theirs alone;
They're orphaned and left helpless as a test—
    In secret, I am with the ones I've blessed.
I'm their support and give immunity;
    It is as if they are all part of me.
They are my men of cloth—beware, good son!
    They are a million and yet they are one.'
If this were not true, tell me then how could   85
    Moses stun Pharaoh with a piece of wood?*
Or Noah, with just one curse, make the sea
    Submerge the East and West so easily?*
If not, could Lot have razed down to the ground
    All of the towns and settlements around?*
Towns just like paradise were caused to turn
    To a black Tigris—find their trace and learn!
Near Syria you'll find remnants still of them
    As you pass southwards to Jerusalem.
Numerous Prophets dealt to generations   90
    God's punishments for their abominations.
If I continue with this speech today
    Mountains will turn to blood without delay;
They'll bleed, then go back to their solid state,
    Though you can't see them, you blind reprobate!
Blind men who boast they have the clearest vision
    See just the camel's hairs with fine precision.

Man, through his greed, inspects it hair by hair;
    Then dances for no reason like a bear.
Dance where you'll break your self, then with full trust   95
    Tear off the plaster from your wound of lust!
Real men whirl on the battlefield, not here;
    They dance in their own blood and feel no fear.
They clap when they escape the self's control;
    They dance once they've escaped the carnal soul.
Their minstrels play the tambourine within;
    Seas surge with foam, excited by their din.
Though you can't see them, leaves on every tree
    Hanging from branches clap in ecstasy.
You can't see leaves clap and you cannot hear—   100
    You need the heart's ear not the outward ear.
Block the head's ear from lies and mockery
    To see the soul's own city vividly.
Mohammad's ear heard secrets through each word:
    God said, '*He is an ear.*'* Have you not heard?
He is entirely ear and eye, and he
    Feeds us like suckling babies generously.
The truth is boundless—let's return again
    Back to the elephants and those warned men.

Continuation of the story about those who bothered the young elephant

'The elephant smells breath,' the sage then said,   105
    'And feels men's stomachs if they seem well fed
Until she finds her child's last resting place—
    Her force and vengeance then they'll have to face!'

You eat the flesh of God's slaves every day
    By backbiting, and so you'll have to pay.
Beware, for the Creator smells your breath
    And only the sincere escape from death.
Later, inside their graves, those who now sneer
    Will be found out by Monker and Nakir.*

You cannot pull your mouth back from those two,   110
    Nor sweeten fetid breath produced by you;
And there's no make-up there to hide behind,
    Nor way to flee from truth for your small mind.
Their heavy mace so many times will pound
    On heads and backsides of each babbler found.
Just think what Azrael's huge mace could do
    Even if now its form is far from view.
Sometimes these maces' scary forms are seen—
    Every man who is sick knows what I mean:
'Tell me, dear friends,' a very sick man said,   115
    'What is this sword that's pointing at my head?'
'We can't see it,' they say, 'It's your delusion!'
    No, this is death and it is no illusion.
It's not imaginary; even the sky
    Becomes transparent, fearing it will die.
The sick man can see swords and maces swing
    While he hangs his own head down, whimpering;
He sees them aim at him most threateningly,
    Even if no one else's eyes can see.
When greed leaves him he then will gain sharp sight;   120
    When this man bleeds to death his eyes grow bright—
What tragic timing to see at that stage,
    Yet blind before due to his pride and rage.
Such birds which sing too early or too late*
    Are those which people will decapitate.
Your soul each moment struggles hard with death—
    Think of your faith as though it's your last breath.
Your life is like a purse, and night and day
    Are counters of gold coins you've put away:
The counter takes all coins out one by one,   125
    Then there is an eclipse of the whole sun.
If you should take and not put back, it's clear
    That even mountains would soon disappear.
Once you've breathed out—breathe in a breath the same
    Till through '*bow down, approach!*'* you reach your aim.
Struggling to finish work is a mistake
    Apart from work which is for your faith's sake.

You want to go without being ready, though
   Your deeds are barren just like unbaked dough.
You cannot build your tomb with these alone: 130
   Materials such as plaster, wood and stone.
Dig a grave for yourself with purity—
   In His existence bury vanity!
Become His dust with yearning at your death,
   So that your breath is nourished by His breath.
A shrine with domes and turrets won't impress
   The mystics who could not care for them less.
Look at the men in satin clothes out there—
   Does his fine satin make him more aware?
His soul is now in torment, torn apart;   135
   Scorpions of grief have settled in his heart.
He may appear embellished from outside,
   But there are desperate, bitter thoughts inside,
While those who wore a patched-up dervish cloak
   Had sweet thoughts and used sweet words when they spoke.

Resumption of the story about the elephant

The sage continued, 'Heed well my advice,
   So that your souls won't pay a heavy price.
Be satisfied with leaves and grass! Don't hunt
   Instead a stumbling baby elephant.
I've done my duty conscientiously—   140
   If you heed me you'll gain felicity.
To pass on this advice is why I came,
   So I might spare you from regret and shame.
Don't let yourselves be led astray by greed
   Or torn up from your very roots—take heed!'
The sage then said, 'Farewell!' and walked away.
   Their hunger doubled each hour of that day
Until they noticed near the road ahead
   A baby elephant which looked well fed—
Like drunken wolves out on a desperate hunt,   145
   They ravaged totally that elephant.

One of the group did not partake and said,
   'That man's advice keeps ringing in my head.'
Those words prevented him from eating too—
   Old wisdom gives new fortune thus to you.
The rest collapsed and quickly fell asleep
   While he stayed up like shepherds with their sheep.
He saw a scary elephant appear;
   She saw him act as guard and so drew near
And sniffed three times to smell his mouth and face,   150
   But didn't sense a murderous scent's trace.
She circled him some more then went away;
   That elephant queen didn't make him pay.
She smelt the lips of all the sleepers then
   And guilty smells still lingered on those men,
Revealing that they had devoured her child,
   So she immediately grew very wild:
Each one of them she fiercely tore apart,
   Feeling no doubt at all inside her heart.
She then threw in the air each of those men—   155
   They split apart on crashing down again.

Drinker of people's blood, get out of sight
   Before blood relatives should come and fight.
Their wealth is similar to their blood of course,
   Because their wealth is taken too by force.
The mother elephant, consumed with hate,
   Will gain her vengeance on all those who ate.
When you take bribes, you eat her child up too—
   The mother's vengeance will soon strangle you!
You can tell devious people by their smell,   160
   And elephants can smell kin just as well.
One who smells scent from Yemen easily
   Is bound to notice falsehood's smell on me:
Mohammad once smelt scent from far away,*
   So, from our mouths, he can smell ours today.
He smells our scent and yet he never tells;
   To heaven rise both good and rotten smells.

Your sin's stench rises up while you are sleeping
 Until it strikes against the furthest ceiling.
It's carried in your foul breath up from here   165
 To the breath-smellers in the highest sphere.
The stench of greed, conceit, and lust as well,
 Through speech will seem just like an onion's smell.
'I swear I've never eaten them,' you claim,
 'I've given garlic up too just the same.'
The breath which you emit within this speech
 Wafts through the nostrils of all men in reach—
Your prayers too by their own smell are denied;
 Through tongues, corrupt hearts are identified.
'*Begone!*' is the reply such prayers receive;   170
 The cudgel drives off men who would deceive.
But if the meaning's true, God won't reject
 Your words, though how you speak is incorrect.

In the sight of the beloved, a mistake by a lover is better than the good deed of a stranger

Belal, the first muezzin, was sincere,
 But he would mispronounce the call '*Come here!*'*
So some said, 'Prophet, there's too much at stake,
 While we expand, to let pass this mistake.
O Messenger, bring a muezzin please
 Who won't call out with such inaccuracies.
At our religion's birth, no person should   175
 Be left to mispronounce "*Come to the good!*" '*
The Prophet boiled with rage and then revealed
 Some of the graces which had been concealed:
'To God, Belal's "*Come!*" sounds much better than
 A thousand "*Come!*"'s from a well-spoken man.
Don't make me angry or I might begin
 To tell about the things you hide within!'
If your breath doesn't smell sweet during prayer,
 Seek a pure-hearted person everywhere!

God's command to Moses: 'Call unto me with a mouth which has not sinned!'

God said, 'Moses, you have to pray to me   180
    With a mouth free from sin for sanctuary.'
'But I have no such mouth, God!' Moses said.
    'Pray then with someone else's mouth instead.
When have you sinned with mouths of other men?
    To call "O God!" use mouths of others then!
Do it in such a way that their mouths pray
    For you each night and every single day!
Using a mouth which is completely sinless—
    Another man's mouth—start to beg forgiveness!
Or strive to make your own mouth pure instead   185
    And make your spirit sharp, one step ahead.'

Remembering God is pure: when purity
    Arrives defilement is obliged to flee.
Things flee their opposites, and so the night
    Disappears when the sun emits its light:
When His pure name is what a mouth should say
    Impurity and worry cannot stay.

Explanation of how the supplicant's mentioning of God's name is the same as God's saying, 'Here I am!'

'*Allah! Allah!*' a Muslim would repeat
    Until, through prayer, his pious lips grew sweet.
Satan said, 'That's too much! You've yet to hear   190
    To your "*Allah!*" the answer "*I am here!*"
From His throne no responses will come down,
    So why still chant "*Allah!*" with that deep frown?'

That Muslim's heart broke and he hung his head low,
  But then he dreamed he saw Khezr in a meadow.
Khezr asked him, 'Why don't you chant any more?
  Do you regret the prayers you sent before?'
He said, '"*Here I am!*"* won't come as reply;
  God has rejected me, so this is why.'
'Your "*Allah!*" is God's "*Here I am!*" call too,   195
  Your need and pain God's messenger to you:
God says, "Your struggles were our moves to meet,
  Approaching you and setting free your feet.
The noose of Our Grace formed your fear and love;
  To your '*Allah!*' '*Here I am!*' rings above." '

The souls of stupid men are far from prayer
  Because to pray 'O Lord!' is not their share.
Their mouths and hearts are closed up with a seal,
  So they can't moan to God of pain they feel:
God gave to Pharaoh riches, and then he   200
  Boasted about his might and majesty;
In his whole life that monster felt no pain,
  So that to God that wretch could not complain—
God gave to Pharaoh all of this world's wealth,
  But didn't grant grief, sorrow, and ill health.
Pain is much better than the wealth men hoard
  For it leads you to pray hard to your Lord.
To pray without pain means you are depressed;
  To pray in pain means that with love you're blest.
Such love's expressed by holding your voice in,   205
  Remembering your actual origin,
Which makes your voice pure when you finally pray:
  'O God, to Whom we turn, send help our way!'
Even a dog's whine can have some attraction,
  For everyone through love finds some distraction:
The dog of Sleepers in the Cave spurned carrion,
  Then feasted as the lofty kings' companion;
Till Resurrection it drinks at that place,
  Without a bowl, water of mystic grace.*

Many look like that dog but have no name— 210
   They down that drink in secret all the same.
Submit your life for one cup's sake, my son.
   Strive and be patient till the battle's won.
Patience is not a difficult demand:
   Patience, the key to joy, makes hearts expand.
Patience and prudence you'll need to ascend;
   For prudence, patience is a needed friend.
Some plants are poisonous—think before you bite.
   Prudence gave all the Prophets power and light.
Just worthless straw will jump with every breeze— 215
   How can the wind make mountains feel unease?
From every side a monster calls you near:
   'Brother, if you desire the path, come here!
I'll show the way and travel by your side,
   For on the secret path I am the guide.'
He's not a guide and doesn't know the way—
   Joseph, don't head towards the wolf today!*
Prudence will save you from a cheap seduction
   By worldly traps which lead to your destruction.
This world is neither beautiful nor sweet, 220
   But in your ear, like spells, it will repeat:
'Come as my guest—you're worthy of a throne.
   My home's yours; you're just like one of my own.'
Prudence would say, 'My stomach feels unwell,'
   Or 'This world's graveyard pains me more than hell,'
Or 'I've a headache which won't go away,'
   Or 'I'm invited somewhere else today,'
Because the world gives only sweets that sting;
   Many sores and discomfort they will bring.
If it gives gold coins to a fish, first look 225
   And you will see it's all bait on a hook.
What is bestowed by tricksters who deceive?
   Rotten walnuts are all that you'll receive;
Their rattling sound will lead your brain astray
   And they think intellects are easy prey.
Your purse and kit-bag are all you require;
   If you're Ramin, Vis is your sole desire.*

Your true Vis and beloved is your essence,
    While outward things are banes which form a nuisance.
Prudence means, on receiving invitations,   230
    You don't think 'They love me' and buy flirtations.
They are like hunters' whistles used as bait—
    The hunter blows, then, camouflaged, he'll wait.
He'll even show a dead bird to pretend
    It is the mournful calling of a friend.
Foolish birds think it is one of their kin
    And gather round—he will soon flay their skin.
The bird with prudence is the sole exception—
    It isn't fooled by flattery and deception.
Imprudence leads to much repentance, friend.   235
    The following will help you comprehend.

How the villager tracked the townsman and invited him with much pleading and flattery

A townsman from among the urban gentry
    Had got to know a bumpkin from the country,
And every time that country bumpkin could
    Visit he would stay in his neighbourhood:
He would stay two or three months as a guest
    At work and at his home, where he would rest,
And anything that he found necessary
    The townsman would provide without a fee.
The bumpkin asked the townsman, 'Why not make   240
    A trip to my home village for a break?
By God, bring all your children—we have room.
    In springtime you can watch the flowers bloom;
In summer ripened fruit is such a sight,
    And I'll be at your service day and night.
Bring your whole family and your retinue.
    Stay in our village for a month or two.
In summer, all admire the countryside
    With farms and tulip fields on every side.'

The townsman promised, 'On the next occasion,'   245
   But many years passed since that invitation.
Each year the bumpkin would repeat, 'Remember
   Your promise! When will you come? It's December!'
The townsman made the same excuse each year:
   'A guest is visiting; I must stay here.
Next year, if I can I will find a way
   To take time off work for a holiday.'
The villager said, 'All my family
   Await yours, my good man, so eagerly.'
Just like a stork that bumpkin would appear   250
   And settle on that townsman's land each year.
That gentleman would generously spend
   His wealth to welcome him as a true friend;
The last time, for three months that man prepared
   So many feasts with no expenses spared.
The bumpkin asked the nobleman from shame:
   'How many promises? Is this a game?'
'I'm keen to come,' the townsman then replied,
   'But all depends on what God should decide.
A man is like a sailing-boat: each day   255
   He waits for God to send some wind his way.'
The villager would plead repeatedly:
   'Come with your children. View the scenery!'
He took his hand three times, to make him swear,
   Saying: 'Give me your word that you'll come there.'
After years of repeated invitations
   And promises with more procrastinations,
The townsman's children said: 'Dad, take a break!
   Even the moon and clouds have trips to make.
That poor man feels indebted still to you—   260
   You went to so much trouble and he knew.
He wants to try to pay you back as best
   He can, by hosting you there as his guest.
In secret, many times he let us know
   By saying, "Children, try to make him go!"'
The townsman said, '*Sebawayh*, this is true,
   But those you're kind to could be harming you!'*

Love is the seed which sprouts in the last instance;
   It might have rotted while kept at a distance.
Companionship is a sharp sword one wields—   265
   Like winter, it will devastate all fields;
Companionship is like the spring's arrival—
   It brings immeasurable growth and revival.
Prudence is fearing bad fate: when you see it
   You'll have at least enough time then to flee it.
The Prophet said, '*Prudence means being suspicious*';
   Each step could hide a new snare that is dangerous.
The plain looks clear and level, but beware!
   Don't recklessly step on a deadly snare.
'Where is the snare?' ask scoffing billy-goats—   270
   They'll fall into the snare up to their throats!
You who demanded 'Where?', turn here your face—
   You saw the pasture, not the lurking-place.
Unless it is a cunning hunter's snare,
   Would you expect to find a sheep's tail there?
You who walk fearlessly above the ground,
   Look at the bones and skulls now strewn around.
The next time that you pass the graveyard's gate
   Ask the bones to recount to you their fate,
In order to observe and benefit   275
   From knowing how blind drunks fell in the pit
Of their delusion. Look on carefully
   Or hold on to your cane if you can't see!
Lacking prudence and guidance as your cane,
   Take as your guide an eye, or else remain
Without that cane or eye and forced to hide
   Instead of standing there without a guide.
Walk forward like the blind do, bit by bit,
   To dodge the dog and to avoid the pit.
Trembling, each puts his foot down with great care,   280
   Fearful lest he should fall into a snare.
You fled from smoke to fire, and for the sake
   Of scraps of food you're now food for the snake!

Story of the People of Sheba and how God's bounty to them
made them disobedient, and how misfortune visited them owing
to their disobedience and infidelity, and an explanation of the
virtue of gratitude and fidelity*

You've not heard Sheba's story, or instead
    You have perceived just sounds from what was said.
The mountain can't perceive the echo's sounds,
    Let alone reach the meaning it expounds;
It makes a clamour but lacks brain and ears—
    When you fall silent its sound disappears.
God gave the People of Sheba rest and ease,   285
    Palaces, orchards, and great luxuries;
Those wicked ones then showed ungratefulness
    And proved much worse than dogs in faithfulness.
If at your door a dog receives food, then
    It strives to please when passing by again;
It will stand by your door and serve as guard,
    Even if circumstances make that hard—
It will stay by your door due to that food,
    Deem choosing others sheer ingratitude.
And if a stray dog enters in a town,   290
    The local dogs give it a dressing down,
Saying, 'Go back home! One must never part!
    To pay back kindness you must pledge your heart.'
They'll bite it saying, 'Go, immediately.
    Don't leave unpaid their generosity.'
You drank life-giving water at the door
    Of mystics, till your eyes could see once more.
And you've gained gratitude and selflessness
    With ecstasies from their door's huge largesse,
Yet, due to greed, you have since shunned their door   295
    And wander bear-like now around each store—
You hope to find mere gravy-soaked fresh bread,
    But all the donors' pots hold fat instead.
'Fat' means a soul which grows and is enlightened;
    Thereby the plight of desperate men is lightened.

How the afflicted would gather every morning at the door of Jesus' cell in the hope of being healed through his prayer

Jesus' cell's the Sufi's table-spread:
    Don't shun that doorway, heed well what I've said!
From all around each morning people came,
    Those dressed in rags, the blind ones and the lame,
To Jesus' cell's doorway in petition,   300
    So, through his breath, he'd free them from affliction.
Once he had finished his own litany
    That godly man would come outside and see
Weak and afflicted people all around,
    Hoping his doorway is where cures are found.
'Afflicted people, all your needs,' he'd say,
    'The Lord has granted mercifully today,
So walk without a struggle, properly,
    To His forgiving generosity.'
Like camels once their knees have been untied   305
    All suddenly stood up from far and wide
After his prayer, and they'd run self-assured
    Back to their homes now they felt they'd been cured.

You've found your own afflictions similarly
    And from the mystics gained the remedy:
Often your limp would disappear again,
    Your soul would also be relieved from pain.
Tie up your legs and feet, forgetful one,
    Lest you become lost just as they have done—
Forgetfulness and lack of gratitude   310
    Made you forget that you've gained special food.
The way is blocked now to keep you apart,
    Since you've made weary every mystic's heart.
Find them and beg forgiveness desperately
    Just as a heavy cloud weeps bitterly,
So that their roses bloom in your direction
    And ripened fruits burst forth for your selection.

Rush there now! Don't act worse than dogs, you knave,
  You fellow slave of that dog in the cave!*
Since even dogs at times advise another,   315
  'Attach your heart to your first home, my brother.
Cling to the door where you first ate a bone
  And pay the debt for kindness that was shown.'
They'll bite it till politely that dog goes
  Back to its first home, where it thrives and grows:
They bark, 'Rude dog, return immediately!
  Don't be your benefactor's enemy.
Just like the door-ring that's attached to it
  Cling to that door, prepared, alert and fit.
Don't ever break the pledge of loyalty.   320
  Don't spread disloyalty so thoughtlessly.
It's through their loyalty that dogs earned fame,
  So don't shame them and give them a bad name.
For dogs, disloyalty's dishonourable
  So how can you think it's allowable?
God too has taken pride in faithfulness:
  Who is more true than me to promises?
Shunning God makes loyal men turn treacherous—
  God's rights come first, ahead of all of us.
Even your mother, whose rights we all know,   325
  Owes much to God for your own embryo:
Inside her body He created you;
  In pregnancy, He gave her comfort too.
She felt you joined to her as a new part—
  His providence pulled what was joined apart.
God's made a thousand mechanisms too,
  So that your mother gives her love to you.
God's rights come first before your mother's, friend—
  Only a donkey fails to comprehend!
Your mother and her nipples He created,   330
  And it was due to Him your parents mated.
Lord, Whose beneficence lives on forever,
  Yours is what I do and don't know together.
You've ordered us, 'Remember God! My rights
  Do not expire with passing days and nights.

Recall the kindness I showed you that day—
 In Noah's ark I kept you from harm's way,
That time when to your ancestors I gave
 Sanctuary from the storms and each fierce wave;
Like fire, an all-consuming flood emerged;   335
 Even the tops of mountains were submerged—
I saved you and did not desert you then,
 Inside your ancestors among those men.
Now that you've risen to the top, could I
 Strike you down, wasting all my work thereby?
Why mix with such unfaithful men today
 And, through sick thoughts, like them fall far astray?
I am immune to infidelity
 And negligence, so why think bad of Me?
Take all these sick thoughts back to where they came—   340
 You're two-faced, joined with men who are the same.
You have found many comrades—where are they?
 You know the truth is they have gone away.
To heaven soared your good friend of true worth;
 The wicked one fell underneath the earth.
Now you remain here, helpless, in between
 Like camp-fires where a caravan has been—
So seize the hem of one who can transcend
 Dimensions like above and under, friend!
He doesn't rise like Jesus used to soar,   345
 Nor, like Korah, fall into earth's deep core*—
He's with you here now, then beyond space when
 You leave behind wealth to seek God again.
He can clean up the worst contaminations
 And treats as faithful your abominations:
His scolding for bad actions is direction
 To lead you from your flawed state to perfection.'

When you neglect your litanies, you feel
 Contraction's* pain and heat, which prove it's real:
This is God's own corrective punishment,   350
 Which says, 'Don't stray from our old covenant,

Lest that contraction turn into a chain,
   Or shackles for your feet grow from your pain:
Your mental pain will soon be visible,
   So don't ignore this as dismissible!
Contraction after sins may hurt you now—
   At That Hour it will be a chain somehow!
If you block Our Remembrance from your mind
   *We'll send a hard life and We'll make you blind.**
So when a thief takes someone's property   355
   Contraction gives his heart pain inwardly:
'I wonder what that is?' the thief then says—
   The victim's pain caused by your wicked ways.
When he stops feeling his contraction's shame
   The winds of perseverance fan each flame.
The heart's contraction brings the thief's arrest
   As every truth is soon made manifest.
The pangs turn into gaol and gibbets, so
   The pang's the root from which such branches grow;
The root was hidden—now it's manifest: 360
   Contraction is the root which sprouts the rest.
When the root's bad, strike it until it's gone
   Or weeds will grow and ruin your fine lawn.
You've felt contraction—find the remedy,
   Since from the roots grow branches of the tree;
You've felt expansion*—quickly water it
   And share its fruit with each associate!

The remainder of the Story of the People of Sheba

The Sheba people lacked maturity,
   Ungrateful for God's generosity.
As one example of their thanklessness,   365
   They'd quarrel with their Lord, the Generous,
Saying: 'We don't need kindness now from You.
   Why irritate us with kind things You do?
Do us a favour: take away Your kindness.
   We don't want eyes, so cause us to have blindness!'

The Sheba people would then also say:
    '*Stay out! Give flaws! Take beauty far away!*
We don't want mansions, orchards with fine trees,
    Beautiful girls, security and ease.
We don't like neighbours who reside too near,   370
    Preferring deserts with wild beasts men fear.'
In summer, Man wants winter to be sent,
    But if the winter comes he's not content,
For he is never pleased with his conditions,
    Neither when poor nor when he has provisions.
Ingratitude! May he be killed today!*
    When he gains guidance he throws it away.
The self is like this—it is better dead:
    '*Kill yourself!*'* God, the Most Sublime, has said.
It's a three-pointed thorn—how then can you   375
    Prevent this one from pricking into you?
Burn the thorn with the fire of shunning lust!
    Cling to the Friend's kind hands, which you can trust.
When they'd exceeded all the boundaries,
    Saying: 'The plague is better than the breeze',
Their counsellors then warned the multitude
    To save them from depraved ingratitude—
They aimed to kill them rather than take heed,
    Sowing perverse ingratitude's bad seed.
The world seems very cramped when fate decrees,   380
    And halva gives mouths painful injuries.
The Prophet said, '*Fate can reduce the size*
    Of open space, block vision from your eyes.'
And fate can put upon your eyes a seal,
    So they can't see the kohl salve which can heal.
Galloping riders raise much dust—that made
    It hard for you to cry out for some aid.
Head for the horseman, not the dust! Keep running
    Or you'll lose out due to that horseman's cunning.
'The one whom this fierce wolf devoured', God said,   385
    'Saw its dust—why did it not cry for aid?
Could it not recognize the fierce wolf's dust?
    Without such knowledge, why graze there with trust?

Sheep can smell dangerous wolves from yards away
    And so they scamper every which way;
The lion's scent is known to a sheep's brain,
    Which tells them to stop grazing on that plain,
But of wrath's lion's scent are you aware?
    Turn back! Return to caution and to prayer!

That group gazed at the wolf's dust all the same;   390
    They stayed until the wolf of terror came.
Enraged, it tore apart those sheep, whose eyes
    Had closed to wisdom's shepherd and his cries.
They never came though he called frequently,
    But threw dust in his eyes contemptuously,
Saying, 'We're better shepherds—go away!
    We're each chiefs—we can't follow what you say.
We're not for God, but for the wolf to eat,
    Fuel for the fire, not modesty's fine meat!'
There was a heathen pride inside their brains;   395
    The crow squawked loudly over their remains.
Digging a pit designed for the oppressed,
    They fell in and cried out, 'Alas!', distressed.
They tore the coats of Joseph, and each crime
    Of theirs came back to haunt them in good time.
Who's Joseph? Your God-seeking heart of course,
    Chained by your self, like prisoners, by force;
A Gabriel you have tied up with a tether
    And now you tear his wings and pluck each feather.
You bring a roasted calf for it to eat   400
    Or even straw, as if that is a treat,
Saying, 'Eat up! For us, this is some spread!'
    Its nourishment is meeting God instead.
Due to this tribulation, grief, and pain,
    You've made it turn to God now to complain:
'Save me from that old wolf, dear God!' it cries.
    'The hour is near; have patience!' He replies,
'From them I will get justice now for you.'
    Except God who can order justice? Who?

It says, 'My patience has worn thin, my Lord,   405
  Kept far from Your face, which I have adored.
I'm Ahmad, left as captive of those Jews,
  Saleh in Thamud's gaol, due to their ruse.*
Giver of joy to souls of prophets, please
  Kill me, or call me back, or come! Don't tease!
Infidels can't bear missing You as well—
  *"Would that I'd been mere dust!"** they loudly yell.
The opposite sort even feel this way—
  How can Your own then bear to be away!'
God says, 'All right, pure one, but listen too.   410
  Be patient: patience is the best for you.
It will be dawn soon. Hush! Don't wail and roar.
  I'll strive for you, and you need strive no more.

Remainder of the story about the townsman going to the village at the invitation of the villager

Enough of this! Turn back! No longer roam!
  The bumpkin took the townsman to his home.
Now put the Sheba people's tale aside.
  Tell how the townsman reached the countryside.
The country bumpkin used some flattery
  To weaken his resolve most cleverly:
Repeated pleading played tricks with his mind,   415
  Clear water turned thus to the murky kind,
And due to his own children's powerful sway
  When they sang in approval, '*Let us play!*'*
Like Joseph, whom, because of fate's selection
  '*Let's play!*'* stole from his father's close protection.
That's gambling with one's life, not having fun;
  It's cunning, fraud, and lies rolled into one.
If something drives you from your sweetheart, friend,
  Don't heed it, for it brings loss in the end;
Though it should offer gains a hundredfold,   420
  Don't leave the treasure's owner for some gold!
But heed how God rebuked some of the best—
  Companions of the Prophet failed this test:

In straitened circumstances, during prayer
    They had a dream, and right away rushed there:
'We void our prayers lest others step ahead
    And all the discounts go to them instead.'
The Prophet, though, continued praying then
    With one or two unwavering, yearning men.
God said, 'By bargain discounts' drums, how can   425
    You be led far from this most holy man?
For mere wheat you have scampered madly there,
    And left the Prophet standing during prayer.
In hope of wheat, you've sown a futile seed;
    The Messenger of Truth you all should heed.
His company's worth more than wealth and playing;
    See who it is you left back there still praying!
To your greed was it not made manifest
    That out of all providers I'm the best?'
He who's placed nourishment in every grain,   430
    Won't let your trust in Him be all in vain.
For wheat's sake you've abandoned that One who
    Has sent the wheat down from the sky to you!

The invitation of the falcon to the ducks to come from water to the desert

A falcon tells a duck, 'Leave water, rise
    To see the lovely plains with your own eyes.'
The wise duck tells him, 'Falcon, disappear!
    Water's our fortress, where we're safe from fear.'
The devil's like the falcon—ducks, beware
    Not to stray from your fortress to its snare.
Say to the falcon: 'Go away! Turn back!   435
    Keep your hands off us! Don't you dare attack!
Infidel, keep your invitation—we
    Will not fall for your clever sophistry.
This fort is ours, the lovely plains for you.
    We turn your offer down—you keep that too.
While there is life, food's found inside this world.
    Where there's an army banners are unfurled.'

The townsman gave profuse apologies,
 To answer that most wicked bumpkin's pleas:
He said, 'I have important work to do—   440
 If I come now, it won't be then seen to.
The king asked me to fix a situation;
 He hasn't slept and waits in expectation.
I do not dare neglect the king's command;
 I can't fail him—you surely understand.
An officer each morning and each night
 Asks me to show the way to put it right—
Should I instead come to your village now
 And make the sultan fiercely knit his brow?
How would I cool his anger and survive?   445
 To come means burying myself alive!'
Scores of excuses came thus from this man,
 But they weren't in accord with God's own plan.
Though all the atoms in the world should plot,
 Next to decrees from heaven they're worth naught.
How can the earth escape now from the sky,
 Or hide itself from it? Let's see it try!
When something comes from heaven, earth has no
 Refuge, recourse, nor other place to go.
If fire should rain down on it from the sun,   450
 It lies back and accepts what it has done;
And if a massive deluge should rain down
 To flood and then destroy each single town,
Like Job, earth would submit to its decrees,
 Saying, 'I'm captive—you do as you please.'
You who are part of earth, don't disobey.
 When you see God's decree, don't turn away.
'*We made you from mere dust*,'* you've heard ring round,
 So act just like dust and don't turn around.
God said, 'Look how I sow the seeds with care—   455
 It's lowly, then I raise it up from there.
Adopt the practice of humility
 And I'll give you the most nobility.'
Water moves from above below; from there
 It will evaporate back to the air.

Grain went down into earth originally,
    Then, as corn ears, it sprang up suddenly.
Into the earth sink seeds from all the fruits
    Then raise their heads up from their buried roots,
As from the heavens bounties all descend,   460
    To serve as fruit for pure souls, my good friend;
When, with humility, they come down, then
    They'll form a part of living, fearless men:
Such things turn into human qualities
    And gaily soar beyond the Pleiades.
'We came down from the living world,' they say,
    'And from this low state we've returned today.'
All atoms, moving or just stationary,
    Say, '*We're returning to Him*'* constantly;
The *zekr** and praise by atoms, which are hidden,   465
    Send constantly a clamour up to heaven.
The time a spell-like song was sung by fate
    A bumpkin trapped a townsman in checkmate.
Despite his firm resolve, once he was mated
    That journey led him to where grief was fated.
He had relied on his own firm resolve,
    Something a tiny flood could still dissolve.
When fate looks out from heaven, you will find
    Intelligent men can turn deaf and blind,
Fish will get flung about then by the sea,   470
    And flying birds get snared so easily;
Genies will go back in their bottles then,
    And Harut back to Babylon again;*
Only if you embrace fate can you flee
    From fate and being slain by destiny.
Embrace your fate itself to find release;
    Your clever tricks won't win you inner peace.

Story of the People of Zarwan and how they schemed to pick
the fruit in the orchards without being troubled by paupers*

    You've read about the Zarwan nation—now
        Why keep on seeking out schemes anyhow?

Scorpion-like men would scheme plots to deprive   475
  Paupers from food they needed to survive.
These men conspired their wicked plots all night,
  Putting their heads together out of sight—
They whispered secretly while sitting near
  To try to make sure that God wouldn't hear.
Can clay conspire against the potter's art?
  Can one's own acts be hidden from the heart?
'*Does not Your Maker know your wish?*' God said,*
  '*Whether your prayer's sincere or false instead?*'
How should those sneaking out one morning keep   480
  Hiding from One who knows where they will sleep?
He has already charted and can view
  The stations where he'll mount and dismount too.
Unblock your ears of heedlessness and heed
  The separation felt by hearts that bleed!
When you hear tales from such a person, you
  Are giving alms to that lovelorn one too.
You'll hear about his heartache in this way,
  This noble spirit's trials while trapped in clay:
That pure one's in a house that's smoke-filled here—   485
  Open a window now by giving ear.
Then, it will breathe again, and struggles cease—
  That bitter smoke within will then decrease.
Wayfarer, sympathize with us one time!
  If you are travelling to the Most Sublime.
This dithering is like a gaol or wall,
  Not letting your entrapped soul move at all.
One thing draws you this way, one thing that way—
  'I am the right path!' each of them will say.
This is an obstacle on God's path, friend—   490
  You're blessed if your feet easily can ascend,
Taking the right path with no vacillation.
  If you don't know the way, choose emulation:
Track the deer's footprints left on this dry land
  And you'll eventually reach its sought musk gland.
If you dare, brother, to walk now on fire
  By this means you can reach realms that are higher;

Why fear the ocean's waves or foam? You've heard
    God say, '*Do not fear!*' to you—heed His word!
Remember '*Do not fear!*' when fear descends*—
    He'll send bread since He's sent its basket, friends!
Fearless men will reserve for God their fear;
    Anguish fills those who fail to circle here.

495

The townsman's journey to the village

The townsman got prepared then for the ride,
    And his resolve flew to the countryside.
His wife and children started soon to pack,
    Loading their baggage on the oxen's back,
Then rushed towards the village, clamouring:
    'We'll taste their hand-picked fruit first like a king.
Our destination's a sweet pasture, where
    We have a fine host who is kind and fair;
He begged us to go countless times, not once,
    And planted saplings of benevolence.
From that fine host's huge stock we'll soon bring back,
    For our own town's long winter, things we lack.
He'll give his orchard to us as a whole;
    He'll make a place for us inside his soul.'
Hurry to profits or it will get late!
    Intellect warns though, '*Don't yet celebrate!*'
Seek profit which comes from the King of Kings;
    God warns not to rejoice in other things.
Mildly rejoice in what God sends your way,
    For gifts can all distract you far away.
Delight in Him, not in another thing—
    They are like winter, while He is the spring.
Everything else attracts to fling you down,
    Be it a throne, a kingdom, or a crown.
Rejoice in suffering, for that's union's snare—
    Decline means progress in this strange affair.
Suffering's like treasure and its mine's your pain,
    But teaching children this can be in vain:

500

505

510

When children hear the word 'game', they all race,
    Just like wild asses, quickly to that place.
Blind donkeys, hidden traps, await this side.
    Much blood's shed here with nowhere left to hide.
The bow stays hidden, but the arrows fly—
    A hundred strike your youth now from the sky.
You must step in the heart's own plain today—
    No opening is found in bodily clay.
The heart is where one can find safety, friend,   515
    And rose gardens with fountains that don't end.
Night travellers turn towards the heart and go
    Where you'll find trees and springs which freely flow.
Avoid the country—it makes fun of you.
    It steals your wisdom's light and splendour too.
The Prophet warned: 'Countryside will prepare
    Your intellect's grave if you settle there.'
Stay in the countryside one day or night,
    For one whole month your wisdom won't feel right:
For one month you'll possess stupidity—   520
    What can be reaped from wild hashish? Tell me!
Spend a whole month out there and you will find
    You'll stay for ages ignorant and blind.
What's countryside? Shaikhs short of union's station
    Who're still embroiled in proofs and imitation.
Near Universal Intellect, sense still
    Is a blind donkey circling for a mill.
Set this aside—follow the tale's form here:
    Leave the rare pearl and opt for a wheat ear;
If you can't go that way, then choose this way;   525
    Take wheat if you can't take the pearl today.
Take its form, though it's crooked, my dear friend.
    It leads to inner depths still in the end.
Each human's start is with a form, then later
    The soul comes, which is beauty in behaviour;
Form is each fruit's original beginning—
    After that comes sweet taste, its actual meaning.
At first, the tent is made, or else it's bought,
    Then they invite a Turkman to that spot:

Your form's the tent, the Turkman is your essence;   530
    Your form's a ship, the sailor is your essence.
End this talk for a moment, for God's sake,
    And let the townsman's ass's bells all shake!

The merchant and his family go to the village

The townsman and his children packed their things
    And galloped out on steeds, as if on wings,
So joyously across the countryside,
    '*Travel to gain!*' they'd shout as they would ride.
The moon becomes, through travelling, Kaykhosrow*—
    How else could it become like him and grow?
Travel can turn a pawn into a queen   535
    And bring to Joseph outcomes he'd foreseen.*
Their faces all got sunburned then by day;
    By night, through stars they worked out the right way.
To them, the ugly route looked very nice;
    Love of the country made it paradise.
Sweet-lipped ones can make bitterness turn sweet;
    The rosebush makes thorns seem a lovely treat.
Bitter plants, through the Loved One, turn to dates.
    Houses seem bigger with the right housemates.
Many a fine youth bore sharp thorns, so soon   540
    He'd win a rose-cheeked girl fair as the moon.
Many a porter broke his back, all for
    The moonfaced sweetheart whom he valued more.
The blacksmith made his face black, so by night
    He'd earn a kiss from one whose face is white.
The trader stands till nightfall in his store,
    Because a lovely figure fills his core;
The merchant travels by the land and sea
    Through love for one who stays home patiently.
Whoever longs for something that is dead   545
    Really hopes for a living thing instead.
The carpenter will focus on mere wood,
    So for his sweetheart he'll make something good.

Struggle then for a living lover too,
  One who won't die within a day or two.
Don't choose a base man as companion—
  His friendship's borrowed, not to count upon.
Where now's your closeness to your parents, friend?
  Closeness to anyone but God must end,
And this includes your wet-nurse and your tutor   550
  As no one else is truly your supporter—
Your love of milk and nipples didn't last,
  Nor your dislike of school once in the past.
That was like sunlight shining on a door,
  That trace returned back to the sun once more.
When sunlight's rays fall on things from above
  Then those things stir within you passionate love.
Your love for such existents, truth be told,
  Arises from God's covering them with gold.
But, when gold leaves them, copper's what will stay—   555
  With senses sated you'll throw that away.
Step back now from its gilded form! Speak less,
  In ignorance, of its attractiveness
Because that beauty's borrowed, and you'll see
  It hides an ugly, foul reality.
Gold flees from base coin to the mine, its source—
  You now should follow gold and take its course.
Light rays flee from the wall back to the sun—
  Head to the sun, which is the perfect one.
Drink water only from the skies, since you   560
  Have not found in canals what will stay true.
Wild wolves are lured by sheep's tails and don't know
  About the source which formed them down below.

They rushed, deluded, to the countryside,
  Imagining gold was neatly wrapped inside.
They danced and laughed away so merrily
  Whirling around each water-wheel they'd see.
Whenever they saw birds which flew ahead,
  Eagerness for the village filled each head.

And they would fondly kiss each person's face   565
    Coming towards them from that sought-out place:
'You have seen our beloved's face,' they'd say,
    'So you're as dear as our own eyes today.'

How Majnun petted that dog which lived in Layli's neighbourhood*

Just like Majnun who'd pet a dog and kiss
    And croon then over it—they'd act like this.
Majnun would humbly circle it and pour
    Rose syrup in its bowl from his own store.
'Majnun!' a person watching called one day,
    'Why do you always act so mad this way?
Dog's muzzles touch filth everywhere they go,   570
    And they lick their own genitals below.'
He gave a long list of the dog's flaws too—
    About wise men fault-finders have no clue.
Majnun replied, 'You just see form and size.
    Come here and view beyond those through my eyes!
For it's a talisman sealed by the Lord—
    It is the guard-dog watching Layli's road.
Look at its soul—that dog can recognize!
    Its choice of where to live shows that it's wise.
It is the blest dog of the cave to me.*   575
    It shares in all my grief and agony.
That dog of her lane—I'd not give one hair
    From it to lions, though trapped in their lair.
Lions are slaves to Layli's dogs, so I
    Think there's no point in saying more. Goodbye!'
If from mere outward form you can transcend,
    You'll reach such heavenly gardens, my good friend.
When you've smashed your own form, then this will bring
    Knowledge of breaking forms of everything.
You'll smash then every form that still awaits—   580
    Like Ali, you'll dislodge those Khaybar gates.*
Form duped that townsman with a simple brain,
    For he accepted words that were all vain,

And rushed with joy to flattery's own snare
   As birds rush to the bait that tempts them there:
The bird deemed it a gift like some fine seed,
   But it was not a gift—it was sheer greed.
Little birds, lusting for the bait, feel joy
   And fly towards what is a mere false ploy.
That townsman's joy if I were to relate,   585
   Wayfarer, I fear that I'd make you late.
I'll be brief: when a village came to view
   It was the wrong one—he set off anew.
Village to village, he went round and round,
   Not knowing where the right one might be found.
Without a guide, a two-day trip will take
   A hundred years, so don't make this mistake.
Those on the Hajj without a proper guide
   Fall low like these fools who'd grown stupefied.
Without a teacher, one took up a craft—   590
   His work was so poor everybody laughed.
From East to West, to be born is so rare
   If there aren't any parents over there.
A man who earns grows wealthy, but it's rare
   For someone to find treasure lying there.
The Prophet's body was like soul—where can
   We find one whom *Kind God taught the Qur'an?**
'*He taught with pen*'* as intermediary
   To all attached to body generously.
The greedy are forbidden this, my son,   595
   So slow down! Only greedy fools would run.
The journey's toil drained that man from the town
   Like landbirds falling where they could soon drown.
All of them grew sick of the countryside
   And sweet-talk from that bumpkin with such pride.

The townsman and his group reach the village, but the bumpkin
is nowhere to be found

When finally they stopped, a month had passed,
   All food consumed, steeds breathing now their last.

That evil bumpkin had deliberately
   Continued to make them face difficulty.
By day he'd hide his face from them, lest they   600
   Fed from his orchard and declined to pay.
A face so full of evil and cruel lies
   Should be kept far away from good men's eyes!
Demons are perched like flies on such vile faces,
   As if they are the guards of sought-out places.
When you should see that face they'll set on you—
   Don't look! At least don't smile back if you do.
Concerning such a face have you not read—
   '*We'll drag him by the forelock!*'* God has said.
They asked and found that man's house finally,   605
   Then hurried to his door like family.
At once the door was bolted from inside,
   Making the townsman mad at what he'd tried.
It wasn't now the time to get aggressive:
   Trapped down a well, there's no point being abrasive.
They stayed there by the door for five full days,
   Freezing at night, then burned by the sun's rays.
Their staying wasn't mere stupidity—
   They had naught left: it was necessity.
When forced, good men might join those fit for hell;   610
   If starved, lions eat carcasses as well.
The townsman saw him and called out, 'Hello!
   This is my name and I am so-and-so.'
He would reply, 'Maybe? I can't be sure
   Who you are—dirty foe or friend who's pure.'
The townsman then would say, 'I see a brother,
   Like at the last hour, fleeing from another!
I am the one from whose rich table you
   Ate all the fine food that you wanted to.
I bought those goods that sunny afternoon;   615
   A secret shared with more than one spreads soon:
All know about the kindness shown by me—
   Past dinner guests should show humility.'
He answered, 'Nonsense! Why is it you came?
   I don't know where you're from or what's your name.'

A violent storm began on the fifth night—
    Even the sky was stunned at such a sight.
The townsman, who could not take any more,
    Screamed, 'Call your master!' as he banged the door.
After a hundred calls, the man came out: 620
    'Gentleman, tell me what you've come about.'
'I now renounce each single previous claim
    And all that I presumed when I first came.
Five years of suffering I've felt these five days,
    Standing unsheltered from the sun's hot rays.'
A sole injustice from a friend or brother
    Is worse than millions of them from another,
Because the victim won't expect injustice
    From those who normally would show him kindness.
Some acts seem harsher therefore to men's eyes   625
    Because they are both wrong and a surprise.
He added, 'Sun whose grace now fades from view,
    Shed my blood—I'll say it's allowed to you.
This rainy night give us a place to stay
    And gather your reward on Judgment Day.'
'There is the gardener's shelter,' he replied.
    'At night he usually stands as guard inside,
Carrying bow and arrow just in case
    The wolf should wander up towards that place.
If it's of use, tonight call it your own;   630
    If not, find somewhere else! Leave me alone!'
'I would be grateful if you should bestow
    That place to me with arrows and a bow.
I won't sleep but I'll guard your vines instead,
    And if the wolf shows up, I'll shoot it dead.
You two-faced man, don't leave us here again
    On ground that's sludgy due to pouring rain!'
The townsman and his family then went
    To that cramped hovel which they had been lent.
Like piles of locusts, they were forced to lie   635
    Together lest a huge flood should pass by.
They cried, 'O God!' throughout that desperate night,
    'This is what we deserve. It serves us right.'

This is what's earned if you befriend the base
 Or treat such people courteously with grace.
This is what's earned by those who from sheer lust
 Should stop revering noble people's dust:
Licking the dust that pure men leave behind
 Earns more than vines of vulgar men you'll find;
Following mystics who're enlightened brings   640
 More gain than if you lord it over kings.
Apart from drum rolls, from the kings on earth
 You won't gain anything that has real worth.
Next to the spirit, townsmen seem like muggers.
 So what are bumpkins? Naught but worthless failures.
This is what's earned when you don't use your brain—
 You hear the ghoul close by, yet you remain.
The time that true repentance takes possession
 Of your own heart, there's no point in confession.

With bow and arrow in his hand, held tight,   645
 He sought the wolf out, looking left then right.
The wolf had hypnotized him; he'd search there,
 But of his inner wolf stay unaware.
Each gnat became a wolf, and every flea,
 So they could bite now much more viciously.
There was no chance to drive the vile gnats back
 From fear the cruel wolf might launch an attack.
The danger of the wolf caused consternation
 As well as fear of more humiliation
By that cruel bumpkin on that chilly night—   650
 They gnashed their teeth while their souls burst with fright.
The figure of a wolf then suddenly
 Appeared behind a hilltop they could see.
That townsman put an arrow in his bow
 And shot the animal down like a foe.
It farted loudly as it slowly fell—
 This made the bumpkin shake his fists and yell:
'You wretch, that was my ass's colt! He died!'
 'No, it's the wolf,' the townsman then replied.

'It has the features of a wolf; you can   655
   Observe this clearly from its form, good man.'
'The fart it let off told me it was mine;
   It is like telling water from good wine—
You've killed my ass colt claiming you're a friend!
   May you be cursed with farting that won't end!'
He said, 'Observe more carefully. It's night—
   Distinctive features are now veiled from sight.
Things look strange and one's sight's inaccurate;
   At night, not all men's sight is adequate.
It's night with clouds and rain—and all these three   660
   Combined cause visual inaccuracy.'
'For me it is a clear day all the same:
   My ass colt's arse—from there that loud fart came.
Among a thousand, I can tell that fart
   The way that travellers tell their bags apart.'
The townsman leapt up, unperturbed, and held
   The bumpkin by his collar, as he yelled:
'Idiot thief, you're lying or you're blind!
   You've smoked hashish and opium both combined.
How can you tell your ass's fart at night   665
   When you can't recognize me in the light!
He who, at midnight, easily can tell
   His colt, can recognize a friend as well.'

You act like mystics in ecstatic highs,
   Throwing dust in munificence's eyes,
Claiming: 'I've lost myself! I'm unaware!
   My heart lets none but God to enter there.
What I ate yesterday I can't recall;
   My heart loves deep perplexity—that's all.
I'm both sane and insane through God—it's bliss,   670
   And I'm excused when selfless just like this.'
Men who drink date wine or eat carrion can
   Still be excused by law despite the ban.*
If drunk or high, one can't divorce or trade:
   One's like a child, absolved—one's debts are paid.

A hundred vats could not cause drunkenness
    Like that from scent blown from His holiness.
The horse is legless—it won't rise at all.
    How can such men be held responsible?
Who would put on an ass colt heavy loads   675
    Or try to teach the Devil Persian odes?
The load is taken off when it is lame,
    As God has said, '*For blind men there's no blame.*'*
'I see through God and of myself I'm blind,
    So I'm absolved of sins of every kind.'
You boast of dervishhood and selflessness,
    And holler like one drunk in God, no less,
Saying, 'I cannot now tell land from sky'—
    God's jealousy's test, though, proves that you lie.
Your ass colt's fart has brought you such deep shame,   680
    Showing you still exist despite your claim.
This is how God can put to shame a fraud;
    This is how fleeing prey is caught by God.
A million tests await for anyone
    Who claims, 'I am the captain!' Heed this, son!
Even if simple men can't understand,
    The adepts know what proof they should demand.
A wretch may claim to be a tailor, but
    The king will throw before him silk to cut:
'Make a fine robe from this that's bound to stun!'   685
    This test will show him up to everyone.
If one did not test bad men, on that day
    Effete men would seem Rostams in the fray!
Even if they wear armour, one soft blow
    Will make them feeble captives of the foe.
A breeze can't shake one drunk in God awake
    When he won't wake for the Last Day's blast's sake.*
The wine of God is true and strong, my friend—
    You've drunk mere yoghurt and wish to pretend.
Jonayd or Bayazid you claim to be:*   690
    'Drunk, I can't tell an axe now from a key.'
Through fraud, how will you hide sloth, lust, and greed?
    Trickster, when will you finally take heed?

You claim to be Mansur Hallaj, and set
    Aflame the cotton of the friends you get:*
'I can't tell Omar and Bu Lahab apart,*
    But still at night I know my ass's fart!'
Only a donkey would believe that's true,
    Making itself both blind and deaf for you.
Don't claim you're travelling on the mystic way—   695
    You spoil the path. Rubbish is all you say.
Fly back from fraud to intellect. Don't lie!
    How can false wings enable you to fly?
Your claim to be God's lover is an act,
    For you make love with demons now in fact.
On Resurrection, lovers shall be tied
    With those they love and then be brought outside—
You now act drunk and witless—tell me how?
    Where is your wine? You're drinking our blood now.
I do not recognize you—go away!   700
    'I am love-crazed like Bohlul,' you still say.
Nearness to God is just a dream you claim;
    To you the plate and potter are the same.
You don't know that the saint's proximity
    Means miracles and powerful majesty:
David turned iron to wax*—please understand
    Wax turns to iron if placed in your vile hand.
God is near all and gives them food to eat;
    Love's revelation comes to His elite.
Proximity's of various kinds, my son—   705
    Mountains and goldmines feel rays from the sun,
But mines of gold have a proximity
    That's never fathomed by the willow tree;
Dry and fresh branches both are near the sun—
    How should the sun be veiled from either one?
The fresh branch bears fruit, even if no nearer—
    It feeds you ripe fruit, so it is superior.
From nearness to it, branches that are dry
    Gain nothing—they will quickly rot and die.
Don't be the kind of drunkard who invents it—   710
    On sobering up from his act, he regrets it.

No, be a drunkard whose wild drunkenness
　　Makes intellectuals feel so envious.
O cat, you've caught a mouse that's now half-dead—
　　With powerful wine one catches lions instead.
You've drunk the empty glass of fantasy—
　　Don't reel like those who're drunken mystically.
Just like a drunk you're staggering about—
　　You're in this realm—you've not found a way out.
The time you find a path that leads you yonder　　715
　　Swing your head side to side, then dance and holler.
You're fully down here—not another breath!
　　Don't agonize as if you've tasted death.
If Khezr-souled ones who don't fear death should state
　　They don't know creatures, that's appropriate.
You salivate for what's not really there—
　　You fill your bag of selfhood with hot air,
Then, with one prick, you'll empty and fall flat—
　　May no wise body get as fat as that!
In winter, you make pots from snow, but they　　720
　　Will not last, holding water, for one day.

How the jackal fell into the dyeing vat, became multi-coloured, and claimed to the other jackals that it was a peacock

A jackal strayed into the dyeing vat
　　And stayed in there for such a long time that
Its skin was dyed. When finally it came out,
　　'I'm paradise's peacock!' it would shout.
Its coloured fur had gained a pretty splendour
　　And sunlight would reflect upon each colour.
It saw itself as golden, red, and green,
　　And stepped out proudly, eager to be seen.
The others asked, 'What has got into you?　　725
　　You've grown deluded and exultant too.
Due to this glee, you're snubbing us for once—
　　Where did you find this twisted arrogance?'

One of the jackals asked, 'Are you a fraud?
　　Or are you really feeling bliss through God?'
To climb the pulpit you have used deceit;
　　Your babble saddens everyone you meet.
You've not gained any ardour, though you've tried,
　　And so you've acted shamelessly and lied.
Ardour is for a Prophet and God's Friend;　　　　　　730
　　Impudence suits impostors who pretend,
To draw men's eyes towards themselves with pride,
　　Then claim, 'We're blissful!' though they're glum inside.

*How a boaster greased his lips and moustache every morning
with the skin of a sheep's tail, and came out to his associates,
saying: 'I've eaten such-and-such!'*

A poor man found a sheep's tail, which he used
　　To grease his moustache, to leave men confused:
He mingled with the wealthy, whom he'd tell:
　　'I've feasted at a party—can't you tell?'
He'd then touch his moustache as if to say:
　　'There's grease on my moustache—all look this way!
This is the proof that what I claim is true;　　　　　735
　　The food I ate was rich and tasty too.'
His stomach would in silence then reply:
　　'*God ruin all the schemes of those who'd lie!*
Your boasting has engulfed me now in flames.
　　May your moustache be pulled out for your claims!
Beggar, your ugly boasts are blocking me
　　From aid from generous men with sympathy;
If you had shown the ailment and not played,
　　By now a doctor's cure would have been made.'
God said, 'Don't move perversely ears or tails;　　　740
　　The truthfulness of truthful men prevails.'*
Wet-dreamer, don't sleep curled up in that state!
　　Show what you have! *Be steadfast and be straight!**
Admit your flaws or else at least refrain
　　From boasts—your tricks will kill you. They're your bane.

Even if you've got hold of gold, stop talking!
   Touchstones await along the path you're walking,
And there are, for these touchstones, more tests too
   To make sure that their own state's always true.
'From birth to death,' God said, and thus made clear,   745
   'Each one of them is tested twice a year.'*
Test upon test awaits, my friend—don't rest
   So chuffed that you have passed the smallest test.

How Bal'am ben Ba'ur felt secure for God had tested him and he had passed well

Bal'am Ba'ur and Satan both became
   Debased at the last test that finally came.
This man craves wealth, as his claims indicate;
   His belly slams his moustache, though, irate,
Saying: 'Show what he's hiding with that face.
   He has consumed me—God, give him disgrace!
All of his body parts are now his foes—   750
   He boasts of spring while they feel winter's woes.'
Boasting repels the kindness men might show,
   Severs the branch from where it used to grow.
Be silent, if you can't say what is true—
   You'll then see mercy and enjoy it too.
His belly now was his moustache's foe;
   It prayed in secret so he wouldn't know:
'O Lord, disgrace this braggart who is base.
   Bring generous people's kindness in his place!'
An answer came then to the belly's prayer;   755
   Its neediness's fire produced signs there.
'Though you be sinners and idolaters,'
   God said, 'I answer all petitioners.
Hold steadfastly to prayer and weeping too,
   As, from the ghoul, this will deliver you.'
His belly pledged itself to God that day—
   A cat then snatched that man's sheep's tail away.
His family chased that cat to no avail.
   Fear of being scolded turned that man's child pale;

He came towards his father in the crowd,   760
    And caused him to lose face by saying aloud:
'That sheep's tail that you use each break of day
    To grease your lips and moustache in that way—
A cat came by and snatched it suddenly;
    I chased it, but it was too fast for me.'
Those present laughed from sheer amazement then,
    And pity in them was soon moved again—
They each invited him to eat his full,
    Sowing, in his soil, seeds so merciful.
When from the nobles he saw honesty,   765
    He shunned pride to become Truth's devotee.

How the jackal which fell into the dyeing vat pretended to be a peacock

That multi-coloured jackal came one day
    And tapped a critic's earlobe twice, to say:
'Everyone, look at me and all my colours.
    An idol like me dazzles idol-lovers!
Just like a rosebush, I am beautiful
    And colourful—bow down, be dutiful!
Behold my splendour, radiance, hue and glory!
    "Pride of the world", "Pillar of faith"—they suit me.*
I'm now the theatre of God's grace for you,   770
    The Tablet where divinity's shown too.*
Jackals, don't call me "jackal" any more!
    Have you seen one as beautiful before?'
Those jackals gathered, moths to a bright flame—
    To be their candle was that jackal's aim:
'What fitting name can we call you? Tell us,
    Peacock, with Jupiter's auspiciousness!'
They then said, 'Peacocks of the soul display
    Their tails inside the rose garden, don't they?
So can you do that too?' He answered, 'No,   775
    To reach Mena there's a long way to go.'*
'Can you squawk like a peacock then instead?'
    He answered, 'No.' 'You're not one!' they all said.

'The peacock's cloak comes from beyond the skies—
How can you gain that through false claims and lies?'

Comparison of Pharaoh and his claim to divinity with that jackal who claimed to be a peacock

Like Pharaoh, proudly, you now wish to pass
    Lord Jesus, but you fly just like an ass!
Pharaoh was a vile jackal's child like that,
    But he fell into status and wealth's vat:
Whoever saw his wealth and status bowed;   780
    He bought fake worship from those who'd been wowed—
That ragged beggar got intoxicated
    By the stunned looks of those who had prostrated.
Wealth is a snake which has a deadly poison;
    Accepting people's worship is a dragon.
Pharaoh, don't act as if you've majesty.
    Jackal, don't act like peacocks. We can see!
If peacocks should encounter you one day,
    You'll seem a fool—no feathers to display!
Moses and Aaron were like peacocks who   785
    Displayed their feathers straight in front of you.
Your ugliness and shame were brought to sight
    And you fell head first from a lofty height.
The touchstone showed that all your coin was base—
    The lion's gone; a dog's now in its place.
You ugly, wolfish dog, do not put on
    A lion's skin through greed—you fool no one!
The lion's roar will test you, for you lied—
    A lion's semblance with a dog inside.

Exegesis of 'You will know them through the corruption of their speech'*

God told the Prophet, 'Vile hypocrisy   790
    Has a clear sign that you'll see easily:

A hypocrite,* though huge and causing terror,
   Has warped speech that will spare us all from error.'
When you buy earthenware pots, customer,
   You test them out, to see which you prefer—
Why do you tap them first on the outside?
   To check there are no cracks on the inside.
A cracked one sounds distinct from one that's not—
   This is the herald stood before the pot:
The sound tells you about its true condition;   795
   Verbs show the verbal noun's own definition.
The subject of a trial has filled my mind—
   About Harut's tale trials always remind:

Story about Harut and Marut and their boldness during the trials from God

I've shared a little of this tale before,*
   One small tale from a hundred thousand more.
I wished to speak of truths deemed mystical,
   But I've been held back by an obstacle.
A little of it will be told again—
   One leg of a huge mammoth we'll explain.
You must heed Harut and Marut's own story   800
   Then we'll be servants of your face's glory!
They got drunk through observing God; they'd view
   With awe the marvels that the Lord would do.
Such drunkenness comes slowly, so imagine
   Drunkenness caused by mystical ascension!
That drunkenness came from his snare's small bait—
   Imagine at His feast what fills each plate!
The pair were drunken and freed from the noose,
   So they gave screams that lovers can produce.
One test and ambush still stood in the way—   805
   Its wind blew mountains, as if straw, away!
This turned them upside down despite their wings—
   How can a drunk be conscious of such things?

To him a ditch and prairie are no different;
  He'd stroll in pits and ditches too, indifferent.
The goat runs up the mountain's slope, to find
  Some food that's safe to eat with peace of mind.
While gathering some grass it suddenly
  Will witness a new trick from God's decree:
It glances at the mountain opposite   810
  And sees a she-goat who seduces it.
This goat gets bleary-eyed and starts to run,
  Leaving its mountain for the other one.
To this drunk goat, it's less than going round
  A drain-hole which in a small hut is found:
Thousands of yards to it seem like one yard—
  Drunkenly, it thinks jumping there's not hard,
But when it jumps, it falls between the pair—
  Two mountains with a gap, and no net there.
From hunters to the mountain it had fled,   815
  But its own sanctuary now will leave it dead.
Between the mountains, hunters sit and wait
  For God to bring about His wondrous fate—
Hunting of goats is like this usually,
  Otherwise they'd elude their enemy.
Though Rostam had great honour and stood tall,
  Lust would ensnare him still and make him fall—
From lust's strong stupor you must break away!
  Observe it in the camel clear as day!
Know also that this worldly drunkenness   820
  Compared with that of angels is worth less:
That drunkenness would stun this weaker kind—
  Why should the angels pay it any mind?
Until you have drunk pure, sweet water too,
  Briny water's the sweetest kind to you.
One drop of heaven's wine would tear away
  Your soul from this world's wine they serve today.
Imagine then the angels' drunkenness,
  And spirits made pure by the Glorious,
Whose hearts, at just one whiff, have all been hurled   825
  Towards that wine, smashing vats of this world,

In contrast to those kept far, who breathe sighs
    Like infidels in graves, all blocked from eyes,
Those who've lost hope of both worlds and have sown
    Thorns ceaselessly, to spread woe like their own.
Harut and Marut drunkenly then said,
    'We'd rain like clouds on land, and then we'd spread,
In this place of injustice, equity,
    Devotion, justice, and pure loyalty.'
The Lord's decree said, 'Stop!' when they spoke thus,   830
    'The traps in front of you are numerous.
Don't boldly head to deserts full of pain.
    Don't blindly go to Kerbala's dry plain.
For due to bones and hair from all the dead,
    A traveller's feet can't find the path ahead:
Bones, guts, and hair fill the whole road, my friend.
    Wrath's sword's brought many things there to their end.'
'My servants walk serenely!' God has said,
    'Since they're connected to my special aid.
Who'd walk upon thorns when his feet are bare   835
    Without a pause to think and to beware?'
Their ears were closed—God spoke to no avail—
    Then blocked up by hot-headedness's veil.
All closed their eyes and ears except the few
    Who'd fled their selves and had been born anew.
What opens eyes but sheer grace from above?
    What pacifies your rage apart from love?
May no one ever toil and forgo rest
    Without God granting triumph. God knows best.

Story about Pharaoh's dream of Moses' arrival and his thoughts about how to avoid this

Pharaoh's work was without God's aid, and so   840
    It came apart however much he'd sew.
He had one thousand court astrologers,
    Skilled sorcerers, and dream-interpreters.

He dreamed that Moses would be born that year
   And then destroy that kingdom he held dear,
And so he asked them, 'What can I now do
   To stop this dream I had from coming true?'
They answered, 'We'll together form a plan
   Preventing his birth like a highwayman.'
Before the night on which his birth was due,   845
   These men thought then the best course to pursue
Was bringing to the public square that day
   The royal throne and footstool on display,
Proclaiming, 'Welcome, Israelites, the king
   Summons you from where you've been lingering,
So he can show to you, unveiled, his face
   And treat you well, to earn from God His grace.'
Those captives weren't allowed, at his insistence,
   To look at him before, except from distance;
If they should come across him travelling round,   850
   By law they'd have to lie and face the ground:
The law decreed, 'No captive is allowed
   To see the ruler's face of which we're proud.
Whenever they should hear his heralds call,
   Each has to put his face against a wall.
And if one sees him, he's a criminal—
   He'll earn the harshest punishment of all.'
Each Israelite longed secretly inside
   To see that face—Man craves what he's denied.

How they summoned the Israelites to the main square as a trick to prevent the birth of Moses

The heralds called, 'Head to the public square,   855
   For you may see the king and his gifts there!'
On hearing these words, every Israelite
   Thirsted and yearned to see this longed-for sight.
They swallowed all the lies and planned to go,
   So each prepared himself for the big show.

A story

A cunning Mongol once said suddenly:
  'I'm seeking an Egyptian, so help me!
Bring the Egyptians here, so that I may
  Identify the one I want today.'
When each one came 'It's not you,' he'd declare.   860
  'Go and sit in that corner over there.'
All of them were assembled in this fashion,
  Thus they tricked then beheaded each Egyptian.
Such is the bad luck for those who don't care
  To heed the one who gives the call to prayer:
Those men were tempted by the trickster's call—
  Take care, well-guided one, that you don't fall!
And heed the cries of poor and needy men
  Lest your ears heed the trickster's cries again.
Though beggars be both greedy and uncouth,   865
  Among such gluttons seek the men of Truth.
Pearls are among the pebbles; just the same
  Glory is found when one has gone through shame.

The Jewish men began to stir at dawn,
  And rushed out to see what was going on.
Pharaoh, through cunning, lured them to that place
  And there he showed them all his beaming face.
He gave gifts and showed friendship to each man,
  Then promised them the world, as rulers can.
Finally, he said, 'By God, I wish tonight   870
  You'd all sleep in the square until first light.'
They answered, 'If you wish, we all will stay
  For a whole month—we'd dutifully obey.'

How Pharaoh returned from the square to the city, glad to have separated the Israelites from their wives on Moses' night of conception

The king returned so pleased with the deception:
    'They're far from wives on the night of conception.'
Emran, his treasurer, was present too,
    Attending Pharaoh as companions do.
Pharaoh told him, 'Emran, sleep by the gate.
    Don't dare go near your wife to copulate!'
'I'll sleep at this gate,' Emran then replied,   875
    'And think of how to keep you satisfied.'
For Emran was as well an Israelite,
    Though he was very dear in Pharaoh's sight.
He never thought Emran would disobey
    And do what would cause him the most dismay.

Emran makes love to the mother of Moses and she becomes pregnant

Pharaoh left, Emran slept then by the gate.
    His wife at midnight came, though it was late.
She kissed his lips and lay down, pressed so tight
    Against him, rousing him from sleep that night.
Emran woke up and saw his own wife there   880
    Kissing him fondly in the open air.
Emran asked, 'Why did you now come to me?'
    She said, 'Out of desire and God's decree.'
Romantically, he pulled her to his side
    And didn't try at all to stem the tide:
They made love, and when he ejaculated,
    'This is no trivial thing,' he intimated.
'A spark was born when iron was struck on stone
    To burn the Pharaoh and all he might own.
I'm cloud, you're earth: Moses was cultivated.   885
    God is the King and we've both been checkmated.

Wife, checkmate, and success come from the King,
     Not us, so don't blame us for anything.
What Pharaoh feared most somebody would do
     Happened the moment I made love to you.'

After they have made love, Emran advises his wife to pretend she hasn't seen him

Don't say a word about our time last night
     Or else we'll suffer from an awful plight.
The outcome in the end will be made clear
     Just as its signs are shown already here.
Suddenly from the area of the square   890
     Loud human cries began to fill the air.
The Pharaoh rushed out barefoot, terrified:
     'What's all the noise that I could hear inside?
What uproar is it that we all can hear
     And which would fill the demons too with fear?'
Emran said, 'Long live Pharaoh! Every Jew
     Is celebrating surely due to you.
Your gifts have filled them with such happiness,
     That they now clap and dance, delirious.'
'Maybe that is the case,' Pharaoh then said,   895
     'But it brings deep suspicions to my head.'

Pharaoh is scared of the uproar

'This tumult has disturbed my soul,' said Pharaoh,
     'And aged me through its bitter grief and sorrow.'
Pharaoh paced to and fro all night so torn
     Like women hours before their child is born.
He kept on saying, 'Emran, all these screams
     Are troubling me and I will have bad dreams.'
Poor Emran lacked the courage to confess
     That he had had sex that night nonetheless,
That his dear wife had come to meet him here,   900
     So that the tale of Moses would appear.

The time a prophet is conceived his star
  Shines in the sky and is seen from afar.

The appearance of Moses' star in the sky and the astrologers' shrieking in the square

Moses' star appeared then in the sky,
  Confounding Pharaoh and the schemes he'd try.
When day broke he told Emran, 'Go, find out
  What all that uproar from the square's about!'
Emran rode there and asked, 'Why do you bawl?
  Last night the Pharaoh couldn't sleep at all.'
Astrologers with heads bare and clothes torn   905
  Kissed the ground solemnly like men who mourn.
Their voices too were hoarse like mourning men
  From moaning and lamenting too much. Then
Each pulled his beard out, smeared his face with mud,
  And gashed his head, as his eyes filled with blood.
He said, 'Is all well? What's all this commotion?
  Does this year show already an ill omen?'
They begged forgiveness and said, 'Noble sir,
  Fate's hand has made us all its prisoner.
Fortune has dimmed, as all our efforts failed—   910
  Pharaoh's foe was conceived, so he's prevailed.
Last night that boy's star could be seen, so we
  Are filled with terror and anxiety.
The prophet's star shone in the sky so clear,
  While we all wept tear after star-like tear.'
Happy inside, but acting sad instead,
  Emran screamed, 'All is lost!' and beat his head.
He acted stern and angry, as if serious,
  And showed a temper like one who's delirious.
He spoke like a barbarian, with no care   915
  About expletives though crowds gathered there,
Pretending he was bitter and dismayed—
  Such fine backgammon moves Emran now played.
He faced the crowd, 'Have you tricked our king, men?
  When will your treachery and greed stop? When?

You lured down here the ruler of our nation
 And now you've caused him deep humiliation.
You said, with hand on heart as guarantee:
 We will release you from anxiety.'
The king heard this and started then to bawl: 920
 'Traitors, without delay I'll hang you all!
I made myself a laughing-stock for you,
 And squandered wealth on you most vile foes too,
So that last night each single Israelite
 Would lie alone, with wives far out of sight;
With no result, I've lost wealth and good standing—
 Was that "help"? That is not my understanding!
For years you've gained robes and remuneration,
 Consuming more wealth than a whole new nation—
Was this your reading through astrology?   925
 You seem like lying, greedy pigs to me!
I'll tear you up and set you all aflame,
 Cut your ears, nose, and lips off—you're to blame!
I'll make you firewood, for you're such a waste!
 Past pleasures will now leave an awful taste.'
They said, 'O lord!' and bowed down at his feet,
 'The Devil this time made us taste defeat,
But we have warded off for years all kinds
 Of harm—what we've done boggles people's minds.
This act deceived us, and he's been conceived: 930
 Sperm shot out and by one womb was received.
We seek forgiveness and won't miss a thing,
 Up to the day of his birth, noble king.
We'll watch out for that day for all we're worth,
 Preventing this way his expected birth.
If we don't solve this, send us to our graves!
 To your thoughts and opinions we are slaves.'
For nine whole months, he'd count each day to see
 His foe slain by the spear of destiny.
Whoever tries to strike at realms beyond   935
 Falls upside down; his spilled blood forms a pond.
If soil should try to pick fights with the sky,
 It would turn barren and its plants would die.

If paintings punch their painter, all they do
   Is self-harm, losing all respect they knew.

Pharaoh summons women with newborn babies to the square
as the next part of his plot

After nine months the ruler brought his throne
   Out to the square and made this order known:
'Women, go with your babies to the square!
   All Israelites must come out and stand there.
Your men gained robes of honour just last year   940
   As well as gold when they chose to appear—
Women, this year is your turn to acquire
   Through fortune everything that you desire.
Fine robes of honour wait for worthy women
   And gold caps for the heads of all their children.
Each woman who has this month given birth
   Will gain from Pharaoh treasures of much worth.'
Women came out with children, and they went
   Joyfully straight towards the royal tent.
Each one who'd given birth just recently   945
   Came unaware of Pharaoh's treachery.
When all the women finally gathered round,
   His men took the male babies that they found,
And chopped their heads off, saying: 'That is so
   A foe does not survive and chaos grow.'

How Moses was born and officers came to Emran's house and
revelation came to Moses' mother, saying: 'Cast Moses
into the fire!'

Emran's wife, who'd borne Moses, kept away
   From the commotion on that dreadful day.
Pharaoh sent midwives to men's houses, so
   They could investigate and let him know:
They pointed out, 'She has a child in there—   950
   Why didn't she come out then to the square?

That pretty woman who lives on this street
  Has a newborn child, but she's been discreet.'
Officers came; she followed God's command
  To put him in a stove with her own hand.
Then revelation came from the Divine:
  'This boy's from Abraham's most blessed line.
And, *fire be cool!* Protect this holy child.
  This fire's bright flames will not be hot and wild.'*
Due to these words from God she now felt calm,   955
  Placing him there, and fire caused him no harm.
The officers went off without success;
  Informers stayed suspicious nonetheless:
In front of Pharaoh they condemned the way
  The officers searched, eyeing extra pay—
They said, 'Go, officers immediately,
  And search each of the rooms more carefully.'

Revelation came to Moses' mother, saying: 'Cast Moses in the water!'

'*Cast him in water!*' revelation said,
  'Have faith and don't tear out your hair in dread!
Cast him into the Nile and trust in me—   960
  I'll bring him back unharmed assuredly.'
This discourse has no end. Vile Pharaoh's plots
  Entangled his own legs and feet in knots.
He killed a million children brought outside,
  But Moses was at home, unseen inside.
This tyrant must have turned insane and blind
  To kill all embryos that he could find.
The plot of unjust Pharaoh was a snake,
  Devouring plots the other kings could make,
But one much greater had now come to view,   965
  Which gulped his plot down, swallowing Pharaoh too.
It was a snake—Moses' rod was made
  Into one which devoured his through God's aid.*
There's one upon another till the end—
  The end is to Him.* Don't you comprehend?

And That One is an ocean with no shore,
 While all the rest are torrents and no more.
Although they're snakes, each trickery and plot
 Next to '*None but God*' is in truth worth *naught*.*
My explanation has now reached the end.   970
 It now must fade; *God knows the right course*, friend.

What was in Pharaoh is inside you too,
 But your snakes hide inside pits far from view;
Inside you are sick traits which are the same,
 Although on Pharaoh you pin all the blame.
If men say they're your traits, you'll turn belligerent,
 If someone else's, you'll remain indifferent.
What ruins you? The self that is abhorred—
 It leads you off the path, far from the Lord.
Your fire does not have Pharaoh's kind of wood, 975
 Or else it would shoot flames too like fire should.

Story about the snake-catcher who thought a frozen snake was dead, tied it up, and brought it to Baghdad

Listen now to a chronicler's old tale
 For hints about this mystery through its veil:
A hunter went up to the hills one day
 To catch a snake with spells that he could say—
Whether the seeker's slow or fast, my friend,
 He will find what he's seeking in the end.
Strive hard in seeking and search far and wide,
 For, on this path, to seek is a fine guide.
Though you should be hunchbacked, uncouth, or lame, 980
 Keep seeking Him, crawl even to your aim!
By smelling scents, by silence, or by speech,
 Catch whiffs of the great King you wish to reach.
Jacob told his sons, 'Search for Joseph please
 Beyond all borders and all boundaries.

Search using all your senses, vigilantly;
   Wherever you go, seek him out for me!'
Of God's pure spirit *you must not despair.**
   Like one who's lost his son, search everywhere!
Use your mouth to ask people for a lead,   985
   Then listen, all ears, so you can take heed;
When sweet scents come, then smell in that direction,
   For you're familiar with that higher dimension;
When you receive a kindness, seek a way
   To the pure source of kindness straight away—
These lovely things are all from a deep sea;
   Ignore the part, view the entirety!
Mankind's wars aim for goodness actually;
   Strength from God points towards the Tuba tree.*
Men's rages are all for the sake of peace: 990
   Restlessness leads to rest once it should cease.
Each blow aims to give comfort, not distress;
   Complaints help us to value thankfulness.
Find a way from a mere part to the whole,
   From one thing to its opposite, wise soul!
Wars aim to bring you peace and harmony;
   This hunter sought a snake for company.
He caught it to gain an associate
   To care for, though it won't reciprocate.
That man searched for a big snake even though   995
   The hills he climbed were covered then with snow.
He saw a massive serpent that looked dead,
   But still filled up his trembling heart with dread.
To find a snake the hunter looked around,
   But one dead serpent was all that he found.
The snake-catcher will hunt just to amaze
   Stupid, impressionable people of these days:
Man is a mountain—how should he be dazzled
   By a mere snake unless his brain has frazzled?
Man doesn't know himself well, obviously—   1000
   He's fallen down from wealth to poverty,
And Man has cheaply sold himself—once rich
   With satin now mere rags are what he'll stitch.

A million snakes and mountains are in awe
   Of him, so why desire the snake he saw?
The snake-catcher took that dead-looking serpent
   To Baghdad to create there some excitement.
He dragged the serpent round for a mere trifling,
   Though it was huge, like pillars of a building:
'I've brought to you a serpent that is dead.   1005
   I suffered much in hunting it,' he said.
This man thought it had died up on the hill,
   Unaware that the snake was living still.
It had got frozen in the wintry snow;
   It only looked dead, but he didn't know.
This frozen world is called 'inanimate';
   'Inanimate' means frozen and inert.
When Resurrection's sun appears, you'll see
   The body of this world move restlessly.
Moses' rod had here a transformation;*   1010
   The intellect thus learnt about creation.
Since God created you from lumps of clay,
   Recognize every lump that comes your way:
The dead are here; beyond one finds the living—
   They're silent here, beyond though they are talking.
When from beyond He sends them down, it's clear
   Since rods turn into serpents over here.
Mountains sang David's Psalms at His command;
   Iron would melt like wax in David's hand.*
The wind would bring what Solomon conveyed.*   1015
   The sea would understand what Moses said.*
The moon saw Ahmad point;* wild flames would turn
   For Abraham to roses and not burn.*
Just like a snake, the earth gulped Korah down;*
   The pillar learnt to moan and earned renown.*
Stones gave Mohammad a salute one day;*
   To John the Baptist mountains once would say:
'We've sight and hearing, and we feel elated,
   Though silent with the uninitiated.'*
You watch the surface of inert things, blind   1020
   To those inert things' souls which lie behind—

Leave the inert realm now for that of souls,
 Hear chatter come from this world's particles.
You'll hear God's praise when those inert things shout;
 Interpretation won't lead you to doubt:
Your soul lacks light to see what I've reported,
 So to interpretation you've resorted:
'It can't be glorification that you hear;
 That claim is self-delusory. This is clear.'
But now the marvellous things that you perceive   1025
 Lead you to praise God and do not deceive.
Therefore, since that thing prompts you to His praise
 That pointer talks in some analogous ways.
This is the view of the Mu'tazilite*
 And that of people who lack mystic light.
If you've not gone beyond the senses, you
 Will find the unseen realm then out of view.
This discourse has no end. The hunter would
 Groan loudly as he'd drag his snake like wood.
That showman wished to go to Baghdad, to   1030
 Attract huge crowds by showing something new.
He set his stage up next to their great river,
 Causing a hubbub on what he'd deliver:
'A snake-catcher has brought a serpent here!
 He caught a wondrous, rare beast most would fear!'
Millions of naive people came to see,
 Gathering as prey to his stupidity.
They all came for the show, and he would wait
 For further simpletons to congregate—
The bigger the crowd that can be attracted   1035
 The bigger the payment that can be exacted.
A hundred thousand idiots gathered there,
 Forming a circle with no room to spare,
Women with men together, as they say
 Will happen on the Resurrection Day.*
Once he began his famed show, eagerly
 The people craned their necks so they could see.
The serpent that had frozen was beneath
 Numerous kinds of covering and sheath;

With thick ropes it had been bound by that man   1040
   Who'd executed cautiously his plan.

While the expectant crowd faced a delay,
   The hot sun of Iraq then shone that way.
The sunshine warmed the serpent to remove
   The coldness of its parts so they could move—
Once seeming dead, it now became revived,
   And stirred, surprised, proving it had survived.
That serpent's sudden movement caused much more
   Amazement in the audience than before:
They started screaming in perplexity,   1045
   And then en masse the crowd began to flee.
The serpent burst its ropes, then all around
   There echoed a most frightening cracking sound.
Once it broke free, it then slid on the floor
   And, louder than a lion, began to roar.
Many were killed among those still around,
   And from the dead they formed mound after mound.
The snake-catcher was paralysed with fear,
   Wondering: 'What have I brought down with me here?'
A blind lamb woke a wolf, and unaware   1050
   It went to Azrael, who waited there:
That serpent made one mouthful of that fool—
   Not hard for those who, like Hajjaj, are cruel.*
It coiled itself around this post-like man
   And crushed his bones with one squeeze, like they can.
Your self's a serpent—how can it be dead?
   Through grief and lack of means it froze instead.
If it obtains the same means as vile Pharaoh,
   Whose personal command made the great Nile flow,
Then it will set up tyranny like his   1055
   And waylay Aarons and new Moseses.
When weak, that serpent was a little worm;
   Through wealth and status gnats too can transform.
Confine the serpent deep in exile's snow!
   Don't take it near Iraq's sun's melting glow!

As long as it's just frozen, you will be
   Your serpent's morsel when it should break free.
Kill it to be secure from death—don't waver
   Mercifully; it does not deserve a favour,
For when it feels the sun of lust's first ray,   1060
   That wretched bat will rise and fly away.
Declare jihad and kill it with your sword!
   God will give union then as your reward.
When that man brought the serpent with him then
   To warmer climes, it soon felt well again.
It sought to cause harm there inevitably
   Twenty times worse than what you've heard from me.
Without force you desire to keep yours tied,
   Sedated and yet loyal—scores have tried,
But how can this succeed for someone base?   1065
   To slay it you'll need Moses' pure grace:
A hundred thousand people were once killed
   By his snake-like rod doing what God willed.*

How Pharaoh threatened Moses

Pharaoh asked Moses once, 'Why did you then
   Drive to despair and kill so many men?
At your hands they were routed mercilessly:
   They slipped down and were killed for all to see.
They view you as their foe now and detest
   The thought of you—hatred has filled each breast.
You called them to you, but the opposite   1070
   Was the result: they're now more obstinate.
While creeping back from evil caused by you,
   I'm plotting a retaliation too.
Stop thinking you can fool me—none will follow
   When you call them, except perhaps your shadow.
Don't be deluded by what you've achieved:
   You've filled men's hearts with fear—don't be deceived!
You could show many marvels, but still face
   Being the laughing-stock who's earned disgrace.

We've seen deceivers like you who all came   1075
  To Egypt with high hopes but left in shame.'

Moses' answer to Pharaoh concerning the threat he made

'God has no partners,' Prophet Moses said.
  'If He decrees my death, I'll feel no dread.
I am content and thankful, enemy;
  I'm blamed here, but God gives me dignity.
To most men, I'm a wretch and foolish too,
  But I'm approved and loved in the Lord's view.
With words I'll tell you, but in any case,
  Tomorrow God will bring you your disgrace.
God and His slaves have glory and true might—   1080
  Adam and Satan's duel shows I'm right.*
Like God Himself, describing never ends,
  So shut up, turn a new leaf, make amends!'

Pharaoh's reply to Moses

Pharaoh claimed, 'Each leaf follows my commands;
  The book and register are in my hands.
The people of the world now follow me—
  Are you more wise than this community?
Moses, you've boasted that you are the best—
  Don't be deluded and too self-obsessed!
I'll bring the great magicians of our era   1085
  To make your ignorance seem even clearer,
But just two days is not sufficient time,
  So give me till Tammuz* in summertime.'

Moses' reply to Pharaoh

Moses replied, 'That's not allowed for me,
  Since I'm God's slave and follow His decree.

Though you are strong and I lack allies now,
   I am the slave of His will anyhow.
While I'm alive I'll fight you, for I'm brave—
   How can I give God aid when I'm His slave?
I'll fight until the Lord's decree's fulfilled;   1090
   Foes only separate once He has willed.'

Pharaoh's reply to Moses and the coming of revelation to Moses

Pharaoh said, 'You must give more time to me.'
   Moses replied, 'Don't try playing cleverly.'
God sent down revelation then that said:
   'Grant him more time and do not be afraid!
Let him have all the forty days he needs
   And let him think his cunning talk succeeds.
I do not sleep, so let him keep on striving—
   Make him hurry. I'll stop him from arriving.
I'll ruin all his tricks, and I'll decrease   1095
   The things that he endeavours to increase:
When they bring water, I'll set it aflame;
   I'll make his candy bitter just the same;
When they unite in love, I'll spoil that union—
   I'll do such things that they can't now imagine.
Give him the extra time and have no fear.
   Say: "Plan your tricks and bring your army here!"' '

Moses gives Pharaoh more time so he can assemble magicians from the cities

Moses said, 'You've been granted the delay
   By God's command, so I'll be on my way.'
He headed home; a serpent trailed behind   1100
   Like hunters' dogs, affectionate and kind;
Like them it also happily wagged its tail,
   Crushing to dust the rocks along its trail.
It kept inhaling rocks and iron too;
   It chewed the latter easily in plain view!

And then it flew above the zodiac—
    Georgians and Greeks fled, fearing an attack.
It spat like camels—those it fell upon
    Were struck with leprosy's curse from then on.
The gnashing of its teeth left all hearts scared: 1105
    Lions' souls even shivered and despaired.
When Moses reached his home and his own men
    He touched it, then it was a stick again.
He leaned on it next, saying: 'How amazing:
    To foes it's night, to me the sun is blazing.'
Doesn't that army see the world is full
    Of morning sunshine? How incredible!
All eyes are open under such bright rays,
    Yet God seals eyes with power that will amaze.
I am amazed by them and they at me—   1110
    Spring brings both their thorns and my jasmine tree.
I took wine to them from the best I own,
    But when it reached them it transformed to stone.
I took a bunch of roses, but each one
    Transformed its sweet form to a poisonous thorn.
For selfless souls this is their destiny;
    Since they aren't selfless how should these men's be?
A 'wakened sleep' is needed for the sake
    Of seeing special visions while awake.
The foe of such sleep's thought of the creation—   1115
    Your thoughts must sleep to gain true inspiration.
To sweep thought out you need perplexity,
    For it devours all thought and memory.
Whoever is more talented down here
    Is backward inside, though that won't appear.
God says, '*You are returning.*'* To your home
    You'll go like some stray goats which used to roam.
When all the goats should turn around, you'll find
    The one that was in front is now behind.
The lame goat that was last is now ahead: 1120
    Returning makes sad faces laugh instead.
How did this group turn wretched and turn lame,
    Giving up glory, buying instead all blame?

With broken legs they can reach Mecca still
   Through hidden routes to bliss from feeling ill.
They've washed their hearts of sciences today,
   Because that knowledge doesn't know the way.
Knowledge from higher realms is what one needs,
   For to its own root every fresh branch leads.
Not all winged creatures can traverse the sea—   1125
   Divine Truths take you to *His company*.*
So why teach ordinary knowledge then,
   If one must clean it from one's breast again?
Don't seek to race in front. Instead be lame:
   On turning back, you'll lead them all the same!
Wise man, *the last will be the first*—it's known
   The fresh fruit's there before the tree has grown.
Fruit only later comes into existence,
   But it is first, the target in the distance.
Like angels, *'We've no knowledge!'* you should say   1130
   Until *'You taught us'** takes your hand one day—
In this school you don't know your ABC;
   Mohammad-like, through mystic light you'll see.
Though you may not be well known in this land,
   You're none the worse: *God knows best where slaves stand.*
Gold's found in ruined spots that are neglected,
   So that the precious treasure stays protected.
Who would hide treasure somewhere populated?
   'Ease is found under toil,' men have related.

The mind tries to put obstacles up here,   1135
   But strong steeds break their shackles and run clear.
His love's the burner for each single problem,
   As daylight sweeps away each single phantom.
Look for the answer in the same direction
   From which, well-pleasing man, emerged the question.
The road is deep in your heart—find it soon!
   Light *not from East nor West** comes from the moon.
Why beggar-like do you search all around,
   Mountain of Truth, for echoes of your sound.

Seek it from that place where you will appeal: 1140
   'O Lord!' when overcome by pain you feel.
Both pain and death will make you turn your head
   That side, so why not when relieved of dread?
In tribulation, 'O God!' you will pray,
   But, when it's gone, you ask me: 'Where's the way?'
I say this since those men with certainty
   Of God are deep in prayer perpetually.
Those veiled by intellect and doubt you'll see
   Sometimes veiled, sometimes feeling ecstasy;
The partial intellect's sure, then unsure;   1145
   From doubts the Universal One's secure.
Sell skills and logic for perplexity!
   Don't seek Bukhara but humility!
Why am I steeped in speech to this degree
   That now they tell tall tales concerning me?
Through moaning, I seek ultimate negation,
   To then inspire the people in prostration.*
But this is no mere tale if you've experience—
   It shares the state Bu Bakr gained in his presence.*
'*Mere tales of past folk*'* rebels mockingly   1150
   Called the Qur'an—this showed hypocrisy.
Filled with the Light of God, in Placelessness,
   Of past and future one could not care less.
Future and past are relative to you;
   In truth they're one thing, but you think they're two.
One man is someone's son and someone's father:
   A roof is under Zayd yet over Amr*—
Whether it's under or above depends
   On those two persons; it's the same roof, friends.
This discourse is a mere analogy;   1155
   Words can't convey such deep truths adequately.
Water-skin, there's no stream left any more—
   Seal your mouth! Candy's ocean has no shore.

Pharaoh sends people to the cities in search of magicians

Moses returned, left Pharaoh standing there,
    Who summoned counsellors from everywhere.
They said, 'We have magicians, and each one
    In magic is a peerless champion.'
They thought it best then that from all around
    Magicians should be sought who were renowned.
At this point Pharaoh sent his officers   1160
    In all directions to find sorcerers:
An officer was sent with this sole aim
    Wherever there was one who'd earned much fame.
There were two youths like this, whom they reached soon—
    Their magic pierced the belly of the moon,
And they would milk that pale orb in the sky,
    While on a wine jar magically they'd fly.
They'd make the moonlight look like cotton too
    And sell it quickly to those with no clue,
Taking much silver—when buyers grew aware   1165
    They'd slap themselves for falling for this pair.
Of all the stunts they pulled this is a sample;
    They didn't follow anyone's example.
Pharaoh's official message came, which said:
    'Your ruler is in need now of your aid,
Because a pair of paupers formed a menace,
    Marching against the Pharaoh and his palace,
Although they only have one rod at hand,
    Which turns into a snake at their command.
The ruler and his men now feel despair,   1170
    Lamenting helplessly due to this pair.
Through magic surely there are methods to
    Save all our lives from threats posed by these two?'
When this news finally reached those sorcerers' ears,
    Their hearts filled up with longings and with fears,
And, once their veins throbbed through affinities,
    Amazed, they leaned their heads down on their knees—

Just as for Sufis, knees are learning-places:
    They solve the problems each magician faces.

The two magicians summoned their father from the grave and asked his soul about the real nature of Moses

They asked their mother on the following day: 1175
    'Where is our father's grave? Show us the way!'
She led them, so they'd find the route to take.
    They fasted for three days for Pharaoh's sake,
Then said, 'O father, Pharaoh in despair
    Has sent this message to us both, to share
That two men make him anxious—in this case
    Before his army they've made him lose face.
That pair lack soldiers and lack weaponry
    Apart from one rod that scares worryingly.
You've left this world for where pure souls are found,   1180
    Though you appear to be still in the ground—
Our father's spirit, help us understand
    Whether it's magic or through God's command,
A cause for us to bow submissively,
    To benefit from God's own alchemy!
Though we despair, hope draws near to our place;
    Though exiles we are drawn back by God's grace.

The dead magician answers his sons

Through a shared dream their father still could teach:
    'Describing it is far beyond our speech;
To make it plain is not allowed to me,   1185
    Although I see close up the mystery;
But I will show a sign that you can view,
    So that this hidden thing is shown to you.
Lights of my eye, when you go to that place
    Find out first where he sleeps, then that night race,
While that sage falls asleep, close to his side,
    And steal his great rod, putting fear aside:

If you succeed to steal it, that means he
    Is a magician—you'll win easily;
If you're unable to, he's a divine   1190
    Prophet of God and guided, sons of mine.
Even if Pharaoh conquers East and West,
    Moses stays nonetheless of those God's blessed.
Souls of your father, I've conveyed this clue—
    Inscribe it on your heart; God knows what's true.
When the magician sleeps, then logically
    There's no one to perform his sorcery.
When shepherds sleep, wolves feel no threat's around,
    For they're not active when they're sleeping sound.
But how can those wolves hope to reach the sheep   1195
    Whose shepherd's God, when it's known He won't sleep?
God's magic's real and true, and actually
    It's wrong to call that truth mere sorcery.
This is the sign that proves that it's no lie:
    Even if he dies, God will raise him high.'

A comparison between the sublime Qur'an and the rod of Moses, and the death of Mohammad to the sleep of Moses, and those who seek to alter the Qur'an to those two sorcerers who aimed to take away Moses' rod while he was asleep

God told the Prophet once, 'Though you may die
    This teaching won't die, for I've raised so high
Your holy book and miracle. No man
    Can get past me to alter the Qur'an.
In the two worlds I'm always your protector;   1200
    For those who scoff at you I'm their rejecter.
No one can add on or delete a line—
    Don't seek protection then apart from mine.
Each day I will increase still more your splendour
    And etch your lovely name on gold and silver.
I'll make more pulpits also just for you;
    Due to my love, your wrath is my wrath too.
For fear, they mention your name secretly,
    And when they pray they do so furtively.

They fear all the cursed infidels around, 1205
  So your religion now hides underground.
With minarets I will fill all the skies
  And grab rebellious men to blind their eyes.
Your servants will gain power and take towns soon;
  Your realm will seem to stretch from fish to moon!*
We will preserve it till the Resurrection;
  No one will abrogate your great religion.
You're not a sorcerer, My Messenger;
  You're truthful, Moses' inheritor,
And the Qur'an is like his rod for you— 1210
  Serpent-like, it can gulp down falsehoods too.
Even when you lie under soil, each word
  You've uttered will be like the rod when heard.
They'll fail if they should try to snatch your rod,
  So sleep in blessed peace all thanks to God.
Your body sleeps, but, up above, your light
  Has strung a bow to arm you in the fight—
Your light's bow shoots down its all-powerful rays
  At each word the philosopher's mouth says.'
The Prophet managed this, and much more too; 1215
  He slept, but not his fortune, which still grew.

'When a magician sleeps, souls of your father,*
  The work he does will then lack any splendour.'
Both sons then kissed his grave's soil and departed
  To Egypt where they wanted a war started.
When they arrived with that aim over there,
  They looked for Moses' house everywhere.
At that same time coincidentally,
  Moses was sleeping under a palm tree.
The locals pointed them in the right way: 1220
  'Look for him in the palm groves,' they would say.
Among the trees they saw him suddenly
  Asleep but as awake as one can be:
He'd shut his eyes to sleep of course, but kept
  Watch over all things near him as he slept.

Many have eyes awake but hearts asleep—
    What can mere bodily eyes see? Not a peep;
Yet with eyes closed, but an awake heart, you
    Can open hundreds more with which to view.
Wake up if you don't have a mystic's heart.   1225
    Fight to become a seeker, make a start.
But if your heart's awake, then sleep in peace—
    Your own attention to the world won't cease.
'My eyes sleep,' once the Prophet clarified,
    'But there's no sleep-time for my heart inside.'
Watchmen can sleep while their great king's awake—
    Sacrifice all things for the seeing heart's sake!
A thousand couplets can't in full express,
    Dear mystic friend, the pure heart's wakefulness.
When they saw Moses sleeping there stretched out,   1230
    They tried to steal the rod they'd heard about—
The sorcerers rushed for the rod and said:
    'Let's snatch it from behind his sleeping head!'
When they prepared to draw close, then the rod
    Started to quiver through the power of God.
The rod vibrated so much that the pair,
    Through fear, became both paralysed right there.
Then it became a serpent and surged near,
    Making them flee with faces pale through fear.
They kept on falling over due to terror,   1235
    Scampering down the slopes from their own error.
Moses was heaven-sent these men thus learnt,
    By seeing how they got their fingers burnt!
Then diarrhoea and a fever's ache
    Made them both suffer more than they could take.
Immediately they sent a man to Moses,
    So he could ask the Prophet for forgiveness,
Saying: 'We've tried to test you. How should we
    Have dared to try except through jealousy?
We've sinned against the King—please now request   1240
    Forgiveness for us, you whom He has blessed.'
When he forgave them, they recuperated
    And then in front of him they both prostrated.

Moses said, 'Noble men, I've pardoned you.
   From hell you can now feel secure anew,
As if I've never noticed you before,
   So don't beg my forgiveness any more.
Come back a seeming stranger known to me,
   To fight for Pharaoh's side just outwardly.'
They then both kissed the ground and went away,   1245
   Expecting such a circumstance one day.

*The magicians of the cities assemble before Pharaoh and receive
honours and put their hands on their breasts as a pledge to defeat
his enemy, saying: 'You can count on us!'*

When these magicians went back to their ruler
   He gave them both some precious robes of honour,
And also an advance of what he'd give
   Of horses, slaves, and what they'd need to live,
Saying: 'Most worthy men, whose rank is high,
   If you succeed in this next test, then I
Will shower down so many gifts on you,
   That generosity will be stunned too.'
They said, 'King, through your fortune which we hail,   1250
   His work will be destroyed and we'll prevail.
We're champions in this art, and none has hope
   Of standing up to us, for they can't cope.
Mention of Moses has become a chain
   For those complaining: "Not those tales again!" '*

Mention of Moses serves now to contain
   The light of Moses, which is what you'll gain.
God knows, Moses and Pharaoh are in you—
   You must search in yourself to find these two.
Until the end Moses' light will prosper;   1255
   The light's not different, though the lamps may differ:
The lamps and wicks are different obviously—
   Their light's not different though, if you can see.

If you gaze at the glass lamp, you'll be lost:
    It brings on dualism as the cost.
Focus just on the light and you'll break free
    From bodily limits and plurality.
It's due to viewpoints, kernel of existence,
    That Muslim, Jew, and Magian show a difference.

The difference of opinion over the nature and the shape of an elephant

An elephant was brought to a dark building   1260
    By Indians, so they could hold a viewing,
So lots of people would come just to see—
    They rushed into the darkness eagerly.
It was impossible to see it there,
    So people groped to feel it everywhere:
One man's hand brushed its trunk—he said, 'This creature
    Is like a pipe.' He based this on one feature.
Another could feel just its ears—that man
    Believed the elephant was like a fan.
Another felt one of its legs alone: 1265
    'Its shape is like those columns made of stone.'
Another touched its back and then cried out:
    'It's similar to a throne without a doubt.'
When they heard 'elephant' each one conceived
    Only the part that they themselves perceived.
Different perspectives meant discrepancies:
    One called it straight like I's, one bent like c's.
For arguments there would have been no space
    If each had held a candle in that place;
The sensual eye's no better than the hand—   1270
    The whole of it the hand can't understand.
The ocean's eye and foam are worlds apart—
    Leave its foam, use the eye inside its heart!
It's that which sets the ocean's foam in motion,
    But you see foam and no more of the ocean.

Like ships off course we crash against each other
    With eyes in darkness though we're in clear water.
You're fast asleep inside the body's boat—
    Look at the water's water as you float:
Water beyond this water's waves rolls them;   1275
    Spirit beyond our spirits here calls them.
Where were Moses and Jesus when That One
    Watered the meadow of existents, son?
Adam and Eve too—do you even know
    Where they were when God strung His order's bow?
This discourse falls short still, and is deficient;
    The Speech of God alone can be sufficient.
You stumble when one speaks to you from there,
    And if they don't, that's your loss—feel despair!
And when such speech is uttered figuratively,   1280
    You cling onto the form still stubbornly:
You're rooted to the earth like grass, and though
    You nod your head to wind, you still don't know.
You lack the legs with which to move away
    Or pull your own feet from the mud today.
How will you pull your feet out? Your life too
    Is so entrenched in mud—it's hard for you.
When you gain life from God, you'll feel no need,
    And, traveller, you will rapidly proceed,
For when a baby leaves its nurse, it then   1285
    Eats solid food and won't seek hers again.
Like seeds, you're tied to earth's milk—break apart
    And seek true nourishment that's for the heart.
Drink words of wisdom, though they have been veiled
    For you who can't receive the light unveiled,
So that, O soul, you can at least have sight
    Eventually of the unveiled, pure light.
And travel like a star up in the heavens,
    Beyond them too, with God, free from conditions.
That's how you came to being originally   1290
    From non-existence—you came drunkenly.
You don't recall the pathways by which you
    Arrived, but I'll recite a telling clue.

Lose your mind to be mindful! I will tell,
    But close your ears, so you can listen well.
No, you're still in an undeveloped state:
    You live in spring—for summer you must wait.

Noble ones, this world's like a tree, and we
    Are still unripe fruits hanging from that tree.
Unripe fruits cling fast to the branch, because   1295
    They're unfit for the palace with their flaws.
But when they ripen and taste sweet to all,
    Their hold will weaken and they'll easily fall.
When mouths taste sweetness due to special grace,
    The world becomes an unattractive place.
Strictness and bigotry are immature—
    A foetus drinks blood; men deem it impure.
There's more—I'll let the Holy Spirit say
    It to you all without my help one day.
No, no one else will say it to your ear,   1300
    But you: when you are I there's just one here,
Like when you fall asleep and quickly go
    From your self to the higher self you know:
You listen to yourself and yet you keep
    Sensing someone address you in your sleep—
You're not a single 'you', my good companion:
    You are the heavens too and the deep ocean.
Your higher self is complex and profound,
    The Red Sea in which lower selves are drowned.*
And sleep and wakefulness can't limit you—   1305
    Speak no more! *God knows best about what's true.*
Stop speaking, so that you'll hear voices say
    What words and explanations can't convey.
Stop speaking, so from sunshine you will hear
    What books and sermons never can make clear.
Stop speaking, so the spirit speaks for you—
    Don't swim on Noah's ark as your foes do,
Like Canaan who did that and let all know:
    'I don't want Noah's ark—he is my foe.'

'Sit in your father's ark!' Noah implored,   1310
   'Don't get drowned in the flood, wretch—climb on board!'
He answered, 'I know how to swim to shores.
   I've lit a different candle, too, from yours.'
'This is the flood of suffering!' Noah cried,
   'Swimming and your limbs' strength are nullified.
Be silent! It's the wind of wrath and woe—
   No candle now but God's is left to glow.'
He said, 'No, to that mountain I will flee
   From harm; that will protect a man like me.'
'Don't go! The mountain's now like straw—beware!   1315
   Only those whom He loves are safe up there.'
He said, 'When have I listened to your counsel
   That you should hope that I'll now join your circle?
I've never liked the things that you have said
   And in the two worlds I don't need your aid.'
'It's not the time for such disdain, my son!
   God has no family nor a partner—none.
You're acting precious, and it's dangerous now;
   In this court whose disdain counts anyhow?
Neither born nor begetting,* He's eternal;   1320
   He has no father, nor a child, nor uncle,
So how can He endure a child's disdain,
   Or from a father? Have I made it plain?
"Don't have disdain; I'm not born." God has said,
   "I don't beget—don't strut with a proud head.
I'm not a husband; there's no lust in me—
   Woman stop flirting with me fruitlessly.
Bondage, humility, and servanthood
   Alone have worth. Have you not understood?"'
Canaan said, 'Father, you've said this to me   1325
   So often I fear it's insanity.
So many times you've told the people—why?
   You only get a negative reply.
Your tiresome words won't reach my ears—I've grown
   So wise and strong I've made it on my own.'
'What harm can there be?' Noah said, 'Now to
   Heed what your father is advising you?'

He thus kept giving this considerate counsel
  While his son Canaan gave back harsh refusal.
He did not tire from trying to help his son,   1330
  But not one word got through to him, not one.
A powerful wave surged and struck Canaan's head
  As they continued, leaving him for dead.
'Forbearing king!' Noah began to pray,
  'My ass died; your flood swept its load away.
So many times before you promised me:
  "You will escape it with your family."
I pinned my hopes on you and what you'd say—
  Why did your flood now snatch my coat away?'
God said, 'He was not from your family—   1335
  You're white but he was blue—could you not see?
When your tooth starts to suffer from decay,
  It's not a tooth then, so throw it away!
Get rid of what was once yours, so you'll not
  See your whole body then begin to rot.'
Noah said, 'From what's different I am quit;
  He who dies through you isn't separate.
You know that You're the one whom I adore
  And need as pasture needs the rain to pour.
I live through You and do so joyfully,   1340
  Nurtured without an intermediary,
Neither united nor apart—perfection
  Without cause, qualities, or any question.
We're fishes while You are Life's Wondrous Sea,
  And we live through Your generosity.
In thought's cramped corner you can't be contained
  And by cause and effect you are not chained.
Before and after this flood has passed through,
  The One to Whom we call is always You.
I spoke with You, not them, for You're the one   1345
  Who gave the gift of speech to everyone.
I'm like the lover who all day and night
  Keeps his beloved's camp's trace in his sight:
As if he's facing ruins he sits there—
  To whom does he sing then? Is he aware?

For sending us the flood, praise be to You,
　And for removing veils of ruins too,
Because they were so awful—no reply
　Came from them, nor the echo of a cry.
I want such ruins now to answer me though,　　　1350
　The way a mountain can receive an echo,
So I might hear Your name repeatedly,
　Your name, which soothes all souls, has smitten me.
As every Prophet holds a mountain dear,
　So that Your name repeatedly he'll hear.
Low mountains are like stony ground—no house
　Stands there for us—it's fit for just a mouse.
I speak but in response there's no caress;
　The breath of my own speech stays echoless.
Better to join it with the earth instead—　　　1355
　It's no close friend, fit just for you to tread.'
God said, 'Noah, for you I'll gather round
　All men, and raise them from graves underground.
For Canaan's sake I won't let your heart shatter;
　Rather I'll tell you of all things that matter.'
Noah said, 'No, with you I am content;
　If You should drown me too, I would consent.
Go on and drown me, if that's Your decree,
　Which is so dear—I'll bear it happily.
I won't watch anyone, but if I do　　　1360
　It's as a pretext so I can watch You.
A lover of Your craftsmanship, my head
　Is not turned by the things You've made instead.'
The lover of God's craftsmanship earns splendour;
　His craftwork's lover is an unbeliever.

Reconciliation between these following two traditions:
'To be satisfied with infidelity is itself an act of infidelity'
and 'Whoever is not satisfied with my decree should
seek a different lord'

A man asked me this question yesterday
  Because he liked to start disputes this way:
'The Prophet said once, "Being satisfied
  With unbelief is unbelief." Our pride
Said also, "Muslims have to be content   1365
  With His ordainment, knowing it's been sent."
God wills the unbelief, claims one tradition;
  If I'm content, though, that is a rebellion.
And if I'm not content, that has flaws too—
  To reconcile these two, what can I do?'
'The infidelity is what's ordained,
  Not the ordainment by Him,' I maintained.
'So tell apart what is ordained from fate
  Itself—your problems then will dissipate.'
I am content with infidelity,   1370
  Not since it's bad, but since it's God's decree.
It isn't unbelief that it's decreed;
  Don't call God infidel—you must take heed!
Unbelief's ignorance, ordainment's knowing;
  Bestowing does not mean the same as owing.
The writing's ugly, but don't blame the writer.
  He's shown your ugliness, but He is brighter.
The artist's skill lets him display to you
  Both beautiful things and the ugly too.
If I extend the discourse now at hand,   1375
  Cause questions and their answers to expand,
Love's wisdom's savour will leave me today
  And from my service I will quickly stray.

Parable explaining that mystical bewilderment prevents investigation and thought

A greying man once hurried to a barber
   Who was accomplished, standing by his mirror.
He said, 'Remove the white hairs from my beard,
   For I've picked a new wife and need them cleared.'
The barber shaved the whole beard off, and said:
   'I'm busy. You pluck white hairs out instead!'
Mystical pain has no use or concern   1380
   For mere hair-splitting's method how to learn.
A man slapped hard another man one night;
   The other man charged at him for a fight.
The one who slapped said, 'I've a question. Please
   Answer it first, then slap me as you please.
I slapped your neck with a loud crack, so I
   Now have a question—would you clarify
Whether this cracking sound came from my hand
   Or from your neck? Please help me understand.'
The other said, 'I feel so many aches   1385
   I lack the time that contemplation takes.
You who lack pain can contemplate, but we
   Who feel don't waste time on frivolity.'

A story

So few Companions memorized the whole
   Qur'an, though each had fervour in his soul.
When kernels grow to full maturity,
   Their minds will thin and then split suddenly.
The walnut, almond, and pistachio shells
   And their rinds too shrink as each kernel swells:
The rinds decreased as wisdom's kernel grew,   1390
   And the Beloved burns up lovers too.

Seeking's the opposite of being sought.
    Through God's light rays, the Prophet burned to nought.
Displaying attributes of the Eternal
    Burns up the mantle of each thing that's temporal.
When someone learnt a quarter of God's Book,
    Companions said, '*A great one's with us. Look!*'
Combining form with such deep meaning can
    Be only managed by a mighty man.
While drunk how can you mind your manners too?   1395
    That would be too amazing to be true.
When you're without need, to show neediness
    Is joining opposites like strip and dress.
The walking-stick is loved by each blind man,
    Though he's a coffer housing the Qur'an.
One said, 'The blind are coffers filled with text
    From the Qur'an and warning of what's next.'
A coffer filled with the Qur'an's superior
    To one that's empty still in its interior.
But one that's emptied is superior to   1400
    One filled with dirty mice and serpents too,
For when one gains the union that is sought,
    To one the go-between is then worth naught.
Since you have reached your goal, O man of grace,
    Now seeking knowledge would be a disgrace;
Now that you've reached the rooftop of the sky,
    What is the point of seeking ladders? Why
Apart from to help others with instruction?
    Once finished, then the path has no more function.
It's stupid to keep trying to rub clean   1405
    A mirror that's the clearest that there's been.
While sitting with the sultan don't remember
    And seek his messenger or his old letter.

Story about the preoccupation of a lover with reading and perusing a love letter in the presence of his beloved, to which his displeased beloved responds: 'Seeking the proof in the presence of that which it is proving is blameworthy, as is preoccupation with knowledge after reaching the object of knowledge

With his own sweetheart sitting opposite,
   A man took out a letter and read it,
A letter full of verses and laudations,
   Laments, entreaties, and long supplications.
His sweetheart said, 'If this is for my sake,
   Doing this while in union's a mistake:
I'm present with you, yet you read a letter.   1410
   That's not sign of a lover, now or ever.'
He said, 'Although you're present now with me,
   I still don't feel fulfilled yet properly.
The things that I'd perceived in you last year
   Have gone, although I'm now in union here.
I've drunk pure water from this spring, and I
   Have with it now refreshed my heart and eye.
I see the fountain, but the water's gone.
   Maybe a highway robber's moved me on?'
The sweetheart said, 'That means I'm not for you: 1415
   I'm in this place; your sweetheart's far from view.
You are in love with both me and a state;
   You've lost that state, and now it is too late.
I'm not the whole of what's sought by your heart;
   Of what you seek I am now just one part.'
I am His home, not the Loved One within—
   Love's based on cash, not the collection tin.
He Who is One is your Beloved Friend;
   He is One, your beginning and your end.
When you find Him, you'll lose all expectations;   1420
   He's hidden and yet in manifestations.

He directs states; they don't rule Him—it's clear,
 The way the moon determines month and year.
When He commands states, they of course obey;
 Bodies turn into souls when He should say.
One hasn't reached the end if one's dependent;
 One who seeks states is one who's still expectant.
His hand's the alchemy of states; if he
 Moves it, then copper swoons in ecstasy.
Death will turn sweet if He commands it to,   1425
 Nettles and thorns will turn to flowers too.
If you're still tied to states, you're human still;
 You let them make you feel high or feel ill.
Each Sufi is 'the moment's son',* but he
 Who's pure is free from time's grip totally.
States are determined by his will and whim,
 And live through Jesus-like breath breathed by him.
You are in love with states and not with me;
 It's for a state you joined my company.
One who's now lacking, now complete, is one   1430
 That sets, a thing that Abraham would shun;
The one that sets and changes is one he
 Would shun: '*The ones that set aren't loved by me!*'*
The one who's sad now, and now feels elation,
 Is fire then water, prone to transformation.
He is the moon's house, but it is quite obvious
 He's not the moon; an idol's form is worthless.
The Sufi is 'the moment's son' when he
 Clasps time as if his father, desperately.
In love of God the pure one thus gets drowned,   1435
 Beyond states, no one's son, in no way bound.
Drowned in light *never born*—have you forgotten
 That *God does not beget nor was begotten*.*
If you're alive, seek love that's so sublime
 Like this; if not you're bound by changing time.
Leave all your vile and pretty forms behind—
 Look at love and at Whom you hope to find!
Don't worry if you're ugly or you're weak,
 For aspiration's all you need to seek.

Whatever you are, keep on seeking. Try!   1440
   Keep seeking water though your lips are dry,
For your dry lips give evidence that they
   Will reach the water's source as well one day:
Dryness of lips is water's reassurance:
   'You're led to water by all this disturbance.'
Thus seeking's a blest action that can slay
   And wipe out obstacles stood in the way.
To things you long for, seeking is the key;
   It is your army's flag and victory.
This seeking is just like a cock that crows   1445
   When dawn arrives, so everybody knows.
Keep seeking—lack of means should be ignored;
   You need no tools when travelling to the Lord.
Befriend those you see searching, son, and bow
   Your head down in devotion to them now.
By mixing with them you'll turn to a searcher;
   Through conquerors' shadows, you'll become a conqueror.
If an ant seeks the rank of Solomon,
   Don't look down at its effort or poke fun.
Though you have wealth and skill now, were they not   1450
   In the beginning just a wish you sought?

Story about the person who, in the time of the Prophet David, would pray night and day, crying: 'Give me lawful livelihood without struggle!'

In Prophet David's era there was one
   Who'd say before both sage and simpleton:
'O God, grant riches to me through Your grace
   Without a struggle though for me to face,
Since you created me a lazy brat,
   Sluggish and slothful, and so proud of that.
A mule's load is not something one can pack
   On a mere donkey with a feeble back;
I'm lazy, God, created thus by You—   1455
   Grant sustenance through being lazy too!

I'm lazy, dozing in the shade of grace
    And of existence, which You've put in place.
Surely you've sent a means to earn their keep
    To lazy men who always love to sleep?
All who can move will seek a livelihood,
    So pity those who can't move to find food.
Send daily bread to those who feel much grief
    The way that rainclouds bring dry land relief:
Land has no feet, so Your munificence   1460
    Drives clouds there to deliver rain at once.
Babies can't walk, and so their mothers feed
    Them every day with all the food they'll need.
I want my portion to come suddenly
    Without more than a plea to come from me.'
For a long while he stayed this way to pray,
    From dawn to dusk, from night to break of day.
People laughed at his words and raw desire
    To gain without work that would make him tire.
'What crazy things he's saying!' people said,   1465
    'Did someone give him drugs to lose his head?
The way to earn is hard work every week;
    God gave all men skills and the need to seek—
Through those means seek out daily bread! Don't wait
    Expectant, *enter their homes through the gate!**
The Prophet and the ruler of this era
    Is David, whose great skills could not be clearer.
He has much might and pomp; he's been perfected
    By blessings, since by God he's been selected.
The miracles he can perform are countless;   1470
    His flow of waves of bounty is relentless.
No one like him, from Adam till today,
    Sang better than the instruments men play;
At sermons, where huge crowds had congregated,
    By his sweet voice all were annihilated.
His preaching would attract both lion and deer,
    Oblivious to the other one being near.
Mountains and birds would join in when he'd preach,
    Both confidants allowed within close reach.

And he had further miracles: his face　　　1475
　　Shone light that came from far beyond all space.
Despite this might, God made it understood
　　He too must struggle for a livelihood;
Without his weaving chain-mail, naught came down
　　As daily bread, despite his huge renown.
And yet a filthy wretch who's God-forsaken,
　　Attached to earth and kept outside of heaven,
The kind who wishes for material gains
　　Without the need to work or suffer pains,
This giddy-headed fool's come to declare:　　　1480
　　"Without a ladder I'll climb in the air." '
One man would mock him, saying, 'Go ahead,
　　Here comes your harbinger and daily bread.'
Another man would laugh in disbelief:
　　'Give us some of your gift, great village chief!'
But he would not reduce his praise and prayers
　　Due to the people's many jokes and stares.
This man then quickly grew so infamous
　　As one who'd buy food with an empty purse,
Seen as a symbol of stupidity,　　　1485
　　Yet asking God for things still ceaselessly . . .

How a cow ran into the house of one who was praying
importunately. The Prophet has said: 'God loves those who are
importunate in prayer, since the asking from God and the
importunity of the requester are better than what he is praying for'

　　. . . Until one morning while he was still praying
　　With sighs as well as words that he was saying—
A cow ran in his house then suddenly,
　　Ramming the door to break the bolt and key.
Boldly the cow rushed in, but couldn't cope—
　　The man leapt up and bound its legs with rope.
He slit the cow's throat with no hesitation,
　　Mercilessly, without consideration,
Then hurried to the butcher straight away　　　1490
　　To get that man to flay its skin away.

The poet excuses himself and appeals for help

You who, inside me like an embryo,
  Make such demands, help me fulfil them! Show
The way and grant success, or else please stop
  Making demands of me. Please let it drop!
If you demand from one in penury
  Much gold, first give him it, king, secretly.
Without you, poetry each single night
  Would not dare to emerge within our sight;
O Knowing One, rhyme, prose, and poetry   1495
  Are Your command's slaves acting fearfully.
You've made all things as glorifiers of You,
  Inanimates and animate beings too.
In different fashions each one sings Your praise,
  Each unaware of all the other ways.
Most don't believe inanimates can sing
  His praise, though they have mastered worshipping;
Even the seventy-two sects* are without
  Knowledge about each other, plagued with doubt.
When people speaking have no clue at all   1500
  What can a mute door know about the wall?
Of prayers by those who speak I'm unaware—
  How can my ears then hear the mute one's prayer?
The Sunnite has a special kind of praise;
  The fatalists opt for contrasting ways—
Sunnites can't hear the fatalists' glorifications;
  While they can't hear the former's great laudations,
Yet say, 'That one is lost and far astray,
  Heedless of God's command: "*Stand up to pray!*" '
The Sunnite says, 'What does he understand?'   1505
  God has thus made them clash through His command.
He brings to view each of their essences,
  And He makes clear what are the differences.
Each man can tell apart His wrath and grace,
  Whether he's wise or ignorant and base,

But grace that hides in wrath or wrath inside
 The heart of mercy, with no sign outside—
This can be seen by holy ones alone;
 Through mystic touchstones in their hearts it's known.
Mere speculation must fulfil the rest   1510
 Who fly with just one wing towards their nest.

*Explanation that knowledge has two wings and conjecture
one—conjecture is deficient and cannot fly; and a comparison
of conjecture with certainty*

True knowledge has two wings, conjecture one.
 You can't fly with one wing—though it might run,
The one-winged bird falls headlong to the floor,
 Then spurts up just a few feet high once more;
Conjecture's bird jumps up, then falls distressed,
 Hoping with just one wing to reach its nest.
When it breaks from conjecture, knowledge brings
 The answer and it opens up two wings.
After this, *it will travel straight and evenly*   1515
 *Not falling on its face or hobbling feebly.**
Now with two wings, like Gabriel it flies straight
 Without conjecture, hot air, or debate.
If all the world tells it, 'You've fled perdition
 On God's path, following the true religion,'
It won't feel flattered, and its peerless soul
 Won't join with them who would try to cajole.
And if they tell it, 'You have truly strayed,
 Thinking you're mountain-like—you're a straw-blade,'
These taunts won't cause it to succumb to doubt   1520
 And it won't feel hurt to see them walk out.
Even if mountains and the sea should say:
 'You're stuck with being left behind astray.'
It won't have any impact on its brain,
 And neither will the scoffers' taunts cause pain.

*Parable about a man becoming ill owing to him imagining
respect from people and the desire of customers for him;
and the story about the teacher**

A teacher caused his pupils so much stress
    Due to hard toil which led to weariness.
They talked about how they could halt the course
    And make him leave his teaching post by force:
'Since this man's never sick, what can we do   1525
    To make him take days off, and free us too
From toil and from this cage which he would lock—
    This man is hard to budge, like solid rock.'
One of the cunning children planned this way:
    'I'll say: "Teacher, how pale you seem today!
Are you okay? Your colour's turning pale, sir.
    Is it because of fever or the weather?"
The teacher will now wonder if he's sick
    For a while, so we must extend this trick.
Then you, my brother, on entering the gate,   1530
    Ask, "Teacher, are you well? What is your state?"
To make him worry that it might be bad,
    Because, through doubts, an intellect turns mad.
Then, let three fellow classmates of ours follow
    Behind us to express concern and sorrow;
Once thirty pupils have repeated this,
    It will be viewed as fact through witnesses.'
The others said, 'Bravo, sagacious friend!
    May you receive the grace that God should send.'
They all agreed a firm pledge afterwards   1535
    That none of them should try to change the words.
And he gave them an oath to take right there
    Not to divulge the plan he would prepare.
One child's opinion influenced every mind:
    He went ahead; the flock would trail behind.
Intellects have some similar differences
    As human beauty in appearances;

'The excellence of men,' the Prophet said,
    'Is hidden in their tongues.' Don't be misled!

*People's intellects differ in their original nature, and according
to the Mu'tazilites, they were originally equal, with differences
emerging owing to the subsequent acquisition of knowledge*

Intellects varied much originally.   1540
    This Sunni doctrine is our testimony.
Opposing this, Mu'tazilites still claim
    Intellects were all equal and the same;
Differences grew from later education,
    So some know more among the population.
This is false, for a child's opinion can,
    Though he lack the experience of a man,
Produce such thoughts that people very old
    Can't comprehend no matter how they're told.
Excellence in a man's original nature   1545
    Is better than what's gained through struggle later.
Tell me what's best: gifts that God first bestows
    Or hoping one born lame walks when he grows?

How the children make the teacher imagine things

On the next day, the students hurriedly came
    To school with their plan and its clever aim.
They all stood waiting patiently outside
    For their strong leader to go first inside,
For he was after all the great plan's source:
    The head will always lead the foot of course.
Don't seek priority, you imitator,   1550
    Over the source of the sky's light—He's greater.
That boy went in and said, 'Teacher, hello!
    Your face is paler than a day ago.'
'I have no ailments, boy,' the teacher said,
    'Sit down, remove that nonsense from your head!'

Though he dismissed it, still imaginings made
   An impact on his heart, and soon that strayed.
Another pupil said he looked sick too,
   And, due to this, his first misgivings grew.
The pupils carried on till his first doubt   1555
   Increased and health was all he thought about.

How Pharaoh became sick owing to false imaginings caused by people's reverence for him

To Pharaoh all his subjects would prostrate,
   Putting his heart and health in a bad state.
'Lord and king!' said each woman, man, and child,
   And this destroyed him, for he grew beguiled,
Such that he claimed divinity with pride,
   A dragon that could not be satisfied.
The partial intellect leads to delusion
   Because its dwelling place is dark confusion.
If there's a narrow path here on the ground,   1560
   Without concern one follows that path round.
But if you're walking on a high brick wall,
   Though it be wide, you'll worry you might fall.
And when you fall it's due to your heart's tremblings—
   Consider well this fear due to misgivings.

The teacher becomes sick owing to misgivings

The teacher felt weak due to doubt and fear,
   And so took home the things he wanted near.
He raged at his wife, saying: 'Her love's weak!
   I'm gravely ill, yet from her not a squeak:
She didn't warn me of my pale complexion.   1565
   To see me die might be her real intention.
Her good looks made her vain and so aloof,
   Unaware I've come crashing through the roof.'
He reached his house and opened the front door,
   Trailed by the children from the class before.

His wife asked, 'Why so early? Is all well?
   May nothing terrible make you unwell!'
'Are you blind? Look at my pale face again.
   Strangers feel worry that I suffer pain,
While you, here at my house, still fail to see   1570
   My anguish due to your hypocrisy.'
'There's nothing wrong with you, sir,' his wife said,
   'That's only a vain thought inside your head.'
'Are you still questioning me, whore?' he then asked her.
   'Can't you detect the changes and my tremor?
How did I earn a wife who's deaf and blind?
   I'm suffering agony of every kind.'
'Sir, shall I bring a mirror here,' she said,
   'To show I haven't sinned and you're misled?'
'Damn you and damn your mirror!' he replied,   1575
   'You're always filled with spite and must have lied.
I want to sleep because pain fills my head,
   So bring some sheets and quickly make my bed!'
He screamed when she would hesitate a bit:
   'Hurry, for you this job's the perfect fit.'

The teacher lies in bed and grieves due to imaginings of being sick

That poor wife made the bed that he'd sleep in,
   Thinking: 'I'll have to bury this within;
If I speak, he'll accuse me and then curse.
   And if I don't the matter will grow worse.
An evil omen can make men feel ill;   1580
   Although they have no ailment it works still.
The Prophet said, "*If you act sick near me,*
   You'll then become sick in reality!"
If I tell him, he will imagine then:
   "My wife has plans to live alone again,
To throw me out of my home; now she dreams
   Of wicked goals achieved by spells and schemes."'
She made his bed and he retired alone,
   Breathing a deep sigh, voicing a loud moan.

The children were still there, and secretly   1585
    While studying they felt anxiety,
Thinking, 'We're prisoners here, and it's our doing;
    We are bad builders who made this vile building.'

The children made the teacher imagine for the second time that
he was sick, saying that their recitation of the Qur'an would
increase his headache

The clever boy then said, 'Read each good fellow
    In a loud voice—I want to hear you bellow!'
When they read out aloud, he said, 'Good, boys.
    The teacher will feel worse due to this noise;
His headache will increase from noise we make—
    Should he endure more for his small fee's sake?'
The teacher soon confirmed this: 'Go away!   1590
    My headache's worse, so that's it for today.'

How the children got out of school through this trick

They bowed and said, 'O noble man, may you
    Stay far from danger and affliction too.'
They then leapt out and headed home elated,
    Like birds who found the seed for which they'd waited.
Their mothers grew enraged and shouted out:
    'A school day and you play and mess about?
It's study time now, but you run away
    From books and what your teacher has to say?'
Each made excuses: 'Mother, please don't bawl!   1595
    We've done naught wrong; it's not our fault at all.
It's due to heaven's wheel of destiny
    Out teacher has become sick suddenly.'
'That is a trick and lie!' the mothers said,
    'They'd lie for trivial things—don't be misled!
We'll soon see if the teacher's really sick
    And then get to the bottom of your trick.'

The children said, 'Go in God's name, and you
   Will find out whether it is false or true.'

The mothers of the children go to visit the teacher

The mothers went and found him the next day   1600
   Looking as if about to pass away.
He sweated under covers in his bed,
   His hands both bandaged, blankets on his head.
He kept on whimpering, and they would cry:
   '*God give him strength!* On God we all rely.
May you recover, teacher! We all swear
   That of your headache we were not aware.'
He said, 'I too was unaware until
   Those sons of bitches showed me I was ill.
I was oblivious, busy with instruction,   1605
   Not knowing that I had a huge affliction.'
When a man's truly busy, he can't see
   His own pain or perceive his agony,
Like the Egyptian women who were blind
   To their own selves when Joseph filled their mind:
They cut at their own hands, so unaware—
   The stupefied soul cannot see what's there.*
Many brave men in battle have ignored
   The fact their limbs were cut off by a sword,
Still using that same limb while they attacked   1610
   With the belief that it was still intact.
Later each sees his hand's no longer there
   And that blood pours while he is unaware.

Explanation that the body is a garment for the spirit and that the bodily hand is a sleeve for the hand of the spirit, while the bodily foot is the 'boot of the boot' of the spirit

The body you're attached to is a garment—
   Seek the one wearing it; break your attachment!

For souls, God's unity is much more sweet
    And it has different hands and different feet;
In dreams you see those ones and their connection—
    View them as real, not mere imagination.
You have another body, so don't grieve   1615
    When from your earthly one your soul takes leave.

*Story about the dervish who went into retreat in a mountain and
explanation of the sweetness of seclusion and retreat and entering
this station, for God has said in a sacred hadith, 'I sit with those
who remember Me and am friends with those who befriend Me.'
If you are with all, since you're without Me you're without all
If you're without all, since you're with Me then you're with all*

There was a dervish in the mountains who
    Chose solitude for sleep and waking too.
A breeze reached him from God, Lord of Creation,
    For humans he then felt no inclination.
Staying home seems the easiest to some, brothers,
    While travelling comes more easily to some others;
Just as you are in love with mastery,
    That man's in love with ironmongery.
Everyone's made for his own kind of art   1620
    Or work, and leans towards it with his heart.
Your limbs can't move without your soul's command;
    Without wind straw won't race across the land.
If your own yearning is towards the sky
    Like the Homa* unfold royal wings and fly.
But if you lean towards the earth, my friend,
    Lament and mourn from now until the end;
Wise ones lament before in preparation;
    The stupid do it at the destination.
Discern the outcome from the start, so you   1625
    Won't be regretful on the Last Day too.

A goldsmith sees the outcome of an affair and speaks as befits that
outcome to someone who wished to borrow his weighing scales

> A man approached a goldsmith, whom he told:
>> 'Give me your scales, so I can weigh some gold!'
> He said, 'Begone, I have no sieve with me!'
>> That man said, 'Give them! Stop this mockery!'
> He answered, 'I don't have brooms at my shop.'
>> That man said, 'That's enough. You'd better stop!
> Give me the scales that I've been asking for—
>> Don't act deaf or evade this any more!'
> He answered, 'I'm not deaf. I heard it all,   1630
>> So don't imagine I'm nonsensical.
> I heard, but you're a trembling old man who
>> Has shaky hands and a hunched body too:
> Your gold's made up of tiny bits that will,
>> When grabbed by your old, shaky hands, soon spill.
> Then you'll ask, "Fetch a broom, sir, for I must
>> Find my gold that has scattered in the dust."
> And when you sweep, you'll gather dust up too
>> Then say: "I need to take a sieve from you."
> I said the outcome from the very start,   1635
>> And so, farewell! I'd like you to depart.'

Remainder of the story about that ascetic in the mountain
who vowed: 'I won't pick fruit from the trees, or shake the trees,
or tell anyone, neither openly nor in veiled terms, to shake them.
I will eat only windfall'

> On that high mountain many fruit trees grew
>> And countless mountain pears could be found too.
> The dervish up there prayed, 'O Lord, I swore
>> That I will not pick their fruit any more;
> I won't pick fruit from those tall trees at all
>> Apart from what the wind should cause to fall.'
> For love, he kept his pledge so faithfully
>> Until there came the trials of destiny.

This is why God said, 'You all must beware   1640
   To add "If God wills" to the oaths you swear
I give hearts ever-changing leanings, and
   I lay upon each one a different brand;
*Each dawn I have a new activity**
   To busy Me; naught sidesteps My decree.'
'The heart's a feather,' Mohammad once revealed,
   'It's led by the strong wind across the field.'
Wind drives the feather each way you can see:
   Front, back, left, right, and changing frequently.
And one hadith says: 'Deem this heart the same   1645
   As water boiling through a cauldron's flame.'
Each moment it may seem to change its mind—
   Views come from somewhere else to it, you'll find.
So why trust in the heart's opinion, friend,
   And make vows you'll regret much in the end?
This too is the effect of the Lord's will:
   You see a pit, but can't avoid it still.
It's no surprise that birds can't see the snare
   And fall into destruction from the air;
It is surprising when it sees its place,   1650
   But goes into that snare in any case—
With eyes and ears both open, and the trap
   In front, its wings still give an extra flap!

A comparison showing that the shackles and snares of fate,
though actually hidden, are visible through their effects

You'll see in rags one from a noble race,
   Bareheaded now he's had a fall from grace;
He is consumed with passion and feels aimless:
   He's sold his property to leave him penniless.
Losing his household, he's become disgraced
   And walks like someone luckless and displaced.
To an ascetic he says, 'Lord, help me   1655
   For God's sake to make progress inwardly.
I've fallen on hard times through paths I've taken,
   And gold, wealth, and much bounty I've forsaken.

Give spiritual support to me today
　　So I can flee at last from this dark clay.'
He begs like this from everyone: 'Help please
　　To give me what I seek: release, release!'
His hands and feet were free and were not bound
　　In iron, and no guards were then around.
'From which chains do you seek release today?   1660
　　From which gaol do you wish to get away?'
Only one who is pure-souled now can see
　　The hidden chain of fate and destiny;
Though it's invisible it's harder than
　　Prison or iron chains for any man,
Because the ironsmith can break that sort
　　And diggers take out bricks from any fort.
No ironsmiths possess the strength to sever
　　The thick and heavy hidden chain, however.
Mohammad once was shown that by His Lord   1665
　　Wrapped round a throat as *a palm-fibre cord*:*
On Abu Lahab's wife's back he could see
　　Firewood—'*the carrier of fuel*'* was she.
By him alone were cord and firewood seen—
　　To him was visible all that's unseen.
Others must try interpreting, for this
　　Comes from being witless, not through cleverness.
That rich man's son grew hunched due to strong chains
　　And now he weeps before you from his pains,
Saying: 'Pray for me, so I might gain release   1670
　　And flee this hidden chain that gives no peace.'
Whoever sees signs and has understood
　　Can surely tell apart the bad from good.
He knows, but hides this due to God's command;
　　To show God's secrets has been strictly banned.
This talk is endless. That fakir through hunger
　　Became so weak he was his body's prisoner.

The fakir who had made the vow becomes moved to pluck pears from the tree and God's chastisement arrives without delay

For five days wind did not cause pears to drop;
  His hunger's flames soon made his patience stop.
He saw a few pears near a branch's tip   1675
  But held back patiently and made no slip.
Wind caused the branch to bend down suddenly,
  Stoking desire to eat what he could see;
Hunger, weakness, attraction, and fate now
  Made the ascetic finally break his vow.
Once he had plucked fruit from that tree, he'd shown
  He'd grown too weak to keep the pledge he'd sworn,
And then God's punishment came from the skies
  To stretch his ears and open up his eyes.

The shaikh is accused of being linked with the thieves and his hand is cut off

Twenty thieves were in the vicinity,   1680
  Dividing what they'd stolen wickedly,
And the police chief was informed about
  Their place, so his men hunted them soon out.
He chopped off their right hands and their left feet,
  Causing a scene and clamour in the street.
They chopped off the fakir's hand too in error;
  His feet were sought next by the law enforcer,
But suddenly a horseman gave a shout
  To the enforcer, saying: 'Dog, look out!
That's one whom God loves—don't you understand?   1685
  Why did you cut off God's elite friend's hand?'
The man to blame then ripped his shirt in grief
  And rushed off to confess to his own chief.
Then the police chief came regretfully
  And begged: 'I didn't know—God vouch for me!
Absolve me of this sin and its huge price,
  O noble chief of those in paradise!'

Then the fakir said, 'I have earned this blade;
  I know my sin and errors I have made.
I broke my promise to Him in the past,   1690
  So His decree took my right hand at last.
I broke my promise, knowing it was wrong,
  And that caught up with me before too long.
May my hand, foot, and skin and brain too be
  Sacrificed to Beloved God's decree!
That was my lot—I say it's lawful to
  You who did not know; there's no blame on you.
The one who knew is He Whose every whim
  Is executed—who'd try fooling Him?'
Many a bird has flown in search of seed   1695
  And cut its own throat open due to greed.
Many a bird through hunger's awful pains
  Was trapped inside a small cage that restrains.
Many a fish, in distant seas, mistook,
  Due to their greed, a fisherman's rod's hook.
Many a girl with a veiled, pious face
  By throat and by vagina earned disgrace.
Many a learned judge who had men's trust
  Was brought to shame by bribery and by lust.
And Harut and Marut by wine got barred   1700
  From heaven, for which they had striven hard.
This is why Bayazid took special care
  When seeing laxness during ritual prayer.
Then that man with great knowledge sought what was
  The reason—too much water was the cause;
He vowed, 'I'll not drink water for a year!'
  Then God gave him the strength to persevere.
This effort was for his faith; he became
  'Sultan and Pole of Gnostics' and earned fame.
Since the ascetic's hand due to his greed   1705
  Had been cut off, he didn't grieve or plead.
'Shaikh Amputee' was used for him alone;
  His gullet's error thus made him well known.

The miracles of 'Shaikh Amputee' and how he would weave baskets with two hands

A visitor once saw Shaikh Amputee
    Weave baskets with two hands miraculously.
The shaikh told him, 'Your own life's enemy,
    Why peer into my hut so suddenly?
Why did you do this with such haste?' 'From burning
    With my excessive love and passionate yearning.'
The shaikh said, smiling, 'Now, come in my friend,   1710
    But keep what you've seen secret till the end;
Till I die don't divulge what you now know
    Neither to friends nor to a worthless foe.'
Later, more men arrived and they could view
    This amputee's two-handed weaving too—
He said, 'Creator, You know what is best
    And why what I hide You make manifest.'
Then revelation came: 'There were some who
    Due to your handicap rejected you,
Saying, "He could be an impostor, one   1715
    Whom God's disgraced in front of everyone."
I don't want them to lose their faith and way,
    Through false suspicions to fall far astray—
This miracle will make them understand;
    In work hours I give you a second hand,
So that those wretched men with their suspicion
    Won't be rejected from the gates of heaven.
Before these miracles I would console
    You through My essence and make you feel whole—
I gave these miracles for them, not you;   1720
    And I made you a beacon for them too.
You're past being scared about the body's death;
    Severance of limbs can't make you gasp for breath—
Thoughts about severance of your feet and head
    Have left, and a strong shield has come instead.'

The reason for the courage of Pharaoh's magicians in the face of the amputation of their hands and feet

Didn't vile Pharaoh threaten the magicians
    With punishment on earth in the traditions,
Saying: 'I'll chop your hands and feet off, then
    Hang you and show no mercy to you men'?
He thought they were in the same state throughout   1725
    Of fear, distractions, vain thoughts, and much doubt,
Such that they'd shake with fear and with regrets
    Due to the self's imaginings and threats.
He didn't know that they'd escaped from fright
    And sat now at the gate of the heart's light;
Their shadows from themselves they now could tell
    And all were joyful, fast, and sharp as well.
If the sky's mortar were to start to grind
    Them down to bits in this low world, you'd find
That, since they'd seen the source of forms, distress   1730
    About imaginings would hurt them less.
This world's a dream—do not count on one thought:
    If in a dream a hand's lost, that means naught.
If in a dream shears chop off your sweet head,
    It will remain and you will not be dead.
If in a dream you're split in two parts, still
    When you awake you will be sound, not ill.
In dreams, for bodies it won't really matter
    If they are maimed or even caused to shatter.
The Prophet called this world of forms we see   1735
    'The dream of someone sleeping heedlessly'.
Out of blind faith, with this you now agree;
    Mystics see with no intermediary.
You sleep all day, heedless without remorse.
    Shadows are secondary, moonlight the source.
Your sleep and wakefulness are both sleep, friend:
    A sleeper dreams he's sleeping. In the end
He thinks: 'I'm sleeping', but can tell no more,
    Because to have that dream he'd slept before.

When potters break their pots, they can restore   1740
  Their pots and make them perfect as before.
With every step men fear pits if they're blind,
  So they walk out with fears of every kind.
A man with vision of the road ahead
  Detects the ditches and does not feel dread;
His legs and knees don't tremble constantly,
  So hardships won't fill him with misery.
'Arise, Pharaoh! We're not like those before
  Who'd freeze with fear when they heard monsters roar.
Rip up our cloaks! He will sew them again   1745
  Or fewer clothes are better for good men.
Without clothes, worthless foe, we would embrace
  This beauty tightly and feel special grace;
There's nothing better than to be stripped bare
  Of body too—Pharaoh, you're unaware!'

How the mule complained to the camel: 'I fall on my face a lot, and you only seldom do so!'

The mule said to the camel, 'My good friend,
  Going uphill, downhill, and round the bend
You don't fall on your head along the way
  While I keep falling like one led astray;
Repeatedly I fall flat on my face   1750
  Whether I'm in a dry or soaking place.
Tell me the reason for this difference, so
  The way to live my life I then might know.'
It said, 'I see more clearly with each eye
  Than you can see, and mine are very high;
When I reach a high mountain-top, from there
  I see the furthest peaks and feel aware.
The Lord reveals to my eyes clear as day
  All of the depths and heights too of the way;
I take each step with vision through His grace   1755
  And so I'm saved from falling on my face.
You see two steps before you, unaware,
  Though you can see the bait of the next snare:

Are blind and seeing men the same to you*
    In their abiding and their travelling too?
When God inserts in embryos men's souls
    He gives attraction too to particles:
It can draw particles through food, to weave
    The body's warp and woof that we perceive;
Until its fortieth year the Lord will sow   1760
    Desire to draw such particles to grow—
Drawing such particles was taught, my friends,
    To spirits by the Lord who comprehends;
The joiner of these motes is the Great Sun—
    Without food He draws particles for fun:
When you wake from your sleep, he calls back then
    Departed consciousness to you again.
That they've not left Him you will quickly learn,
    When they come back at His command '*Return!*'

How the particles of the ass of Ozayr were assembled after
it had rotted away, through God's permission, and were
reconstituted before Ozayr's eyes

'Ozayr, look at your ass,' a voice would say,   1765
    'You saw it previously in slow decay:
He will collect all parts in front of you,
    Its skull and tail, both ears and both legs too.'
He can unite such parts without a hand:
    Scattered things can be joined by His command.
Consider now a tailor who's so clever
    Without a needle he sews rags together:
No thread or needle sounds impossible—
    He sews and yet no seams are visible.
Open your eyes now—Judgment Day's in view!   1770
    No doubts about it will remain with you.
You'll see My own uniting power entirely
    And not shake when you die from deep anxiety,
Just as, while sleeping, you're secure from fear
    Even though bodily senses disappear—

You do not tremble then with consternation
Despite your senses' clear annihilation.

The shaikh who did not grieve the death of his own children

In former times there was a Sufi guide,
A heavenly candle blazing far and wide,
Just like a prophet with his people, who   1775
Can open paradise's garden too—
The Prophet said, 'Compare the shaikh to me:
A prophet in his own community.'
One morning by his family he was told:
'Good natured one, why is your heart so cold?
Due to your children's death our hearts are torn—
We are bent double as we grieve and mourn.
You don't weep. Why won't you lament? Please start,
Or do you have no pity in your heart?
When you lack pity and seem not to care,   1780
How can we have faith something's still felt there?
Leader, we live in hope you won't depart
And leave us all to perish while apart.
When on the Final Day they bring a throne,
Our intercessor will be you alone;
On such a day when we will be defenceless,
We will depend on you then feeling generous.
Our hands will grip your coat-tails desperately,
That time when sinners lack security.'
'On Resurrection Day', the Prophet said,   1785
'I can't leave sinners with the tears they've shed;
For those who have transgressed I'll intercede,
So that from heavy torment they'll be freed.
I'll spare grave sinners that strong punishment
They fear for breaking their own covenant.
The godly will have no need on that day
For me to intercede there anyway,
But they can intercede—their words will be
Then just like an effective, firm decree;

Burdened men can't bear others' burdens, friend,   1790
   But I'm not burdened—God made me transcend.'
The one not burdened is the shaikh; commands
   Reach him from God like bowstrings in men's hands.
What does 'shaikh' mean? Old man, one with white hair—
   What does white hair mean though? Become aware:
Black hairs denote his self-existence, so
   A single black hair can't be left to grow.
He is a master when his being's not there,
   Whether he has black hair or grizzled hair—
Black hair means human attributes instead   1795
   Of hair that grows upon your chin or head.
Jesus cried in the cradle words of truth:
   'I am a master, though not yet a youth!'*
If human attributes leave partially,
   That's black and white hair, not true mastery;
When not a single black hair can be traced,
   He is a shaikh then whom God has embraced.
If he's with self once all his hair turns white,
   He's not of God's elite who has gained light—
If one hair-tip of his own qualities   1800
   Remains, he's not from where no plain man sees.

The Shaikh excuses himself for not weeping for his sons

The shaikh then told his wife, 'Do not imagine
   That my heart has no pity or compassion.
I feel for infidels too, though their soul
   Remains ungrateful for the Lord's bestowal;
I pity dogs too, wondering on my own:
   "Why are they yelled at and hit with a stone?"
For dogs that bite I pray with this petition:
   "Save him please from his evil disposition!
Watch over these dogs which I have made known,   1805
   So they're not targets that the people stone."'
God brought His Friends to earth, so He might then
   Make them *a mercy to the world of men.*

God's Friend invites men to the special door—
   'Give them complete release, God!' he'll implore.
He counsels them so they will mend their ways—
   And, if this fails, 'God, don't close it!' he prays.
Ordinary men have just particular grace;
   Great men have also Universal Grace—
To Universal Grace their own is tied;   1810
   They have the Ocean's grace as their own guide.
That lesser grace joined with the Universal,
   Take this as your guide—this is no rehearsal.
An individual cannot find the ocean;
   Small pools seem oceans to his faulty vision.
If he can't see the way, how then can he
   Serve as your guide and lead you to the sea?
Once he joins with the sea, then from that moment
   He can lead you like streams or like a torrent.
If now he calls to God, it's imitation,   1815
   Not through His vision, aid, and revelation.
The shaikh's wife said, 'If you now pity men
   Like shepherds with their flocks, tell me why then
Do you not mourn your own son's shortened life
   Now death, the bleeder, has employed its knife?
The proof of sympathy is in the eye—
   Why are your eyes without tears and stone dry?'
The shaikh turned to his wife and said, 'O woman,
   Winter is not like summer—that's for certain:
Whether they're dead or living still, how can   1820
   They ever leave the heart's eye of this man?
Since they appear here clearly in my view,
   Why should I twist my face round just like you?
Though they now be beyond time, still near me
   They keep on playing just as previously.
Weeping is due to separation's pain,
   But joined with my dear ones I still remain.
Others may see them in their sleep, but I
   Can see them while awake with my own eye.
From this world I can hide myself, you see,   1825
   Scattering the senses' leaves all from their tree.'

Sensation's intellect's own prisoner;
   Intellect's spirit's in ways similar—
The spirit sets the intellect's hands free
   And it resolves its problems easily.
Senses and thoughts are like weeds that flow past
   On the pure water's surface where they're cast:
Intellect's hand sweeps those weeds to the side,
   So wisdom can see water which they hide.
The weeds are on the stream as a thick layer—   1830
   Once they're swept off, water can be seen there.
If God did not free intellect's strong hand,
   Due to desire the weeds would then expand,
Covering the water up—then all the while
   Intellect would keep weeping and lust smile;
Once piety has chained desire's two hands,
   God then sets free the intellect's strong hands.
Thus, powerful senses follow your decree
   When intellect's your master totally:
While you're awake God makes your senses sleep   1835
   To make appear unseen things hidden deep
Inside the soul; awake, through dream-like vision,
   You then can open up the gates of heaven.

Story about how a blind shaikh would read the Qur'an
in front of him and regain his vision as he read

Once in the past that shaikh saw a Qur'an
   Inside the home of a blind holy man.
One summer he had been there as his guest;
   Together there the two would talk and rest.
He thought, 'How strange—there's a Qur'an! But why
   When this good dervish lacks a seeing eye?'
Then his bewilderment from this fact grew: 1840
   'No one else comes to visit like I do!
There's a Qur'an on his shelf though he's blind.
   I am not wrong; I haven't lost my mind!
Shall I ask? No. I should stay patient here
   So that, through patience, my aims will appear.'

He held back; for a while he felt unease
    Till he heard: '*Patience is the key to ease.*'

*How Loqman saw Prophet David making iron rings, but
refrained from asking him about it because he bore in mind that
'Patience will lead to the resolving of the question'*

Loqman once came near David and he saw
    Him making rings from iron and felt awe.
He then observed as well that lofty king   1845
    Linking together every single ring.
He'd never seen coat-mail being made before,
    So he was curious to discover more.
'What is this? Shall I ask?' he contemplated,
    'With these joined rings what have you now created?'
Then he reflected, 'Patience is the best
    Approach, and reaches your goals earliest.'
When you don't ask it is made manifest—
    Patience's bird is faster than the rest.
It will take longer if you choose to ask;   1850
    Impatience turns ease to an arduous task.
Loqman stayed silent, so immediately
    David's work was completed, and then he
Put on the coat of mail that he had made
    In front of patient Loqman, who had stayed.
'This garment is so worthwhile, you should know,
    For your protection from each combat blow.'
'Patience is too,' Loqman said once secure,
    'For it protects against pain you'd endure.'
Patience and truth are paired together, friend—   1855
    Read closely '*By the time*'* until the end!
God has made numerous cures, but none can claim
    They've seen a cure like patience all the same.

Remainder of the story about the blind man and the Qur'an

The guest was patient as he'd taken heed
   And so the problem was resolved with speed.
That night he could hear somebody recite
   The pure Qur'an, then saw a stunning sight:
The blind man reading it without a flaw—
   He couldn't wait more, so enquired in awe:
'Amazing! How, blind man, are you reciting?   1860
   How can you possibly see holy writing?
You have read out the verses of your choosing;
   To keep your place your finger too you're using—
Your moving finger proves that I'm not lying:
   You see the script on which you are relying.'
'You who've left ignorance,' that man replied,
   'By God's work why are you now mystified?
I prayed, "You from Whom we seek help in strife,
   I'm hungry to recite as though for life.
I don't know it by heart; when I recite   1865
   Grant my eyes vision through Your Perfect Light.
For that short time return to me my vision,
   So I can read Your Pure Book with precision."
From God then came the cry: "Industrious fellow,
   Who keeps faith in me during every sorrow,
You have good thoughts and live with the desire
   That every moment you might hear, 'Rise higher!'
Whenever you hold the Qur'an to read,
   Or to inspect the texts if you feel need,
I will restore your vision at that moment—   1870
   Venerable man, to me you are important."
He has done this, so every time that I
   Wish to read the Qur'an we magnify,
The One Who misses naught, for He's informed,
   The Noble King by Whom all things were formed,
That Peerless King restores for me my sight
   At once like lamps which brighten the dark night.'

That's why God's Friends will make no protestation:
    For what He takes He soon sends compensation.
If He burns down your vineyard, grapes are sent;   1875
    He sends you joy when He sees you lament.
He gives a hand to someone who's lost his
    And makes hearts filled with grief receive sheer bliss.
Thoughts of '*We won't submit*' have gone away,
    Since what is lost now He will soon repay.
Warmth comes without fire when He should desire,
    So I'm content if He puts out my fire;
When He gives light without lamps, why should you
    Fret if you lose your lamp as fools would do?

Description of some Friends of God who are content with God's decrees and do not pray, 'Change this decree!'

Hear from me now the following description   1880
    Of wayfarers who feel no opposition:
They're different from those saints who supplicate,
    Who sew then tear, alter, and then rotate.
I know these other Friends of God whose station
    Means that their lips are closed to supplication:
Due to contentment that these Friends possess,
    Attempting to change fate's unfaithfulness.
From fate they taste a special ecstasy,
    So it's unfaithful to seek liberty.
God's made His good opinion of them known,   1885
    So they don't wear dark mourning clothes and mourn.

Bohlul questions a dervish

Bohlul once asked a dervish, 'How are you?
    Dervish, please tell me of what interests you.'
The dervish answered, 'How should someone be
    For whom the world's work's done perpetually,
For whose wish torrents and all rivers flow,
    Whenever he should wish the stars all glow,

And for whom life and death are officers
  Who move around whenever he prefers?
He sends condolences at times he pleases, 1890
  Congratulations too as hardship eases;
If he wills wayfarers can move ahead
  Or fall astray inside his snare instead.
In this world no mouth ever smiled, you see,
  Unless it was approved as his decree.'
Bohlul said, 'King, your words are true and blest,
  For in your radiance this is manifest,
This and much more besides, veracious man,
  But please explain as clearly as you can
Such that both wise and foolish people too 1895
  Will readily accept what's claimed by you.
Put it now into words appropriate
  For ordinary men to benefit.'

The perfect speaker offers food for minds—
  His table has food of all different kinds,
So that no guest will be without provision,
  Each finding there the source of his nutrition,
Like the Qur'an, because its seven layers
  Give common folk and the elite their shares.
The dervish said, 'The masses understand 1900
  At least that this world follows God's command:
No leaf will ever drop off from a tree
  Unless it is the King of Fate's decree.
No morsel passes from the mouth below
  Until God tells it, '*Enter!* You can go.'
Men's inclinations form their reins which lead
  The way desired by He Who has no need.
On earth as in the heavens, as you'll learn,
  No atom moves a wing and no leaves turn
Save by the Lord's eternal firm command— 1905
  But how can one make others understand?
Who can count all the leaves there on the branches?
  How can mere speech encompass what is boundless?

Hear this much: the occurrence of each action
   Is just by means of the Creator's sanction,
And once the slave's content with God's decree,
   He then becomes its servant willingly,
Not as a burden, nor for recompense,
   But from his virtuous nature's excellence.
He wants his life for his own sake no more;   1910
   A life of pleasure's not what he lives for.
Whenever God's command is what dictates,
   Life and death are the same to him as fates.
He lives for God's sake and not for mere wealth;
   He dies for God's sake, not due to ill health.
His faith is for God's sake; he aims to please.
   That's not for paradise with streams and trees.
For God too he abandons unbelief,
   Not out of fear of hell, nor for relief,
And not through taking on forced discipline—   1915
   His nature was that way in origin.
He laughs the moment he sees God content;
   He views as sweetest candy fate that's sent.
When God's slave's character takes such a form
   To his command the world must then conform.
Why should he pray to God and remonstrate,
   Saying: 'O Lord, please change this bitter fate!'
His and his children's deaths are not of note
   For him, like something pleasant down his throat;
This faithful man compares their agony   1920
   With how sweets give poor old men ecstasy,
So why should he resort to supplication
   Unless he sees this cause God's satisfaction?
His supplication and his intercession
   Are not due to that pure man's own compassion,
Which was consumed that day when from above
   God lit up the bright lamp of His slave's love.
Love is hell-fire for attributes—that flare
   Has burned his attributes to the last hair.
How can night travellers fathom this distinction,   1925
   Except Daquqi,* who rose in this fortune?

Story about Daquqi and his miracles

Daquqi was so handsome and well dressed,
    Lover of God with miracles so blest.
He walked the way the moon glides by at night;
    Through him night travellers' spirits all grow bright.
For long in one place he would seldom stay,
    Spending in every village just one day.
'If I stay in one place two days,' he said,
    'Love for that dwelling might then turn my head.
Don't be seduced by dwellings, soul, take heed!   1930
    Travel to independence from all need.
I won't attach my heart to one location,
    So it stays pure for its examination.'
By day he travelled and by night he prayed;
    Falcon-like on the king his focus stayed,
Cut off from men, not due to bad within him,
    Nor dualism born of egotism,
Compassionate to creatures, intercessor
    Whose prayers would always soon receive an answer,
Refuge to good and bad and always generous,   1935
    Better than both your parents and more precious.
The Prophet said, 'Dear men, like fathers do,
    Compassionately I sympathize with you.
Because you are all parts of me—why then
    Separate small parts from the whole again?'
Once severed that part's useless. Can't you see
    A severed limb's just carrion tragically?
It's dead unless it joins the whole once more;
    Of life it has no knowledge any more.
Even if it should move, what would that prove?   1940
    The freshly severed limb can also move.
And if the severed part falls, nonetheless
    The whole won't then become a portion less.
One can't explain with words these mysteries;
    Comparisons have their inadequacies.

Resumption of the story about Daquqi

The Prophet once compared his friend Ali
    To lions, though he's different actually.
From likeness, difference, and comparison
    Head to Daquqi's story now—move on!
That jurist–chief for his community   1945
    Excelled the angels too in piety,
Moved with more measure than the moon; how jealous
    Religion felt to see one so religious;
Though he would pray and show much piety,
    He'd seek out God's elite still constantly:
His main aim on his travels was to meet
    For just a moment one of God's elite,
So he would pray while travelling: 'God, let me
    Become familiar with that company.
O Lord, make me a slave who is devoted   1950
    To those whom my heart recognized and noted.
And, God, though they be veiled still from my eyes,
    Make me treat well those I can't recognize.'
God would say, 'Great chief, what love in such pleas
    And what an unquenched thirst in prayers like these!
You have My love—why seek some others' too—
    Why seek a human being when God's with you?'
He'd answer, 'Lord, my secrets You can read.
    You opened to my heart the path of need.
I'm seated in the middle of the sea,   1955
    Yet lust for water from a jug grips me.
Like David, I possess now ninety sheep,
    Yet lust in me for others still runs deep.
Lust for Your love brings glory, rank, and grace;
    Lust for all other things just brings disgrace.'
This manly lust brings gains; it's not the same
    As that of dazzled ones, which just brings shame.
Lust of the manly ones brings them progression;
    Lust of effeminates brings them regression—

The former's part of masculine perfection,   1960
  The latter just disgusts and earns rejection.
There is a hidden mystery right here, one
  For which to Khezr's side Moses would soon run
Like someone thirsty who's insatiable—
  Don't settle when much more's attainable!
This court is limitless, so now disown
  And leave your proud seat—this path serves as throne.

The mystery behind Moses seeking Khezr despite the perfection of his Prophethood and proximity to God

Learn now from Moses the Kalim's sound ways
  And witness what, through yearning, this man says:
'Though I have Prophethood, which ranks so high,   1965
  I seek Khezr now to clear self from my eye.'
'Moses, your people you have left behind
  And, dazed, a special man you aim to find.
You're free from fear and hope, a king who's strong,
  How long will you keep seeking him, how long?
What's yours stays with you—this you understand;
  O sky, how long keep roaming on mere land?'
Moses said, 'Please hold off reproaching me:
  Don't waylay sun and moon to that degree!
To *where the two seas merge** I'm heading nearer,   1970
  To follow the true sultan of the era.
I will make Khezr a means to my goal, friend,
  Or pass on a night journey with no end.
With wings I will fly on for years to come—
  What are mere years? For a millennium!
I'm heading out—do you think it's not good?
  Love of God is worth more than love of food!'
This discourse has no end. Narrate for me
  The thrilling tale about this Daquqi.

Resumption of the story about Daquqi

Daquqi, may that man by God be blest,   1975
    Explained, 'I roamed a while from East to West;
Out of love for the moon for years I wandered
    Unaware of the path and so bewildered.'
'Barefoot on thorns and rocks why do I tread?
    I am bewildered, selfless, off my head.
Don't look at just these two feet on the ground—
    It's by their hearts that lovers move around:
When through its sweetheart it's intoxicated,
    The heart can't tell then where the path's located.'
Bodies can be described as 'long' or 'short';   1980
    The spirit's path though is a different sort.
Your foetus gained an intellect—no station,
    Nor any footprint, marked this elevation.
The soul moves round beyond both time and space;
    The body learnt from it in the first place.
He's left behind all bodily motion now;
    Seen in a body, he's free anyhow.
He said, 'I sought out ardently one day
    The Light of God in humans, just one ray,
To find an ocean in a drop, or one   1985
    Atom that can envelop the whole sun.
By the time that on foot I reached the shore
    It was by then approaching night once more.

The apparition of what looked like seven candles in the direction of the shore

I noticed seven candles from a distance
    And rushed towards them through my own persistence.
Each candle's flame's light stretched so beautifully
    Up to the heavens, as if over me.
Bewilderment filled me and then it led
    Its wave to surge above my reasoning's head.

Candles had been lit up of a rare kind,   1990
   Yet people's eyes to them are somehow blind—
People sought lamps despite the candles' radiance
   While they were lit up, thereby showing ignorance.
Blindfolds covered their eyes, which left me shocked—
   By "*He guides whom He pleases*"* they'd been blocked.'

The seven candles then appeared as one candle

Then suddenly I could see with my eye
   Seven become one, cleaving the whole sky;
The one turned into seven flames anew.
   My drunkenness and stupefaction grew.
There were connections too between each candle   1995
   Beyond what words express and brains can handle.
Things that you can perceive with just one look
   Can't be expressed in speech or in a book;
Ears, even after years, will never see
   Things that in flashes you sense inwardly.
Return *to yourself*. Since this has no end,
   I can't find praises fit for You to send.*
I ran much closer, curious now to see
   These candles' clues about divinity.
And I became astonished while I raced,   2000
   And witless, falling down due to my haste—
There in the dust for some time I remained,
   Unconscious, with my yearning uncontained,
Until my wits returned and I could stand
   And move without a body in this land.

How those seven candles appeared as seven men

The seven candles seemed then to my eye
   As seven men; their light reached to the sky.
Next to those rays, daylight looked dark as night.
   Their brightness overwhelmed all other light.

Those candles become seven trees

Each took a tree's form then to my surprise,   2005
    Their greenness blessing my astonished eyes—
So many leaves kept branches out of view,
    So many fruit that covered its leaves too.
Their branches stretched beyond the lote tree's place*
    In heaven—in fact, they reached beyond all space.
Their roots stretched down into the earth's deep core,
    Beyond the ox and fish and then some more.*
Their roots more so than branches formed a smile;
    One's brain is stunned by such shapes all the while.
After bursting them open, beams of light   2010
    Spurted out from each single fruit in sight.

How those trees were kept hidden from the eyes of people

More wondrous was that millions of men
    Passed by this desert and the plain just then,
But they spent their time chasing shadows and
    Even made shades from rugs across the land;
They didn't see the shadows of these trees—
    I spit on such distorted eyes as these!
God's wrath had sealed these people's eyes, to bar
    Them from the moon—they just see a small star,
And just a mote instead of the sun's rays,   2015
    Though they don't lose hope of God's generous ways.
The caravan lacks food, yet fruit that's ripe
    Drops off the tree—God's magic's a strange type.
Thirsty men fought, and never paused to wonder,
    Over such rotten fruit, as though fine plunder,
While every leaf and bud of that same tree
    Screamed out, *'Would that my people now could see!'*
From every tree rang out the cry, 'Come here
    Towards us, wretched people, while we're near!'

God's strong possessiveness then told the trees: 2020
  'We've sealed their eyes. *There are no sanctuaries.*'*
If someone told them, 'Head that way to find
  The trees which will fill with delight your mind.'
They would have said, 'There's some poor wretch again—
  Divine will's made that drunkard turn insane.
His brain has rotted like an onion, due
  To ecstasies and trials of hardship too.'
And that man would have stayed there saying, 'How odd!
  What is the veil that blinds these people, God?
The intellectuals, each with an opinion,   2025
  Won't take one step in the correct direction.
Their obstinate minds make them all insist
  That no such trees can possibly exist.
Am I the one who is insane instead,
  Or has the Devil put things in my head?
I rub my eyes each moment, wondering how
  And ask myself if I am dreaming now—
How can it be a dream? I ate the fruit,
  So I can't doubt it's real. There's no dispute.
When I see the deniers turn away   2030
  From this most lovely orchard every day,
Suffering poverty and neediness,
  Spending their lives on what is valueless,
And lusting after one leaf from a tree,
  These destitute ones sighing heavily,
Millions of them now having fled on foot
  From these great trees and all their special fruit,
"Have I gone mad?" I ask repeatedly,
  "Have I touched trees that are imaginary?"'
Read '*Not until the Prophets felt despair*'   2035
  And '*Thought they'd been denied*'* did aid come there.
Recite it with *tashdid*,* or otherwise
  The Prophets would themselves be veiled by lies.
The Prophets' souls lapsed into doubting then
  Due to denials by the wicked men.
After the doubting our aid came in time:
  'Renounce them for the soul's tree and then climb!

Eat up the fruit and give each man his lot—
    Each moment wondrous sorcery's being taught.'

The people say, 'Amazing—what's that sound   2040
    In this plain where no trees or fruit are found?
Deceiving words of the intoxicated
    Which say, "Near you huge orchards are located?"
We've rubbed our eyes yet see no orchards here,
    Just desert and a harsh path most would fear.
Amazing how they prattle on in vain!
    Why should they do this? They should all explain.'
I answer back, 'What marvel, what surprise!
    Why has the Lord put seals upon their eyes?'
In a dispute Mohammad was stunned once;   2045
    Bu Lahab had the same experience.
But there were differences between the two—
    What matters is what that Great King will do.'
Daquqi, silence! Rush ahead from here—
    Why harp on where there's not a single ear?

The seven trees become one

'Seven trees merged as one,' Daquqi said,
    'As I, who was so lucky, moved ahead.
Each moment they kept changing: seven then one.
    Perplexity from this left me undone.
Then I saw all the trees perform the prayer,   2050
    Forming, like an assembly, one row there:
One tree in front who led the prayer; the others
    Standing behind and worshipping like brothers.
Their standing, bowing, and prostrating then
    Left me amazed—they acted just like men.
Then I recalled God's words, which I'll relate:
    "He told the stars and trees to all *prostrate*."*
These trees did not have waists to bend, nor knees—
    What an assembly formed here by mere trees!

The inspiration from above came down: 2055
　"Are you bewildered still, man of renown?"

The seven trees become seven men

'After a long while these trees turned to men
　Seated before God, Who's unique. I then
Kept rubbing hard my eyes and wondered who
　These seven lion-hearts were and what they do.
Once I had neared them on the path I'd taken,
　I greeted them, alert, no longer shaken.
Then to my salutation they replied,
　"Daquqi, noble men's great source of pride!"
How did they recognize me instantly   2060
　When they had not before set eyes on me?
Quickly they read my mind just like a book
　And gave each other a brief, furtive look.
They answered me with smiles, then: "Our dear friend,
　Too hidden still for you to comprehend?
How can the secret of where's left and right
　Be hidden from a God-drunk heart's clear sight?"
I thought, "Their gaze is on realities,
　So how do they know names, forms such as these?"
"If a name disappears from saints," one said,   2065
　"They are effaced, not ignorant instead."
Then they said, "We would like to follow you,
　Our holy friend, and copy what you do."
I said, "Okay, but give me some time, please.
　Time's passing makes me face some difficulties,
Which your companionship that has much worth
　Could solve as grapes grow from the nurturing earth
And seeds with kernels graciously consort
　With dark soil to form life of a new sort—
In that soil it was able to efface   2070
　The self and not to leave behind a trace;
Effacement changed it from a closed-up seed:
　It opened and expanded, rode its steed.

Once it shed self and faced its origin,
    Form left, display of meaning could begin."
They nodded then to say, "At your command!"
    Causing a flame in my heart to be fanned.
There, for a stretch of time I meditated
    With that group, and from my self separated;
My soul escaped to freedom from time then   2075
    Because time is what turns youths to old men.'

All change is due to time, therefore if you
    Are freed from time, you're free from changing too.
If you spend time beyond time, you will see
    Your attributes all vanish totally.
Of timelessness time has no clear perception,
    For it sees no way out but mystification.
In the realm of this search, each one is tied
    Inside a stable that's been specified.
Each stable has its trainer—no admission   2080
    Is given to deniers without permission.
If lust makes one break out, it sticks its head
    Into the stable of the rest instead—
Immediately strong guards will then appear
    And drag it by its halter back from here.
My friend, if you don't notice those guards still,
    Look at your choice opposing your own will:
You make a choice, but your own hands and feet
    Will not respond—you're trapped and can't compete.
Have you tried to deny the guards their role,   2085
    Renaming them 'threats from the carnal soul'?

Daquqi goes forward to act as the leader

Daquqi, this talk has no end—run fast
    Before the prayer's allotted time has passed:
Unique man, do the dawn prayer that is due,
    So that the day can be adorned by you.

Leader with clear sight, to have this position
   The prayer leader must have perfect vision:
It's disapproved by law to pray behind
   A congregation leader who is blind.*
Though he be well trained at the highest school,   2090
   Clear sight is better even in a fool,
Because the blind man can't avoid pollution—
   Sight is the best means to avoid confusion.
The blind man cannot see dirt in his way—
   May no believing man turn blind, I pray!
The outwardly blind is impure outside,
   The inwardly blind is impure inside;
Outward impurity is washed away,
   The inward kind increases day by day—
It only can be washed by tears the moment   2095
   Inner impurity becomes apparent.
God has called infidels 'unclean'—it's clear
   Outward uncleanliness is not meant here:
Infidels' outward faces aren't impure;
   Their faith and ethics are what's meant for sure.
The outward kind's smell wafts from yards away,
   The inward kind's from Syria to Rayy.*
Its smell will reach the sky and then still rise
   Up to the houris and to paradise.
I speak to suit your own capacity,   2100
   Seeking one who perceives things perfectly.
Perception's water, body the jar it fills,
   And when the jar breaks all the water spills.
The jar has five big holes that you can't fill
   With water or with snow, try as you will.
The order '*Shut your eyes!*' has come, but you
   Have still not done what you've been told to do.
Your mouth, through speech, steals what you understand;
   Your ear soaks it away like driest sand.
Your other holes act in a similar way,   2105
   Drawing your hidden wisdom all the way.
If you take water from the sea without
   Replacements, then a desert soon spreads out.

It's late now, otherwise I'd give tuition
    About replacements and such substitution,
Such as where they've arrived from to the sea
    After some being used up previously.
A million animals drink from this source;
    Clouds carry water on a different course.
The sea then draws replacements, but from where?   2110
    The ones with proper guidance are aware.

We've started this book's stories hastily,
    So they're unfinished in this Masnavi.
Hosam, the heavens haven't brought the birth
    Of such a king who could have equal worth.
You've seldom entered in our souls, and they
    Feel so unworthy when you come their way.
How often I had praised those of past days.
    You were the only one I meant always:
A prayer knows its own home: whoever's name   2115
    You use in prayer it reaches its true aim.
God gave us parables to hide this praise
    From those who don't deserve to know these ways.
Though this praise seems unworthy, still be sure
    That God accepts *exertions of the poor*.
He will excuse it, though it seems deficient,
    For, from blind eyes, two drops are deemed sufficient.
The moon and birds know this obscurest route
    By which I've praised this man of good repute.
Thus, sighs of envy of him will decrease   2120
    And envy's teeth's attempts to bite will cease.
A jealous man won't find his dreamt-up goal,
    A parrot can't fit in a mouse's hole.
His image is made up—don't judge too soon:
    It is your eyebrow's hair, not a new moon.
Beyond both realms I send praise gratefully.
    Write 'Daquqi steps forward' now for me.

Daquqi steps forward to lead the congregation in prayer

Praise to the Prophets blends in combination
　　With praise to righteous men and salutation;
The praises are commingled as one whole   2125
　　Just like jugs emptied into one large bowl.
The focus of all worship is the One,
　　So all of the religions must be one;
All praises reach God's light eventually;
　　With men and forms their stay is temporary.
Who can you praise but He Who is deserving?
　　Still those astray will follow their own reckoning.
When light reflects across a wall, just think,
　　For all those rays the wall serves as a link;
The moon appeared inside a well one day;   2130
　　A lost man poked his head inside to pray.
When the reflection went back to its source,
　　He lost the moon and stopped prayer in remorse—
The moon was the real object of his praise
　　Although he faced the moon's reflected rays.
To the moon, not reflections, praise belongs,
　　But it is unbelief when it's done wrong.
Through unbelief that bold man was misled:
　　He thought the moon was down below instead.
By idols people too became distracted,   2135
　　Then felt ashamed that on their lusts they'd acted.
Fancies feed lust and lead you far away
　　From Truth, where you should face each time you pray.
What pulls you to a wish you should now see
　　As wings which take you to reality.
Your wings drop off when you try to appease
　　Your lust—you lose control and that wish flees.
Preserve your wings, don't let lust start a fire,
　　And then ascend on wings of true desire.
People think they are doing pleasing things   2140
　　When, for a fancy, they tear off their wings.

I need more time to properly explain,
　　But I am poor and must stay quiet again.

The group follow behind Daquqi

Daquqi stepped ahead to lead the prayer—
　　In front of satin, silk stood that's more rare.
Those kings then followed him just like a herd
　　Of camels, waiting on his every word:
Once they'd said the *takbir*,* they all then fled
　　This world like sacrifices, with no head.
'Prayer leader, hear the meaning that is true: 2145
　　"God, we now sacrifice ourselves to you."'
While making sacrifices they exclaim
　　'*God's great!*'* While slaying self you do the same!
Ishmael's the body, Abraham the soul
　　Which utters the *takbir* in the slayer's role.*
Desire destroys the body in the end;
　　'*Bismillah*'* sacrifices it, my friend.
They stood in rows before God then to pray
　　And have their deeds weighed as on Judgment Day.
They shed tears as they stood before God then,   2150
　　Just as on Judgment Day do fearful men.
God asks then, 'What have you brought Me, in view
　　Of all the respite that I've granted you?
In your life what have you at last achieved?
　　For what have you used food that you've received?
With what have you worn out your radiant eyes
　　And all your other senses? Don't tell lies.
You've used up all your senses and your mind,
　　So what's your gift from that realm left behind?
I gave you hands and feet as good as tools—   2155
　　They didn't come down by themselves, you fools!'
Millions of harsh and painful messages
　　Come from the Lord that day to you like this.
While standing up in prayer, their bodily parts
　　Bend down, as out of shame their bowing starts.

Due to the shame, which all the while gets stronger,
    They lose the strength to stand up any longer.
Then the command arrives: 'Lift up your head
    From bowing down and answer what God's said!'
Each lifts his head up; he who's earned disgrace   2160
    Falls back down like a snake flat on his face.
Then orders come: 'Lift your head from prostration!
    Relate your deeds for our communication!'
He lifts his head up one more time, and then
    That shamefaced one falls on his face again.
God says, 'Lift up your head now and relate
    Your deeds to me, as I interrogate.'
No longer with the strength to stand at all
    Because these awesome words have struck his soul,
He kneels down under such a heavy load   2165
    And God says, 'Speak up clearly! Give what's owed.
Where is your thanks for what I gave to you?
    Show me that wealth and all your profit too.'
He turns his head right for the salutation*
    To souls of Prophets and men of high station
As if to say: 'Please intercede for me,
    For I'm stuck in this mud and wish to flee!'

*Explaining how the salutation towards the right at the
Resurrection indicates dread of being examined by God
and the appeal to Prophets for help and intercession*

The Prophets say, 'No cure's left any more.
    Solutions and the means were here before.
You're an untimely bird, unlucky one,   2170
    Leave us alone, stop bothering everyone!'
Then the man turns his head the other way,
    Left, to his kin: 'Be silent!' they all say.
'Give the Creator, God, your own reply.
    Who are we to? On us do not rely.'
With no cure either side, that helpless heart
    From its own depths is quickly torn apart.

This poor wretch now despairs of everyone
   And joins his hands to pray to God, the One:
'I've now lost hope in everyone but you,   2175
   The First, the Last, the Ultimate One too.'
When you next pray, observe these signs we've shown,
   That make what's coming to you clearly known.
Bring the chick out now from the egg of prayer,
   Don't peck at it without respect or care!

During the prayer Daquqi hears wails from a boat that is about to sink

Daquqi led the prayer as said before,
   Performing it at long last by the shore.
The congregation all looked very fine
   Behind the chosen leader, all in line.
His gaze changed its direction suddenly   2180
   On hearing, 'Help! Help!' coming from the sea.
He saw a ship there in a perilous state,
   Suffering, while tossed by waves, an ugly fate.
Huge clouds, enormous waves, and a black night—
   Three darknesses, shipwreck fears too in sight.
Like Azrael, a fierce wind suddenly
   Tossed the waves left and then right violently.
The men on board almost lost consciousness
   And they raised desperate cries in sheer distress.
In mourning then they beat their heads as well,   2185
   Turned faithful now, even each infidel;
They promised and made heartfelt vows right there
   To God on that hour while engaged in prayer.
Bareheaded in prostration lay these men
   Who never had faced Mecca until then.
'That worship's pointless,' these men used to say,
   But saw the power of life in it today;
They'd now lost hope in every man that lives,
   Including parents, friends, and relatives—
Renunciants and hedonists equally   2190
   Turned pious as cruel men in agony.

There wasn't a solution anywhere;
    When all else fails one knows it's time for prayer.
On every prayer of theirs and desperate sigh,
    Black smoke rose up from them towards the sky.
Just then, the Devil yelled as a fierce foe:
    'Dog-worshippers, you've two banes: death and woe!'
Hypocrites and deniers, that will be
    The final outcome of your destiny.
And then your eyes will weep, as your mistake   2195
    Made you become a devil for lust's sake.
You won't recall how God helped you that day
    Of peril, when you all had lost your way.
These words came from the Devil to deceive—
    A good ear is required still to perceive.
Mohammad, Pole and Sea of Purity,
    Told us before about this accurately:
That stupid men see at the very last
    What wise men saw at the first stage they passed.
Though at the start it may have been concealed,   2200
    To wise men at the start it is revealed;
Its start's concealed, but ignorant and wise
    Both later see its end with their own eyes—
Stubborn wretch, if you can't see it today
    When did your prudent mind get snatched away?
What's prudence? Viewing this world with suspicion,
    Expecting grief to come all of a sudden . . .

The conceptions of the prudent man

. . . As when a lion grabs a man, and then
    Drags him back through the jungle to his den—
What will he think while being dragged away?   2205
    Religious expert, think that way today!
Fate's lion drags to jungles souls inside
    All people trade has left preoccupied;
Those who fear poverty in this same way
    Are totally submerged in brine today.

If they'd instead fear poverty's creator
　　They would see everywhere the wealth and treasure.
All of them, fearing pain, fall in its essence,
　　They seek existence but find non-existence.

Daquqi's supplication and intercession for the deliverance of the ship

And when Daquqi saw that scene of woe,   2210
　　His pity stirred and tears began to flow.
'O Lord, don't look at just their deeds,' he prayed,
　　'Beloved, please give them a hand in aid.
O You Whose hand controls both land and sea,
　　Bring them ashore, back to security.
O Generous, Merciful, Eternal One,
　　Overlook wicked things they might have done!
O You Who've given eyes and ears for free
　　And intellect and wisdom needlessly,
Giving before it had been earned, though You   2215
　　Have faced ingratitude and error too,
You can forgive the major sins we bring,
　　Great Lord, beneath the shelter of Your wing.
We've burned ourselves because of lust and greed;
　　We've learned from You this prayer we make in need—
We deeply honour You for teaching it
　　And for the lamp that in the dark You've lit.'
He prayed these words as he was standing there,
　　Like mothers do for children in their care.
Tears then began to flow out of each eye;   2220
　　While unaware, his prayer rose to the sky:
The prayer of him who isn't self-aware
　　Differs: not him but God recites that prayer.
God says the prayer, for this man is effaced:
　　Its answer comes from God too, if it's traced.
Without an intermediary in creation
　　How can one fathom such a supplication?
God's slaves are merciful and are long-suffering;
　　They show God's nature while they are reforming,

Generous without a bribe, and helpful too,　　　　2225
　　Remaining in the worst times just as true.
Seek out this group before you're next distressed,
　　Afflicted man, judge them a treasure-chest.

The hero's breath released the ship, but they
　　Thought they'd done it themselves still anyway,
They thought at this most dangerous moment still
　　Their arrow struck the aim through their own skill.
Foxes' legs save them during hunting season,
　　They credit though their tails for no good reason,
And play with them so fondly, thinking: 'They　　2230
　　Saved our lives in the ambush yesterday.'
Fox, save your tail from brickbats. A mere tail,
　　When you have no legs, is of no avail.

We're foxes, Friends of God our legs who save
　　Us from so many dangers that are grave.
Our subtle scheming is our tail, and we
　　Make love to it each day continually:
We wag our tails with our argumentation,
　　To dazzle men and win their admiration.
We want to dazzle people constantly　　　　　2235
　　And lustfully grab at divinity,
To rule hearts with mere spells—but there's a hitch:
　　We can't see that we're stuck deep in a ditch.
You wretch, you're in a ditch despite your airs—
　　Keep your nose out of other men's affairs!
Once you have reached a lovely garden, you
　　Can then lead other people up there too.
You live in the material world's cramped gaol,
　　And try to guide the rest to no avail.
You serve the donkey, kissing its backside　　　2240
　　Yet try to lead us to that place with pride!
Serving God didn't suddenly appear
　　In you, so how did lust for rule reach here.

You have tied cords around yourself just to
    Make everyone say 'Bravo!' now to you.
Fox, leave this tail of tricks and cunning things—
    Entrust your heart now to the mystic kings.
A lion's protection guarantees you meat,
    So don't rush to a carcass now to eat!
You'll start to love God at that moment, soul,   2245
    When you move like a part back to its whole.
God said, 'We watch the heart and do not pay
    Heed to the form of water and mere clay.'
You answer, 'I too own a heart, you know.'
    Real hearts are higher than God's own throne though:
There's water in dark mud across the land,
    But that's not suitable to wash your hand,
For it's been spoiled by mud, so don't you start
    To claim your heart is also a real heart.
Hearts loftier than the heavens are possessed   2250
    By Abdals and the Prophets, not the rest.
Cleansed of soil, theirs is purified and it
    Has grown to be complete, immaculate.
Abandoning soil, it has now reached the sea;
    It's oceanic—from soil's gaol it's free.
Our water, though, is trapped in mud today—
    Ocean of mercy, draw us out of clay!
The ocean says, 'I'd drag you here somehow,
    But you pretend you are sweet water now.'
Your own pretence blocks you—give up that view   2255
    And come out into me, as I draw you.
Water in mud desires to join the sea,
    But mud still pulls its feet back stubbornly—
If water frees its feet from mud's grip, then
    Mud is left dry, and it is free again.
What draws from mud the water, friend of mine?
    Attraction to the mystic sweets and wine.
There is a very similar kind of lust
    For rank and wealth in this low realm of dust:
Each one of these makes you intoxicated   2260
    And hangovers come when your lust's frustrated;

The hangover's ache proves your drunkenness
   Originates from sources valued less.
Don't take more of such things than you must do
   Or they'll soon conquer and rule over you.
You turned away; 'I have a heart!' you cried,
   'I am in union, with needs satisfied.'
Water in mud once turned away and said:
   'I am pure water—why should I seek aid?'
You reckoned that polluted thing a heart   2265
   And from the mystic lords kept it apart;
That thing loves milk and honey—do you feel
   It should be counted as a heart that's real?
Sweetness is the heart's shadow, so of course
   Each sweet thing gets this from the heart, its source.
The heart's the essence and the world is just
   Its accident, for which no heart can lust;
Can hearts love wealth and status like a fool
   Or be the captive of a muddy pool?
Or worship vain thoughts and imagination   2270
   For the sake only of good reputation?
The heart's naught but an ocean of pure light;
   It's where you see God—how can it lack sight?
The heart's not owned by everyone around,
   But just one person—where can he be found?
Forget those crumbs, seek a complete heart, friend!
   So yours will be a mountain in the end.
The heart encompasses all being; you'll see
   It scatter gold through generosity—
It scatters blessings through its own volition   2275
   From God, to reach the world's whole population.
All gold that the heart scatters is collected
   By those whose skirts are ready and corrected;
Your skirt's your desperate need for God, no less—
   Don't place in it your store of wickedness,
Or else it might get torn by that mistake—
   Then you won't tell a real coin from a fake.
You've filled your skirt with worldly stones, a few
   Being gold and silver, just as children do.

They are imaginary, since there's no gold;   2280
  Your skirt got torn and grief increased tenfold.
How can a stone be seen as a mere stone
  By children till their brain makes this fact known?
The *pir** is wisdom, not mere greying hair,
  Which cannot reach their realm beyond compare.

That group disapprove of the supplication and intercession
by Daquqi and fly away, disappearing beyond the veil over
the Unseen. Daquqi becomes bewildered, asking: 'Did they
disappear into the air or into the ground?'

Once the ship had been rescued fully there
  The congregation finished then their prayer.
They started murmuring what soon grew clearer:
  'Who was that busybody interferer?'
Each one of them would speak up critically,   2285
  Hidden then from the ears of Daquqi,
Saying, 'It wasn't me who made that prayer
  To God to save that boat with special care.'
One added, 'That prayer leader through despair
  Interfered by performing such a prayer.'
Another said, 'You're right; it seemed to me
  Exactly as you've thought it all to be.
He interfered because grief left him pained,
  And tried now to oppose what God ordained.'
Daquqi thought, 'When I now looked behind   2290
  To try to find out what was on their mind,
I couldn't see there any of them—they
  Had somehow all just disappeared away:
Neither above, below, the left, or right,
  I couldn't spot them anywhere in sight,
As if they were such pearls that melt away
  Without a footprint or dust tracks that stay.
That moment they'd all entered in God's dome—
  Into which meadow did that flock then roam?
I stayed perplexed and wondered how God hid   2295
  That group from my eyes suddenly as he did.'

The way that fish dive into streams—they too
    Became concealed so quickly from his view.
He grieved the loss of them for many years,
    And out of longing shed so many tears.
We might well think, 'How should God's slave be seeing
    Alongside God his fellow human being?'
The ass collapses here, for you saw all
    Of them as merely flesh and not of soul.
The whole affair is ruined, immature man,   2300
    For, like the vulgar, you saw them as human.
You looked at them in wretched Satan's way
    When he said, 'I'm of fire, while he's of clay.'*
Close your Satanic eye for just one moment!
    On seeing external forms why be insistent?

Stop your sore eyes from streaming—don't despair,
    Daquqi, seek such men out everywhere.
To gain good fortune seeking is the start;
    Paths open when your wish consumes your heart.
Detached from this world, with no thought to spare   2305
    For it, and cooing dove-like to ask, 'Where?'*
Veiled one, consider well this observation:
    God linked '*I'll answer*'* to Man's supplication.
The prayer of the pure heart is ailment-free;
    It reaches the Great Lord of Majesty.

*A further explanation of the story about the one who, in the time
of David, sought a lawful livelihood without exertion or toil,
and how his prayer was answered*

I'll now recall for you an earlier tale:
    A pauper day and night would moan and wail,
Begging God for a lawful sustenance
    That won't require hunts, work, or effort once.
About some of its aspects I have told,   2310
    But the postponement has become fivefold.

We'll mention it now too—where can it go,
    When, from the clouds, God's wisdom pours below.
The owner of the cow screamed furiously:
    'You who have shown my cow such cruelty,
Explain to me why you have murdered her;
    For once be decent, stupid pilferer!'
'I faced the Lord's direction', that man said,
    'And begged him in my prayer for daily bread.
My old, decrepit prayer drew a response: 2315
    I killed it as that was my sustenance.'
The owner grabbed his collar violently,
    Then punched his face a while impatiently.

The two adversaries go before David

To Prophet David he then dragged the pauper,
    Saying, 'Come with me wretched, stupid robber!
Leave your proofs, bastard! They will not convince.
    Wake up again! Use some intelligence!
What prayer? What are you mumbling now at me?
    Do not insult and mock my dignity!'
'In saying that prayer', then the pauper said,   2320
    'Inside I've suffered; a high price I've paid.
I'm sure my prayer was answered in that way,
    So beat yourself, foul-mouthed one! Go away!'
The owner shouted, 'Muslims, gather round
    To witness drivel from one who's unsound—
For God's sake, how can what belongs to me
    Through prayer become instead his property?
If that were true, the whole world could use prayers
    To claim another's property as theirs.
If that were true, blind beggars could change then   2325
    Into fine princes and rich noble men—
They make such supplications day and night:
    "God give to us!" they beg without respite,
"Unless You give, no one will give at all.
    Opener, open the lock!" the beggars bawl.

Prayer is the means in which the blind must trust,
    But they receive naught but a stale loaf's crust.'
The people said, 'The truth is what we're hearing;
    The other one with prayers is profiteering!
How can prayer be possession's proof and cause? 2330
    When was this part of the Shariah's laws?
Something becomes yours through donation, sale,
    Bequest, and gift, or it's of no avail.
Where is this new law? Cite the page as well!
    Give back the cow or it's the prison cell!'
He looked up at the sky, 'No one but You
    Knows the reality and what is true.
It's You who put inside my heart that prayer
    And raised a hundred hopes inside of there—
My claim's not idle, though that's how it seems; 2335
    Like Prophet Joseph I had seen some dreams.'
Joseph had seen the sun and stars prostrate
    Before him, though that is a servant's trait.
He trusted in his dream, so in the well
    And prison, he sought naught else—time would tell.
That reassurance spared him from distress
    In slavery, blame, and owning more or less.
He would rely on that dream, which shone bright
    Just like a glowing candle to his sight.
When Joseph was thrown down the well, a cry 2340
    Came down to reach his pure ears from on high:
'You will become a king one day, and then
    You'll rub injustice in their face again.'
The One who said this wasn't visible,
    But to the heart He was perceptible:
Much strength, support, and inner peace he found
    Inside his soul due to that speech's sound.
This strength helped him endure contentedly
    Whatever came his way of tragedy.
A feast and rosebush soon replaced that well; 2345
    Abraham's fire changed just like this as well.*
The way Alast's deep question gave a savour
    That keeps believers' hearts content forever;

They never struggle to resist affliction,
   Nor feel upset due to God's prohibition.
Rose syrup shall consume the bitter taste
   Of portions of God's will that they have faced.
But those without rose syrup as digestive
   Will vomit morsels that they find repulsive.
Whoever's dreamed once of Alast's fine day   2350
   Is drunk entirely on devotion's way—
Like drunken camels, he now bears his sack
   Without doubts, flagging, or becoming slack.
His mouth foams too with holy testimony,
   As proof he's drunk and lovesick genuinely.
This camel has become now lion-strong
   Through eating little food for very long.
For the she-camel numerous fasts he'll bear;
   A mountain he'll regard a strand of hair.
One who has not dreamed of Alast meets failure: 2355
   In this world they lack mystical endeavour.
Instead he'll vacillate much, still unclear,
   Thanking God, then complaining for a year,
Forward then backward on religion's way,
   Uncertain, vacillating every day.
I owe you help, so you can understand—
   Listen one moment: '*Did we not expand?*'*

The explanation's limitless, so now
   Let's go back to the man who claimed the cow:
The one who killed it prayed, 'That fake called me   2360
   Blind due to this, and spoke unfaithfully.
When have I ever prayed like blind men plead
   Or shown to anyone but God my need?
To men, in ignorance, the blind make pleas;
   I want just You, You Who make hardship ease.
He's blind, but thinks I am. He cannot see
   My neediness and deep sincerity.
My blindness is because of love, the kind
   Mohammad said "*makes people deaf and blind*".

I'm blind to all apart from God. I see   2365
   Through Him—this is what love makes necessary.
God, You can tell that I'm not blind at all.
   I circle round Your Grace, Pivot of all.
To truthful Joseph, dreams of this rare sort
   You showed and they became his firm support—
Your Grace has shown to me a dream that way;
   My ceaseless prayer was not just pointless play.
Those people didn't know my secret. They
   Consider as mere drivel what I say.
That's their right, for just God knows the Unseen;   2370
   He hides our flaws, but knows all that has been.'
'Look at me! Tell the truth!' the owner said,
   'Why are you looking at the sky instead?
You are deceiving and committing fraud,
   Claiming love and proximity to God.
What nerve you have to face the sky above!
   Your heart is deaf, so how can it feel love?'
This caused a clamour to rise all around,
   While that man put his head down to the ground
To pray, 'O God, don't put this slave to shame—   2375
   Don't show my soul, even if I'm to blame!
You know all aspects—those long nights when I
   In neediness would call on you and cry.
Though this to them has no worth, in your sight
   This is a burning torch that still shines bright.'

David listens to the two adversaries and interrogates the accused

When Prophet David finally came out,
   He asked, 'What is this quarrel all about?'
'Prophet of God, be just!' the plaintiff said,
   'We found my cow in this man's house instead.
Please ask him why he dared to kill my cow—   2380
   Demand an explanation from him now.'
David told him, 'Speak up and answer me:
   Why did you ruin this man's property?

Don't spout out nonsense, but bring evidence,
  So that this case can be resolved at once.'
'O Prophet David,' the accused man said,
  'For seven years all day and night I prayed:
"O God give lawful sustenance!" I'd pray,
  "Which won't need me to struggle any way."
Everyone knows about my wailing, and   2385
  Children can give accounts too, at first hand.
Ask anyone you please, and you'll hear then
  The truth without the need to torture men.
Ask openly, and then in secret too:
  "What did that ragged beggar say to you?"
After all of my groans and constant prayer,
  A cow appeared in my home from thin air.
My eyes dimmed, not because of food, for I
  Instead felt joy my prayer drew that reply.
I killed it, to give it in thanks instead   2390
  To Him Who knows and heard the prayer I said.'

Prophet David gives judgment against the killer of the cow

David said, 'Wash away such talk at once
  And show your argument's firm evidence
Without such proof would you permit me to
  Establish a wrong precedent for you?
Who gave you it? Did you buy or inherit?
  Are you a farmer? How then will you profit?
Earning is just like farming: you must sow
  The seeds to claim the plants that later grow.
You only reap what has been sown by you,   2395
  Otherwise claims against you are all true.
Go and pay that man! Don't lie or pretend!
  Get a loan if you must. My rules won't bend.'
He answered, 'King, when you say I'm to blame,
  Don't you know wicked men said just the same?'

The pauper prayed earnestly to God against
David's judgment

He then prostrated, praying: 'God, please show
   To David's heart my burning, which you know!
Put in his heart what into mine You sent
   Secretly, Lord. You are munificent.'
He wept aloud then, hoping desperately   2400
   That David's heart might feel some sympathy.
David replied, 'You who want back your cow,
   Give me some peace; ease off a little now,
So I can be alone and ask in prayer
   God, Who knows all the facts of each affair.
I'm used to His attention when I pray.
   "*My joy's in ritual prayer*"* fits what I say.
My own soul's window's open; purity
   Brings God's Book with no intermediary.
The Book, the rain, and light all enter in   2405
   My house through it, from where they all begin.
Call windowless homes "hell"—that is their name;
   To make such windows is our faith's main aim—
Don't use your axe to make things other than
   A window like this if you're a real man.
Or don't you know that solar rays in view
   Reflect the Unseen Sun's rays veiled to you.
You've only seen the light that beasts can see,
   So how then was *Man honoured*?* Answer me.
Just like the sun, I'm plunged as well in light   2410
   And can't discern myself, try as I might.
My solitude and going off to pray
   Is just to teach the people here the way.
I'd do things wrongly to make this world right—
   The Prophet's saying "*War's a cheat*" sheds light.
There's no permission, otherwise we'd see
   It pour out of the Sea of Mystery.'
David continued speaking in this way,
   Making men's brains desire to burn away

He felt his collar grabbed at suddenly,   2415
  And heard: 'I don't dispute God's unity.'
He came back to his wits and stopped his speech,
  Then left for a retreat beyond their reach.

David goes into seclusion so that the truth is revealed

David then closed the door. Alone in there
  He hurried to the niche to say a prayer.
God showed him the whole story and he learnt
  Just who deserved to get the punishment.
The litigants came back on the next day,
  Forming a line in front of him. Their fray
Continued as before: each one would scream,   2420
  Cursing the other one to the extreme.

David gives judgment against the owner of the cow, saying he should withdraw his case about the cow, and the owner condemns David

David said to the plaintiff: 'Leave here now.
  Absolve this man concerning your old cow;
Seeing as God has covered up for you,
  Give the right to discretion to him too.'
He screamed, 'What kind of justice? Woe is me!
  Is this new law made for me specially?
Your justice's fame left, and now it flies,
  Perfuming distant lands and different skies.
Blind dogs get treatment that is far more just;   2425
  Mountains, at this, would crumble into dust.'
Like this he kept on cursing publicly:
  'Everyone wake up to this tyranny!'

David gives judgment against the owner of the cow, saying: 'Give all you own to him!'

David then told the plaintiff, 'Stubborn man,
  Give him your wealth as quickly as you can,

Or it will be worse still. I have told you
    So he can't bring your cruelty in plain view.'
He poured dust on his own head, ripped his garment,
    And said, 'You make the cruelty worse each moment.'
He then reproached pure David as before,   2430
    So David chose to summon him once more.
'Since it was not your fortune,' David said
    'Your wickedness will now be shown instead.
You climbed the ranks by shitting as you pass—
    May twigs and hay be saved from such an ass!
Begone! Your wife and children from today
    Will be his slaves. Don't speak, but just obey.'
He slammed a rock against his breast and ran
    Up and down stupefied, a desperate man.
Others came to complain too, unaware   2435
    Of all the hidden facts of this affair.
How could those mocked by lust as if they're straw
    Tell wronged from guilty just by what they saw?
Tyrant and victim are distinguished by
    One who has chopped his self, so it will die.
The tyrant is that self. Insanity
    Will make it be each victim's enemy.
Always that dog attacks a desperate man;
    It wounds such men as wildly as it can.
Lions feel shame, but not dogs. Lions don't prey   2440
    On their own neighbours in a dog-like way.
The victim-killing, tyrant-loving pack
    Harangued him in their dog-self's wild attack—
Confronting David, they said, 'Chosen one,
    Prophet who feels the pain of everyone,
This is unworthy of you and unfair;
    You've punished someone guiltless—don't you care?'

*David resolves to summon the people to a field, in order to
    reveal the hidden truth and end all arguments*

David said, 'Friends, the time has come to show
    You all this hidden secret, so you'll know.

Arise all of you, and we'll go to see   2445
  The truth about this hidden mystery.
There is a huge tree in a certain plain
  With branches arched like roofs to block the rain,
And like a tent with pegs entrenched in mud—
  From its deep roots I sense the smell of blood.
At this fine tree there was a most foul murder—
  This wretched man in cold blood killed his master.
God's clemency till now kept it concealed;
  Ingratitude means it will be revealed.
He paid that master's family no heed,   2450
  Neither on the New Year, nor even Eid.
He didn't try to bring them food at all;
  His debt to them he chose not to recall.
This wicked man because of just one cow
  Knocked his descendants to the ground till now.
He's lifted by himself the veil which hid
  His sin—the Lord had hidden what he did.'
Infidels in this age, when woe prevails,
  Tear open by themselves their own sins' veils.
Wrongdoing is kept secret by the soul,   2455
  Yet the wrongdoer will expose it all,
Boasting, 'Look here—I've grown new horns now too!
  Behold, the bull of hell is in plain view!'

Hands, feet, and tongue testify concerning the hidden truth about the cruel person even in this world

Even here now your hands and feet won't lie;
  About your misdeeds they will testify.
Your conscience then advises you this tack:
  'Divulge what you believe and don't hold back!'
In angry arguments especially,
  It hangs your secrets out for all to see.
Since your adviser was your cruel oppression,   2460
  Which said, 'Now hands and feet give a confession';
And since your secret's witness leads you, then
  While raging for revenge against all men,

The One Who makes your conscience direct you
   Can raise your secret's banner in plain view.
On Judgment Day That One can still create
   More supervisors to divulge your state.
You who've shown spite and cruelty and won't rest
   Will not need this—your nature's manifest.
For cruelty you don't need more infamy—   2465
   They know your fiery conscience intimately.
Your soul each second flashes new sparks out,
   'I'm from the men of fire!' it longs to shout.
I'm part of fire, returning to my whole,
   Not light, which goes to God like a pure soul.*

The one who failed to recognize God now
   Had hidden things because he stole the cow.
He'd taken cows and camels from the other—
   The self's like this—cut your ties to it, brother!
To God he never showed humility,   2470
   And never wept, 'O Lord, do this for me:
Make my own victim happy through Your Grace;
   If I harmed him, give him gain in its place!
If I've escaped, my blood-price then will be
   On You my guardian for eternity.'
For that pearl he won't even give a stone;
   The self's injustice is what we make known.

The People go out to that tree

When all the people finally reached the tree,
   David said, 'Bind his hands fast now for me,
To show his sin and crime to all of you   2475
   And raise the flag of justice right here too.
He left the other's grandfather for dead;
   This slave thereby became a lord instead.
You killed your master, then you took away
   His property—God's shown this clear as day.
Your wife had been his handmaid previously,
   But treated him with you so grievously.

Whatever child she bore from him, each one
　　Is now his heir, each daughter and each son.
You are a slave; your wealth is really his.   2480
　　You sought the law—take it, for here it is.
You killed your master cruelly over there
　　While he kept on appealing, "Please beware!"
You buried then your knife here with much haste,
　　Due to the scary phantom which you faced.
Behold! The weapon and his skull are here—
　　Dig up the ground and it will soon appear.
You'll find etched on the knife this vile dog's name—
　　He'd schemed to harm his master with no shame.'
They dug a hole, as ordered, in the ground,   2485
　　And very soon the knife and skull were found.
They started screaming, shocked at what they'd found,
　　Severing doubt's girdle that they'd tightly bound.
'Come, justice seeker, now!' David then said,
　　'Take your own justice with your vile, shamed head!'

David orders retribution against the murderer after his conviction

David ordered equal reprisals then.
　　God's knowledge can't be overcome by men.
Though we gain from God's kindnesses, He will
　　Expose us if we overdo it still.
Blood never sleeps; in every heart one finds   2490
　　Desire to solve what challenges all minds.
Persistence from God's own preordained plan
　　Brings it forth from the conscience of each man.
They ask, 'What happened to him? He's okay?'
　　Just as the plant will sprout from soil one day,
Boiling of blood provokes investigation,
　　Through pricking consciences and plain discussion.
Once that man's deeds were shown, though none had guessed,
　　The miracle was doubly manifest.
Bareheaded people came from all around   2495
　　And humbly touched their foreheads to the ground:

'We've acted just like the congenitally blind,
  Though we'd seen wonders from you of this kind:
Once you were spoken to by a mere stone,
  Saying: "Take me with you to Saul. Don't go alone!"
You went with just a sling and three stones there,
  Slew thousands with a shot beyond compare:
Your stones would shatter, forming thousands more,
  Each slaying there a foe;* and years before
Iron became wax in your hands when you   2500
  Made chain-mail you'd been specially taught to do.*
Mountains were Prophets through your revelation,
  The Psalms, as experts in their recitation.*
A million inner eyes were granted vision
  And, through your breath, could see realms that are hidden.
That miracle's your strongest—it's abided;
  Eternal life's the gift that you've provided.
This is the heart of every miracle—
  It gives the corpse an everlasting soul.'
The killing of that wicked man too gave   2505
  Life to a world: each was again God's slave.

Explanation of how Man's carnal soul is in the position of the murderer who made a claim regarding the cow, and how the killer of the cow is the higher intellect, and how David represents God or the shaikh, who is God's representative, with whose strength and support it is possible to kill the wicked, and become enriched by sustenance that is neither earned through work nor calculated

Kill your self! Bring the world back from the dead.
  It killed its lord; make it your slave instead.
The one who claimed the cow is self—take heed!
  It dressed itself as a lord fit to lead.
Its killer is your higher intellect,
  Your flesh's slayer which you can't reject.
This intellect's held captive, and its wish
  Is daily bread, without toil, on a dish.
What does its wish from God depend on now?   2510
  Slaying the source of evil: that same cow.

'How dare you kill my cow?' the self will say—
  The self's cow is the body's form in clay.
The master's son, intellect, is in need.
  The murderous self claims mastery's right to lead.
What then is daily bread without toil, friends?
  Prophetic mystic nourishment God sends.
Killing the cow is what this hangs upon.
  The treasure's in the cow—learn, curious one!
I must have eaten something strange last night   2515
  Not to hand all the reins now to your sight.
'I've eaten something' isn't really true—
  All comes from secret precincts down to you.
We look at secondary causes—why
  When we've learnt glancing from His flirting eye?
Above these causes are those that are higher—
  Look only at those causes, which come prior.
Prophets came down to sever lower ones
  And fling their miracles to distant suns.
Without need for a cause, they parted seas;   2520
  Without once farming, they brought wheat with ease;
Through them, sand turned to flour fit for a feast,
  Goat hair to silk as soon as it was fleeced.
Cutting the cause is the Qur'an's aim, friend,
  Through paupers' gains and Abu Lahab's end.
Birds each drop on an army one small stone,
  Defeating all those troops by this alone;
The stones of those birds caused their elephant
  To fall with wounds—that poor beast bore the brunt.*
'Strike the slain man with that cow's tail!'* God said,   2525
  'So in the shroud he'll come back from the dead,
So you'll see him jump up whose throat was slit,
  Seeking revenge from that one who did it.'
In such ways, the Qur'an throughout so well
  Cuts secondary causes off. Farewell!

The meddling intellect's of no avail—
  Become a slave to see this all unveil.

Philosophers are bound by reasoning;
    The pure ride intellect just like a king:
Your intellect's own intellect and it   2530
    Are core and husk which for a beast is fit;
Husks don't attract those seeking kernels, which
    Are lawful for the good, the spiritually rich.
Your intellect needs proof, for it to see;
    That intellect has constant certainty.
Your intellect fills notebooks very soon;
    That intellect spreads light far like the moon.
That one's beyond what's black and white—to start
    The light of its moon rises in your heart.
If power's gained by what is black and white,   2535
    It's from the Night of Power's* star-bright light.
A purse's value is in gold like this,
    Without which every purse is valueless:
The soul is what decides the body's value;
    The soul's worth's fixed by rays God shines upon you.
If souls without rays are alive, would He
    Have said that infidels *are dead*?* Tell me!
Speak, for His eloquence digs out a river,
    So water will reach generations after.
Each generation's brought its own report;   2540
    Still sayings of past sages give support.
The Torah, Psalms, and Bible testified
    That the Qur'an contained the truth inside.*
Seek daily bread without toil, schemes, or price,
    So Gabriel brings you fruit from paradise.
Better still, get it straight from God, my brother;
    Don't make the gardener sow or suffer bother.
Bread has worth since it is His gift to you;
    Without the husk as means, it helps you too.
Bread's taste's hidden; its form's like cloths we spread;   2545
    Without a tablecloth comes God's Friend's bread.
How will the daily bread for which you've tried
    So hard come down, except through your own guide?
When the self sees you walk in harmony
    With him, it will obey then totally.

That slain cow's owner finally confessed
　　On seeing David's breath was specially blessed.
Higher intellect prevails, it must be said,
　　Over your self, with the guide's special aid.
The self's a snake with tricks of many kinds,   2550
　　The guide's face is the emerald that blinds.*
If you want the cow's owner to submit,
　　Drive his self like a donkey, goading it—
When to a Friend of God it should move near,
　　Its long tongue's shortened, so we need not hear.
It has a hundred tongues, which each possess
　　Ten languages, much fraud, and cleverness.
The claimant of the cow's the self: proficient
　　In using proofs, but they are all deficient.
He hoodwinks all the people gathered there,   2555
　　But he can't trick the king who is aware.
The self holds the Qur'an in one hand, brother,
　　With a sharp dagger hidden in the other.
Don't you believe in its hypocrisy!
　　Shun its Qur'an, avoid its company!
It takes you to perform ablutions to
　　A spring, then shoves you in without ado.
The luminous intellect seeks with such skill—
　　How can the dark self dominate it still?
Since it's at home and intellect's the stranger: 2560
　　At its own door a dog's a frightening danger.
But such blind dogs will be obedient when
　　The mystic lions reach their home again.
Ordinary men can't see the self's deceit—
　　Heart inspiration's needed for that feat.
He who is just like it is its associate,
　　But not your David-mannered guide who knows it:
He's been transformed; whoever God should place
　　In the heart's station leaves their form and space.
People have flaws within that will jump out;   2565
　　Flaws will attract each other there's no doubt.
Impostors claim, 'I'm David for our people!'
　　The undiscerning man is their disciple.

The stupid bird hears hunters' whistles and
    Flies to them, as it cannot understand
Or tell what's real from fiction—he's astray;
    Even if he looks spiritual, run away!
To him a graft and what grows naturally
    Are one—he doubts, though he claims certainty.
Even if he's the cleverest of his school,   2570
    Since he can't now discern, he's still a fool.
As deer flee from a lion, run away—
    Don't rush to him like fools might do today.

How Jesus fled to the mountain-top from a fool

Jesus fled to a mountain as if he
    Were being chased by lions ravenously.
Someone pursued him saying, 'It's okay!
    No one is coming. Why then rush away?'
He kept on hurrying and due to haste
    Gave no reply—he had no time to waste.
That man pursued him further, then he shouted: 2575
    'For God's sake, Jesus, whom we've never doubted,
Please stop for just a moment! Won't you, please?
    Your fleeing gives me deep anxieties.
Running up there, from whom do you now flee?
    No lion's in pursuit, no enemy.'
'I'm fleeing from a fool!' Jesus explained,
    'I now must save myself, not be restrained.'
The man asked, 'Aren't you the Messiah then,
    The one who heals all deaf and all blind men?'
Jesus said, 'Yes.' 'And aren't you that king who   2580
    Possesses spells from the Unseen Realm too?
When you chant spells on corpses, suddenly they
    Jump up like lions pouncing on their prey.'
Jesus said, 'Yes, that's I.' 'Don't you create
    Living birds from mere clay with power so great?'
Jesus said, 'Yes.' 'Then, Holy Spirit, who
    Can scare one who can do the things you do?

Who in the world could see these signs you gave
    And not desire at once to be your slave?'
Jesus said, 'By God's holy essence, He   2585
    Who made our bodies made souls previously;
And by His attributes and essence too,
    Which heavens love the way that madmen do,
Since that spell and God's greatest name, which I
    Pronounced on deaf and blind men, ranks so high:
Their power made the mountain split in haste,
    Tearing its cloak apart down to its waist;
They made a corpse revive in just an instant
    And non-existents to become existent.
I have pronounced them over one fool's heart   2590
    Numerous times, but healing just won't start.
He turned to stone and wouldn't change—God knows
    He is now sand from which not one plant grows.'
The man then asked, 'Will you now make it clear
    Why God's name failed to be effective here?
There's sickness here just like those sicknesses:
    It healed before—why didn't it cure this?'
'Folly's disease is God's wrath,' Jesus said,
    'Blindness and such aren't wrath but trials He's made;
A trial attracts God's mercy to such woes,   2595
    But folly only can attract more blows.
That which is branded on him God has sealed,
    So such a person never can be healed.'
As Jesus did, from fools you have to flee;
    Carnage results from foolish company.
The air steals flowing water bit by bit,
    And fools make faith evaporate like it.
They steal your warmth to give you chills—beware,
    They'll sneakily put sharp rocks on your chair.
It wasn't due to fear he fled from reach—   2600
    Jesus can feel secure; it was to teach.
If frost fills all horizons with its chill,
    It cannot harm the sun which rises still.

Story about the People of Sheba and their folly, and how the advice of Prophets has no effect on the foolish

Remember Sheba's people's woe: their breeze,
    Through stupid fools' breaths, filled up with disease.
Sheba resembled that huge city in
    The children's tales passed down among your kin.
Children like telling fables to each other,
    But they hold hidden wisdom too, my brother.
In tales there's idle chatter in some measure;   2605
    One also must search ruins to find treasure.
There once was a grand city, they relate,
    Which only was as big as a side-plate.
It was so huge and broad—what a dominion,
    Extremely big, the same size as one onion.
The people of ten cities filled that place,
    Totalling three, each with a dirty face.
Inside were countless people, but just three
    Raw beggars were in that locality.
(The souls which to the Loved One do not race,   2610
    Though many, count as half through their disgrace.)
One with good vision, but blind totally
    To Solomon and ants' legs equally.
The second could hear well, and was deaf too,
    Treasure which has no gold inside for you.
The third was bare—his genitals he'd show;
    His skirt had such a very long hem though.
'An army's nearing. Look!' the blind one said.
    'I know how many. I see them ahead.'
The deaf one said, 'I've heard the noise near me,   2615
    What they say openly and secretly.'
The naked one said, 'I'm afraid of them,
    For they might want to shorten my long hem.'
The blind one said, 'They're close. Let's not remain
    For we'll be struck and bound then with a chain.'

The deaf man said, 'The noise is louder, so
   My friend it is our last chance now to go.'
The naked one said, 'They'll cut my hem short.
   I'll be unsafe among that lustful sort.'
They went out of that city due to fear   2620
   And hurried to a village that was near.
They found a bird there that was very fat
   Without flesh on it—abject just like that;
A withered bird, which from firm blows from crows
   Had bones like threads with which a tailor sews.
They ate it like three lions on a hunt;
   Each felt as full as a huge elephant.
All three became fat due to what they ate,
   Like three huge elephants all overweight.
And due to the degree that they'd grown fat,   2625
   None could be fitted in this world like that.
With their huge size and big limbs, they escaped
   Through small cracks in the door which now had gaped.
The way to death for creatures is unseen;
   Since it has no place, it then can't be seen.
Look, caravans now follow in succession,
   Through this crack in the door that is so hidden.
You can't find that door's crack, for it's so small,
   Gateway to union, but invisible.

Interpretation of the blind, far-sighted one, the deaf, sharp-eared
one, and the naked one with a long skirt

The deaf one's hope, which of your death has heard,   2630
   But of his own death has not heard a word.
The blind one's greed: all others' flaws he sees
   And speaks of them in all vicinities.
He can't see his own flaws because he's blind,
   Though everybody else's he can find.
The naked one fears his skirt will be torn,
   But who would strike a man with nothing on?
The worldly man is scared and penniless;
   Though he owns nothing, thieves cause him distress.

Naked he came and naked soon he leaves, 2635
    Yet he's distressed and filled with dread of thieves.
At death's hour, dirges then will reach his ears
    And his own soul will laugh at its past fears.
The rich man then finds out he has no gold,
    The clever man no talent, truth be told.
With a child storing peel they are compared,
    Who, like a rich man, for his horde feels scared;
If you take some, he'll cry in misery;
    If you return it, he'll smile happily.
Since he lacks knowledge and is ignorant, 2640
    His tears and laughter are irrelevant.
A man thought he possessed what was just loaned
    And feared to lose what he thought that he owned.
He dreamed that it was all his property
    And feared that there might be a robbery.
Once death pulled at his ears till he would wake,
    He laughed at his fears, seeing the mistake.
That's like the scholars' trembling out of fear,
    Since they have knowledge just of things down here.
Regarding these accomplished scholars, read 2645
    In the Qur'an '*They do not know*'*—take heed!
Each fears that somebody will come and steal,
    Thinking his knowledge is worth a great deal.
He says, 'They're wasting all my time,' but he
    Doesn't have time of value actually.
'They've taken me away from work!' he'll say;
    His soul is plunged in sloth, though, all the way.
'My skirt is long,' the bare man says in fear.
    'How will I get it safely out of here?'
He views the sciences as valuable, 2650
    But still has failed to understand his soul.
He knows the property of every substance,
    But, like an ass, does not know his own essence.
'I know what's lawful and what's not,' he'll claim—
    You don't know if you're lawful—feel some shame!
You know the licit and illicit well,
    But are you licit? You can't even tell.

You know the cost of everything on earth,
  But not what you yourself are really worth.
The lucky and unlucky stars you see,   2655
  But not which one you are, unfortunately.
The point of every science is to convey
  To you who you will be on Judgment Day.
You know the laws and creeds of your religion,
  But how good and how bad is your foundation?
Your own foundation's worth more in the end,
  For finding out your origin, my friend.

Description of the pleasantness of the City of Sheba and their ingratitude

At root the Sheba People were so rotten:
  They'd shun the means to reach God; they'd forgotten
He gave them orchards, fields, and a huge mansion   2660
  On every side for their joy and expansion.
The trees had so much fruit on them that they
  Would fall off on the ground and block the way:
The windfall left the road below so blocked;
  The tons of fruit left travellers very shocked.
Baskets on heads in the vicinity
  Would fill with falling fruits unwittingly.
Wind scattered all those fruits around, not them—
  The fruits filled every person's waiting hem.
Huge branches would hang down so low, and then   2665
  Be brushed by heads of all the passing men.
And due to gold found there in such excess,
  Labourers would wear golden belts no less.
The dogs would trample on cakes good to eat;
  Wolves could get stomach aches from too much meat.
The town and village were now safe from robberies;
  Wolves didn't cause goats any more anxieties.
If I were to record all bounties they
  Were given and which grew more *day by day*,
It would then hinder matters more important—   2670
  The Prophet followed this: '*Be firm and constant!*'*

The Prophets came from God to counsel the People of Sheba

Then thirteen Prophets entered there, so they
    Could guide all of the lost men. They'd then say:
'Give thanks that bounty has been multiplied!
    If waking's steed sleeps, wake it!' these men cried.
'Thanking the Benefactor's necessary,
    So His wrath's door won't open suddenly.
Witness the generosity that's sent!
    Would your small thanks leave others still content?
He gives a head, so it will bow down low,   2675
    And legs to kneel in thanks He will bestow.'
'The ghoul has taken our thanks,' said the men—
    'We're weary now of giving thanks again.
Our weariness with His munificence
    Means we're not happy with obedience.
We don't want orchards, bounties most would treasure;
    We don't want every means and aid to leisure.'
The Prophets said, 'In your heart is a sickness;
    Your knowledge of God therefore suffers weakness—
All bounty from Him turns to more disease;   2680
    Food cannot strengthen men as sick as these.
Stubborn one, many sweet things came for you,
    Then turned unsweet, from pure to dirty too.
You were the foe of all things that were pleasant,
    And everything you touched would turn unpleasant.
Whoever then befriended you was seen
    By your eyes as contemptible and mean.
You viewed as someone who deserved deep reverence
    Whoever kept their distance from your presence.
This is one of that sickness's effects—   2685
    It poisons all things with which it connects.
You must fight that disease off very quickly,
    For it makes sugar seem to your eyes filthy.
Every sweet thing that comes to you will turn
    Unsweet—Water of Life, like fire, will burn.

That sickness aids your death and torment, friend;
    Due to it your own life will quickly end.
Your heart has come alive through kinds of food
    That make your body rot—it does no good.
Through coaxing many have been hunted—they   2690
    Seemed worthless, though, when they became your prey.
When higher intellects become acquainted
    They gain within through love that is untainted;
But when two base selves do this, then instead
    It brings about diminishment ahead,
Because the self soon circles round the sickness
    And very quickly this corrupts your gnosis.
If you don't want your friend to be a foe,
    Choose someone next who knows more than you know.
Since you're sick, through the Simoom-self's effect*   2695
    Whatever you should touch you will infect.
A jewel you'll change to stone; and then if you
    Touch the heart's love, this turns to hatred too.
If you take a pure saying that is wise,
    It soon turns vile and tasteless to your eyes.
You'll say, "I've heard this often. It's old, brother.
    If you're my helper, share with me another!"
If something new should later come to you,
    The next day you'd grow weary of that too.
Uproot the sickness, then each thing you hear,   2700
    Though it be old, will sound new to your ear;
Fresh leaves will grow from that old tale—you'll see
    A hundred blossoms bloom on an old tree.
We're soul-physicians, God's apprentices;
    The Nile *was parted** when its waves saw us.
From other healers we're so far apart—
    They can't see through your pulse inside your heart.
We view it with no intermediary;
    Clairvoyance gives us vantage-points to see.
Those are physicians who give food and make   2705
    The animal soul stronger by mistake—
We are physicians of your deeds and speech,
    Inspired by God's light ray within our reach.

We say, "These deeds will give you benefit,
    But those deeds lead you far away from it.
This kind of talk will help you move ahead,
    But that kind will cause harm to you instead."
Urine is those physicians' evidence,
    Ours revelation from His eminence.
We don't request from anyone a fee—   2710
    God gave us so much gain most generously.
Incurable diseases rush to us—
    Our remedy treats all the illnesses.'

The community demanded miracles from the Prophets

The people said, 'You who claim Prophethood,
    Where's proof you can heal and make bad things good?
Like us you have to sleep and eat, then lead
    Your cattle to the field so they can feed.
Since you're trapped too in water and in clay,
    How can you make our phoenix hearts your prey?
The lure of power and status lures men to   2715
    Make claims that they're new Prophets like you do.
Such lies and boasts will not be well received,
    For we refuse to ever be deceived.'
'This is due to your sickness,' they replied,
    'Blindness is vision's veil, and it will hide:
You've heard our call, but you can't understand
    Or see the jewel we hold now in each hand;
This jewel's a test for people, which we turn
    Around their eyes to see if they'll discern.
Demanding "Where's the proof?" shows you can't see   2720
    The jewel. You're trapped by blindness tragically.
If the sun says, "The day has come—arise!"
    Would you dispute its words as though they're lies?
Would you say, "Where's your proof?" It would reply,
    "Blind one, you should ask God now for an eye!"
If someone seeks a lamp in daylight, that
    Tells us he is as blind now as a bat.

If you can't see, but guess aloud it's dawn,
　　Despite the fact you're veiled, do not let on
To everyone like this about your blindness.　　2725
　　Be silent, wait for God's grace and His kindness!
To ask a man, "Where is the day?" at noon
　　Will draw disgrace to yourself very soon.
Silence and patience draws God's mercy, but
　　Seeking proofs shows you are inadequate.
Accept "*Be silent!*"* so that its reward
　　Will come into your spirit from the Lord.
If you don't want a relapse near Him, then
　　Fling your wealth and your head down, sage of men.
Sell your superfluous speech, buy sacrifice　　2730
　　Of status, wealth, and soul—that is the price
For His grace to sing your praise, and thus make
　　The heavens jealous of the rank you'll take.
When you respect these healers' hearts at last,
　　You'll feel ashamed of doubting in the past.
Removing blindness is beyond all humans,
　　Yet God guides you to honour your physicians—
With all your souls become their devotees
　　And thus be filled with musk and ambergris.'

The people are suspicious of the Prophets

The people said, 'It's fraud and trickery.　　2735
　　How should God make mere men His deputy?
Kings' messengers must be of the same nature;
　　Water and clay's so far from the Creator.
Have we just eaten donkeys' brains, to view
　　As close friends to the Homa gnats like you?
How far apart, like God and earthen clay,
　　Or motes and sunlight which make bright each day.
Where's the resemblance? What connection binds
　　That it should be believed by rational minds?

Story about the hares who sent one hare to the elephant, telling
him: 'Say that you are the ambassador of the moon in heaven
come to warn him not to drink from that spring!' as it is told
in full in Kalila and Dimna*

'This is like when the hare said, "It is true,   2740
   I'm the moon's messenger and partner too":
When all the beasts of chase were suffering
   Due to some elephants near their pure spring,
Deprived of water, they stayed barred so long
   That they devised a trick, since they weren't strong.
From a hill's peak their chief called to invite
   The elephants on the new moon's first night:
"Come here on the fourteenth, elephant king,
   And you'll find evidence inside the spring.
King elephant, I'm the ambassador;   2745
   Remember you can't blame the messenger.
The moon says, 'Elephants begone, and know
   That that pure spring is ours. You must now go
Or else I'll turn you blind most wickedly.'
   I've warned you, so the blame won't fall on me.
Agree to leave the spring—not one more word
   Unless you want the moon to slash its sword.
The proof is that the moon's form splits and bursts
   Each time an elephant comes there who thirsts.
King of the elephants, come here that night   2750
   To see the proof at that spring in plain sight."
The herd's own king came when two weeks had passed
   And drank from that same spring his very last—
On lowering his trunk inside the pool,
   Water splashed and the moon seemed split. The fool
Believed the claim made earlier by the hare
   Because the moon's reflection broke in there.
We're not like elephants that we should fear
   The moon's reflection breaking up now here.'
'Oh dear, our spiritual counsel has instead   2755
   Tightened their shackles!' all the Prophets said.

The Prophets answer their sneering and tell them parables

'Alas that the cure of your malady
    Has turned now to wrath's poison tragically.
Our lamp has made your sight worse by surprise,
    Because God's placed wrath's blinkers on your eyes.
What could we gain from you when we possess
    Dominion higher than the stars no less?
How could the sea of pearls then benefit
    From a mere ship that has been stuffed with shit?
Alas for that blind eye—the sun appears   2760
    As a mere mote, however much it nears.'
Of Adam, who was peerless on that day,
    Satan's eye could perceive no more than clay.*
The devilish eye sees winter when it's spring;
    It's drawn back home still from a different thing.
Fortunes come down to the unfortunate,
    Yet stupidly they turn away from it.
Beloveds come unrecognized, then go
    Unnoticed by the luckless who don't know.
Privation makes men's eyes err tragically;   2765
    What turns their hearts is a bad destiny.
Since a stone idol is a god for you,
    Blindness and curses naturally ensue.
To partner God you deem stone suitable—
    Closeness to God you'll still deny Man's soul?
A dead gnat fits the Homa's company—
    Can't living men then gain God's intimacy?
You merely have concocted that dead thing;
    Living beings are created by the King.
You're lovers of yourselves and what you've made;   2770
    Towards their own heads serpents' tails have prayed.
That tail lacks grace and fortune, and there's no
    Delight or peace in that head even though
The serpent's tail twists round its head—the two
    Both suit each other as all partners do.

In His divine book, Hakim Ghaznavi
    Makes this point, if you listen carefully:
'With what fate has decreed don't interfere!
    The donkey's body suits the donkey's ear.'
Bodies and limbs as well fit with each other,   2775
    As attributes and souls belong together:
Its attribute suits perfectly each soul,
    For God has made it one harmonious whole.
Since God's the One Who put them in their place,
    They match as well as eyes in someone's face.
Ugly or fair, these attributes all fit;
    Any words God writes are appropriate—
*Between two fingers** eyes and hearts of men
    Are in the Writer's hand just like a pen.
The fingers are His wrath and His compassion;   2780
    Their pen, the heart, contracts then feels expansion.
Pen, if you glorify the Lord, please view
    Whose *pair of fingers** is now holding you.
The fingers give you motion and intention;
    Your nib is now at a main intersection.
He alternates, like letters, your heart's states—
    From Him all your intent originates.
Neediness and abasement work alone,
    But not by every pen is this fact known.
Pens only know to their capacity,   2785
    Shown through their good or bad activity.
The hare and elephant tale they would use
    To mix eternity with a plain ruse.

Explanation of why not everyone can give parables, especially those concerning God

Such parables can't be made by your sort
    And then applied to that most holy court.
All parables belong to God, not you,
    Like hidden knowledge and what's in plain view.
What do you know of the disguised intention,
    Baldhead, that cheeks and tresses you should mention?*

Moses thought it a rod once by mistake;   2790
  Its hidden side then showed it was a snake.*
When such a king mistook wood's hidden side,
  How can you see the snares with bait inside?
Moses mistook that past similitude,
  How can mice see who meddle and intrude?
He'll turn to dragons your analogies,
  And they will tear your body up with ease.
Cursed Satan used analogies this way
  And was then cursed by God till Judgment Day.*
Korah's analogy made him sink down   2795
  Into the soil with both his throne and crown.
Deem your analogies as owls and crows—
  Hundreds of households were destroyed by those.

Noah's community said parables in mockery when the ark was being built

Pure Noah built the ark in the parched desert.
  Parable-tellers chose to mock his effort:
'Here in the desert, where one cannot find
  A well, he builds an ark—he's lost his mind!'
Another said, 'I hope your ship can run!'
  'Make wings for it too!' joked another one.
Noah responded, 'This is God's decree   2800
  And won't be foiled by witty irony.'

Story about the burglar who on being asked, 'What are you doing at midnight at the base of this wall?' said 'I'm beating a drum'

Now heed this parable: a thief one night
  Bored into a wall's base while out of sight.
Someone sick was at midnight half-awake
  And heard the tapping sound the thief would make.
He went up to his roof for a good view,
  Then asked, 'Mister, what are you trying to do
At this late hour? I'd like this clarified.
  And who are you?' 'A drummer,' he replied.

'What are you doing?' 'Drumming!' said the thief.   2805
  'Where is its music? That's beyond belief.'
'You'll hear its sound tomorrow, every yell,
  Sigh, exclamation, and lament as well.'
That tale which you just heard about the hare
  Was false, but of its truth you're not aware.

The answer to the parable that the unbelievers relate about
the hare being an ambassador with a message from the
moon in the sky

Find out the secret meaning of the hare
  Who came as an ambassador once there,
Depriving your dumb soul, which hardly thinks,
  Of Water of Life that the great Khezr drinks.
You have perverted its true meaning, so   2810
  Prepare yourself for unbelief's earned blow.
The moon broke in the water's image here
  And that filled all the elephants with fear.
You tell this tale about the spring, the hare
  And elephant whom they could easily scare,
But, blind, raw ones, how does this moon resemble
  A moon that makes us helpless and most humble?
What is the moon, the sun, and the vast sky,
  Intellects, souls, and angels up on high?
Ray of light from the sun what do I say?   2815
  Surely I'm talking in my sleep today?
The wrath of mystic kings has wiped away
  Millions of cities, you who are astray!
Into a hundred bits the mountains split;
  Eclipses made suns helpless, desperate.
The wrath of such men makes the clouds turn dry
  And has destroyed worlds which would reach so high.
Unembalmed corpses, turn around to see
  Where punishment reached Lot's community!*
What's a mere elephant when birds alone   2820
  Could easily pulverize its every bone.

Those *ababil** birds were so weak, but then
   The elephants could not stand up again.*
Who hasn't heard of Noah's flood, my son,
   Or how the troops of Pharaoh were undone?*
The spirit cast them into waves that tore
   Them to a hundred separate shreds and more.
Who hasn't heard of Thamud's fate that day,
   And how the wind swept all the Aad away?*
Look fondly at such elephants that kill   2825
   The other elephants that wish you ill.
Those elephants and kings of tyranny,
   When facing wrath of hearts will always flee
From darkness to more darkness: they forever
   Descend and find no mercy whatsoever.
Maybe the news of good and bad missed you,
   Though everybody else heard of those two?
You claim not to have seen what was made clear,
   But death will open your eyes to what's here.
Suppose the world is filled with splendid light—   2830
   When you sink to a grave as dark as night
No share of those strong rays stays in your view;
   Your window's blocked from generous moonbeams too.
You've sunk down from the tower into the pit—
   Is it the world's fault that you're losing it?
The soul remaining wolf-like stubbornly
   Will not see Joseph's face assuredly.*
David's Psalms reached the rocky mountain's ear,
   But stony-hearted men still couldn't hear.*
May mystic intellects be always blessed!   2835
   And God knows what's the path that is the best.
Believe the Prophets, Sheba's people, and
   The spirit captured by Him, understand!
Believe in them! They're rising suns and they
   Will save you from disgrace on Judgment Day.
Believe them! They are full moons that are radiant,
   Before they meet you at the Hour of Judgment.
Believe them! They're lamps in the dark. Don't mope,
   But honour them; they are the keys of hope.

Believe them! They don't seek your wealth! Don't stray   2840
     Nor try to lead the other men astray!
Abandon Arabic, in Persian say:
     Be Indian slaves of Turks, you men of clay!
Heed testimonies that the kings will tell.
     The heavens do believe—you should as well.

The meaning of prudence and the parable of the prudent man

Observe what was your predecessors' fates
     Or fly through prudence to see what awaits.
What's prudence? Weighing up two plans you see,
     To choose that furthest from insanity.
'No water's on this road,' one person says,   2845
     'And there's foot-scorching sand for several days.'
Another says, 'What lies! Proceed; each night
     You'll find a flowing fountain in plain sight.'
Prudence means taking water just in case,
     Freed from concerns thus from what you might face.
If water is there, pour your own away;
     If not, the stubborn ones will feel dismay.
O children of God's deputy, be fair!
     Be prudent—now for Judgment Day prepare!
That foe showed your forefather so much spite   2850
     Dragging him down to gaol from such a height,
Checkmating the heart's king with frightening ease,
     From paradise down to calamities.
How often did he seize him in the fight
     And pin him down to give him such a fright.
He did this to that champion, so don't view
     Him as a weakling when compared with you.
That envious one could snatch so cleverly
     Both of our parents' crowns and finery.
He left him wretched, bare, and desperate;   2855
     Adam would weep for years, disconsolate,*
Such that a plant soon grew from every tear.
     He wept, 'Why must I stay in Non-being here?'

The Devil's impudence reached the degree
  That he snatched such a great chief's dignity.
Beware, materialists, of him! Instead
  With '*God give me strength!*'* chop off his vile head,
Since from his hideout he now spies on you—
  Beware because he's hidden from your view.
The hunter keeps on scattering seeds around—   2860
  They're seen, but traps are hidden underground.
Wherever you should see a seed, beware!
  Don't let your wings get captured in a snare.
The bird that sees seeds, but opts not to eat,
  Will eat seeds in the realm free from deceit,
Feeling content with that and set free too
  From snares—its wings can move as they wish to.

The unsoundness of the action of that bird which abandoned prudence due to greed and lust

A bird is perched there on the wall again,
  Eyes fixed upon the snare's alluring grain.
It glances at the open field in view,   2865
  But turns around to that snare's grain anew;
This glance and that one battle constantly
  And empty wisdom from birds suddenly.
A different bird puts dithering aside
  And turns to that field where it may abide.
Its happy wings must be congratulated,
  For it's the chief now of the liberated.
Whoever follows it will gain salvation
  Through that security and liberation,
Because its heart's the king of prudent fellows   2870
  Its home is in the rose gardens and meadows.
Prudence is pleased with it and that is mutual—
  Act like this to avoid becoming rueful!
Repeatedly you've fallen in greed's snare
  And let your throat be cut while unaware.
Time and again Compassionate God has freed you,
  Accepted your repentance, brought you joy too:

'*Return like this and we will too,*' He said;
    '*We match your actions with rewards ahead.**
When I draw one to me, I guarantee   2875
    Its mate will follow soon and run to Me.
We've paired all actions with effects—it's clear
    Once one comes soon its partner will appear.'
A raider carries off a man, and then
    His wife trails him to find her spouse again.
You've come once more to this snare, and have thrown
    Dust in repentance's eye—it is your own.
For you once more Forgiving God unbound
    A knot and said, 'Flee now, don't look around!'
When heedlessness's chief one more time came,   2880
    It dragged your soul directly to the flame.
Moth, end forgetfulness and questioning!
    Look just one time now at your own burned wing.
Once you've escaped, to give thanks means not to
    Look back towards the grain that once drew you,
So that when you give thanks, He'll then bestow
    Daily bread free from fear about your foe—
To give thanks for that grace that set you free,
    You must remember God's grace constantly.
How many times, while suffering, you would cry: 2885
    'God, free me from the snare in which I lie,
That I may serve and always act with kindness,
    Then throw dust at the Devil to cause blindness.'

Story about the vow made by dogs every winter: 'When summer
    comes then we'll build a house in readiness for winter'

Wintertime makes a dog's bones draw together;
    They're made so small due to the frosty weather.
'With such a tiny body', he'll then moan,
    'I soon must build a storehouse made of stone;
Once summer comes, I'll build with my own paws
    A storehouse to live in till winter thaws.
But when the summer comes, its bones stretch back   2890
    And that dog's skin is now no longer slack.

It sees itself fill out with its own eyes,
　　Then asks, 'Which house can fit a dog my size?'
It grows and drags its feet to somewhere shady,
　　Now overfed, sharp, cowardly, and lazy.
Its heart repeats, 'You must erect one now!'
　　But it responds, 'How will I fit in? How?'
When you feel pain, your greed's bones then contract
　　Due to the struggles by which you feel racked.
You say, 'I'll build a house in my contrition,　　2895
　　A winter refuge for my own protection.'
But when your pain subsides, and you grow greedy,
　　Like that dog you'll no longer then feel needy.
To thank God tastes more sweet than grace bestowed;
　　Thankers don't chase more or feel something's owed.
Thanking is bounty's soul, bounty its shells,
　　For thanking leads to where the Loved One dwells.
Bounty makes people heedless, thanks aware—
　　Hunt bounty with your thanks to Him as snare!
The bounty of your thanks makes you content,　　2900
　　So you'll give to the poor more than you're sent;
You'll eat your fill of God's meats and sweets too,
　　So begging and going hungry both leave you.

The deniers prevent the Prophets from giving counsel and bring forward fatalistic arguments

The Sheba People said, 'Preachers, it's clear
　　You've said enough, if men have interest here—
God's locked our hearts, so it's of no avail;
　　Over Our Maker no one can prevail.
That Artist has designed us in this way
　　And this won't change no matter what you say;
You're telling pebbles, "Turn to rubies now!"　　2905
　　Or something old to turn brand-new somehow;
Or dust to turn to water, clear and runny,
　　Or water to transform next into honey.
He made the heavens and celestials,
　　The water, earth, and all terrestrials.

He gave skies purity and turning; both
  Water and clay he gave dark hues and growth—
How should the heavens choose turbidity?
  Can clay and water then choose purity?
To each He has assigned a certain course;   2910
  Mountains can't turn to straw through their own force.'

The response of the Prophets to the fatalists

The Prophets said, 'God did make qualities
  That no one can escape; as well as these
He made some that are accidental too:
  A vile man can become thus good and true.
Stones won't transform to gold quite obviously,
  But copper turns to gold through alchemy.
You can't wish sand to turn into a rose,
  But soil can do that—watch as its stem grows.
He's given ailments with no remedy,   2915
  Like lameness and being blind congenitally,
But also those for which cures are in place,
  Like headaches and paralysis of the face.
He made those cures for harmony's sake; pain
  And remedy were not made just in vain.
Most ailments do have their own remedy—
  You'll find it if you seek it earnestly.'

The unbelievers repeat the arguments for fatalism

The people said, 'Listen, our malady
  Is not one for which there's a remedy.
You've uttered spells and counselled us for years,   2920
  Each moment strengthening locks upon our ears—
If it were possible to cure this sickness,
  Then some part of it would now be a bit less.
With hepatitis water's blocked from livers—
  It goes elsewhere, though you drink down vast rivers.

The hands and feet swell so you'll think they'll burst
    Yet all that water fails to quench your thirst.'

The Prophets' next response to them

The Prophets said, 'Despair is a disgrace,
    For there's no limit to God's boundless grace.
With such a Benefactor don't lose hope!   2925
    Cling to His mercy's saddle-straps like rope.
Many a plight was hard on the first day,
    But was relieved as hardships passed away.
After despair, there's still hope, so be wise:
    After the darkness many suns will rise.
I see you're now immovable as rocks
    And on your hearts and ears you have put locks,
But your acceptance isn't our main mission—
    It's doing God's will in complete submission.
He ordered us to do this service, so   2930
    We don't speak for our own sakes what we know.
We have life just to follow His command—
    If he says to, we'd cultivate dry sand.
A Prophet's soul has just God as companion;
    He disregards acceptance and rejection.
He gives rewards for our delivery;
    For Him we'd turn vile like your enemy.
We don't feel tired and weary at His court,
    That, due to distances, we should stop short.'

Weary, with heart closed, is that gloomy person   2935
    Distant from God, as if inside a prison.
The Sought Beloved's with us nonetheless;
    Our souls are grateful for His kind largesse.
Our hearts have fields of tulips and fine roses;
    They block away age and what decomposes.
We stay forever fresh and delicate,
    Laughing, refined, sweet, and immaculate.

A hundred years and one hour, long and short—
　　We've naught to do with measures of that sort.
Length is for bodies and things physical;　　　　　　2940
　　Such measures do not figure for the soul.
For those men in the cave, so many years
　　Was one day free from sorrow, harm, and tears.*
It seemed to them just one day in that story;
　　From non-existence soul returned to body.
When there's no day and night, or month and year,
　　None can feel sated, tired, or old, it's clear.
Non-existence's garden boasts pure selflessness,
　　So from God's grace there is much drunkenness.
Only the one who's tasted truly knows:　　　　　　2945
　　Dung beetles can't conceive scent from the rose.
And if it were conceived, it would have then
　　Faded like everything conceived by men.
Can hell conceive of paradise? Then, how?
　　A fair face can't be witnessed on a sow.
Beware! Don't slit your own throat. Heed my tips,
　　For such a morsel is now near your lips.
I have now brought the hard ways to an end,
　　Making the way so easy for each friend.

The community repeated their opposition to what the Prophets hoped for

'Though you bring for yourselves luck,' they replied,　　2950
　　'You're our bad luck, rejected and defied.
Our souls were free from any cares, then you
　　Hurled us straight into pain and grief anew.
Your warning split a hundred times and more
　　Our concord and agreement from before.
Once parrots eating sugar, through you we
　　Have changed to birds who now think morbidly.
Wherever a grief-spreading tale is found,
　　Wherever ugly rumours spread around,
Wherever doom is forecast and mishaps,　　　　　　2955
　　Chastisements, deformations, and cruel traps,

They fill your parables and dark predictions—
　　Your appetite is to create afflictions!'

The response of the Prophets once more

'Warnings of doom are solidly supported
　　By your own souls,' the Prophets then retorted.
If you are sleeping somewhere dangerous, where
　　A snake slides close while you are unaware
Then someone kind alerts you to it, screaming:
　　'Jump quickly from that snake—don't lie there dreaming!'
And you then say, 'Foretelling doom's not right.'　　　2960
　　He'll say, 'What do you mean? Look in the light!
From such a dark fate I'll whisk you away
　　To my own home, where you can safely stay.'
Like Prophets, he informs of what's concealed;
　　What's veiled to others is to him revealed.
'Don't eat unripe grapes!' if a doctor says,
　　'For they will harm you in so many ways.'
Would you respond, 'Why diagnose such pain?'
　　You'd be abusing someone's help again.
And if astrologers tell you, 'Today,　　　2965
　　Don't plan to do that action, come what may!'
Though numerous times his words have proved untrue,
　　If he's right once, you'll do what he tells you.
Our stars don't have such variability—
　　They're always true and yet you fail to see?
Physicians' and astrologers' opinions
　　Give data, while we draw upon true visions.
We see in the far distance smoke and fires
　　Approaching to burn up all the deniers,
Yet you insist, 'Be quiet and refrain　　　2970
　　From tales of doom—it causes us much strain.'

You who ignore help from the ones who know
　　Will have bad fates wherever you should go.

A snake slides on your back beyond your view,
    And someone on a roof is warning you,
But you say, 'Silence! Don't stress me this way.'
    'Stay happy then; my talk's stopped,' he will say.
When the snake bites your neck, and joy you sought
    Turns bitter, you will scold him then for naught:
'Is that all you could say? Then why not holler   2975
    And with your wailing tear your own shirt-collar?
Or from above throw down a stone at me
    To warn of danger coming imminently?'
He'll say, 'Because you said you'd be annoyed.'
    You'll snap back, 'Well you've left me overjoyed!'
'Chivalrously I warned you,' he'll remind,
    'To help you to escape that awful bind,
But, due to your vile state, you wouldn't see,
    And answered with offence and injury.'
This is the nature of base wretches sadly: 2980
    You treat them well and they will treat you badly.
Through self-restraint make your vile self surrender;
    Kindness is not fit for that cursed offender.
For noble men you should do a good turn—
    They'll give you several hundred in return.
Treat a wretch with much wrath and cruelly
    And he'll serve as your slave then dutifully.
Infidels torture while they're prosperous, but
    In hell they plead, '*Lord, help!*' while desperate.

*The wisdom of the creation of hell in the hereafter and the prison
in this world, so they may be places of worship for the arrogant:
'Come either obediently, or disliking it!'**

The cursed are cleansed when they are met with harshness 2985
    And they become cruel when you show them kindness.
In this way, hell's their mosque for worship—where
    Are wild birds caught apart from in the snare?
For thieves and villains, gaol's a monastery—
    They're mindful there of God continuously.

Worship is mankind's purpose, and so hell's
    The place of worship for one who rebels.
Man has a hand in all things one could mention,
    But worship is his purpose and intention:
'*I made mankind and jinn for just one thing*':*   2990
    No other point but worshipping their King.
Though a book's purpose is its content, you
    Can use it as a pillow easily too!
To serve as pillow was not its intention,
    But guidance, theory, gain, and information.
If you should use a sword just as a nail,
    You're choosing to lose out and not prevail.
The point of Man is knowledge of the Way,
    But each has his own personal way to pray.
'*I've honoured him*' is fitting for the noble;   2995
    '*I've made him weak*' is fitting for the woeful.
Strike villains till they bow down in submission.
    Give to the noble, then watch their fruition.
God's made a mosque here naturally for both;
    The former's hell, the latter's gain and growth.
Moses put up Jerusalem's small gate,
    To force vile men to bow down and prostrate,
For they'd been proud and so imperious;
    Like that gate, hell's a place for neediness:

*Explanation of how God has made the appearance of kings the
means of subduing the proud and haughty who refuse to be subdued
by God Himself, just as Moses built the Small Gate in the walls
of Jerusalem in order for the haughty among the Israelites to bow
down on entering, and say: 'Enter the gate, prostrating yourselves,
and say "God lighten our burden!"'**

Likewise, the Lord has built a small gate too   3000
    From flesh and bones of kings—heed what is true!
Worldly men bow to them so happily,
    Though they won't bow down to God's majesty.
God made a dunghill as their niche to pray—
    It is called 'prince' or 'champion of the day'.

For such a holy presence you're unworthy:
　　Holy men's canes have sugar; yours are empty.
Grovelling before the curs you'll see the base;
　　For lions, grovelling there is a disgrace.
Cats oversee mouse-natured ones; it's clear　　3005
　　Mice don't deserve to fear a lion's near—
Only mere curs of God give them a fright;
　　How should they feel scared of God's suns' strong light?
'*My Lord, Most High!*' the prayer of the greats;
　　'*The lord, most low!*' however suits ingrates.
For lions of the fray mice feel no fear—
　　That's for the mystics who are swift as deer.
You should seek one who's slightly less a beggar
　　And choose him as your lord and benefactor.
Enough! If I explain it all to you,　　3010
　　The prince will rage, because he knows it's true.
The upshot is: 'Treat villains badly, friends,
　　So they will lay their necks down in the end;
If you should treat the wretched self now kindly,
　　Like thugs, it shows ingratitude so blindly.
This is why those who suffer are so grateful,
　　While prosperous men rebel and are deceitful—
With gold-embroidered robes they're proud and rude;
　　With plain cloaks they've a grateful attitude.
Thanking won't grow from blessings and possessions;　　3015
　　It grows instead from pain and tribulations.

Story about a Sufi's love for an empty mealcloth*

A Sufi saw a mealcloth on a hook—
　　He ripped his shirt once he had had a look,
Shouting, 'Behold food of the foodless there!
　　A cure for pains and famines that is rare.'
When his hot fervour boiled and reached the brim,
　　Whoever was a Sufi joined with him.
They shrieked and stamped their feet in ecstasy,
　　Some losing consciousness so drunkenly.

A meddler asked the Sufi, 'Why this mood   3020
   Over a mealcloth which contains no food?'
He said, 'Begone! You've form, but not the essence.
   You're not a lover—go and seek existence.'
Love for the lack of food can sate the lovers
   Who aren't bound to existence like the others.
Lovers have no care for their being at all;
   They profit when they have no capital.
Without wings they can fly to distant lands,
   And win at polo though they have no hands.
A dervish who perceived reality   3025
   Wove baskets though he was an amputee.
Lovers have pitched their tents in Non-existence;
   They're similarly one-coloured with one essence.
To babies sweetmeat's taste is still unknown,
   Though fairies sense it through its scent alone.
But how can men perceive through just a scent,
   When from a fairy they're so different?
From scent that fairy gains a whole lot more
   Than you can gain from a whole sweetmeat store.
Egyptians viewed the Nile as death and blood,   3030
   But to the Jews the same waves were so good;
For them the waves became a road that's paved,
   Yet they drowned Pharaoh, who would not be saved.*

*How Jacob was privileged to taste the cup of the Truth from
Joseph's face and to inhale the scent of the Truth from Joseph's
scent, and the exclusion of his brothers and the others from both
these privileges*

In Joseph's face what Jacob then could view
   Was privileged—Joseph's brothers had no clue.
Through his love, Jacob would have gone to dwell
   Inside the trap they'd dug for him: the well.
His mealcloth had no food in their poor sight;
   Jacob saw it as full through appetite.
You can't see houris with your face unwashed;   3035
   The Prophet said, '*No prayer unless you've washed.*'*

Love's food and drink for souls—that's what is meant
  When saying hunger is their nourishment.
Jacob hungered for Joseph in that instance,
  So his desired food's scent came from the distance.
The man who brought the shirt at rapid pace
  Could not perceive of Joseph's scent one trace,
While Jacob, though a hundred miles away,
  Could sense the scent of Joseph right away.
So many scholars do not have real learning—   3040
  They learn by rote and lack the lover's burning,
But from them others can perceive the scent:
  A common listener too learns thus what's meant,
Because with scholars that shirt's just on loan,
  Like slave-girls with the dealer—not his own:
They're worthless to him if with him they stay—
  He hopes to sell them all on the first day.

The Lord's apportionment sends daily bread;
  One's share won't go to someone else instead.
One man's fine thought brought heaven for a day;   3045
  An ugly thought then blocked another's way—
God has made heaven from one thought, and He
  Made hell's fires from another similarly.
Who knows the way to His rose garden then,
  Or to his furnace, which one of our men?
The heart's guard cannot see well from his view
  From which nook of the soul the thought first grew—
If it had seen its source, it would have sought
  To block the way for each unpleasant thought.
How can its feet reach there when that location   3050
  Lies in Non-being, the furthest destination?
Seize the hem of His grace, O my true kings,
  The way *the blind take ownership of things*.
His hem is His commands and His decree—
  Happy is he who lives obediently.
He lives in meadows with fresh streams that flow,
  While one beside him lives with pain and woe,

Wondering, 'Why does that man feel such savour?'
   The former asks, 'In whose gaol is my neighbour?
Why are you dry when there are springs around?   3055
   Why are you sick still when the cure's been found?
Neighbour, come to this garden now with me.'
   He'll answer, 'I can't come, unfortunately.'

Story about the prince and his slave who loved ritual prayer and
had much intimacy with God through his prayer and invocations

A prince desired to take a bath one dawn
   And shouted, 'Sonqor, wake up now! Come on!
Fetch from Altun the flannel, bowl, and clay,
   We'll both go to the public baths today!'
Sonqor fetched all this list of things at once,
   Then followed him with full obedience.
There was a mosque on this route and near there   3060
   Sonqor heard suddenly the call to prayer.
Since he was keen to do each prayer, he said:
   'Great prince who treats slaves like his kin instead,
Would you mind waiting on that bench for me
   While I perform the prayers deemed necessary?'
The worshippers and the imam who'd led
   The prayers came out once all the prayers were said,
But his slave Sonqor still remained within,
   So then the prince, whose patience now grew thin,
Called, 'Sonqor, why have you not stepped outside?'   3065
   'This Great One won't let me!' Sonqor replied,
'Wait a bit more, and I'll be out of here.
   I heed your words; they're ringing in my ear.'
Seven times they repeated this that day,
   Until the prince could not take more delay.
'He won't let me come to you, noble master!'
   Was every time Sonqor's repeated answer.
Then the prince shouted back, 'The rest have gone;
   Who's holding you there, making you stay on?'
He'd say, 'The same one who's kept you outside   3070
   Has at the same time locked me up inside.

That one who won't allow you now to enter
   Will not let me depart from this mosque either.
The one who won't allow you to step in
   Has shackled this wayfarer's feet within.'

The sea won't let its fish depart from it
   And it won't let land creatures enter it.
The fish's source is water and theirs land.
   Trickery's pointless as are schemes you've planned—
The lock is strong; God is the only opener,   3075
   So strive to be content with full surrender.
If every atom should become a key,
   Still only God can open it—trust me.
Once you put all your schemes and tricks aside,
   You'll find new fortune from your Sufi guide.
Forget your self, to be remembered. Then,
   You'll be the slave who is set free again.

*How the Prophets lost hope of being accepted and approved by the
deniers. God has said, 'Until when the messengers lose hope'**

The Prophets wondered, 'How long shall we give
   These people counsel on how they should live?
How long should one beat iron that's still cold,   3080
   Or waste one's breath when everything's been told?'
Fate is what makes a creature move and turn;
   Teeth sharpen when the stomach starts to burn.
The First Soul brought the Second Soul forth,* and
   Fish start to stink from heads down. Understand
And drive your ass as fast as possible—
   God said, '*Deliver!*'* It's not optional.
You don't know which one of those two you'll be—
   Strive hard till you can see that easily.
When you load cargo on a ship, you do   3085
   That with full trust God keeps it safe for you.
You don't know which of those two—you might drown
   Or else be saved from ever sinking down.

If you say, 'Till I know which one I'll be,
   I won't get on a ship or in the sea;
On this trip, I'll be saved or I'll get drowned—
   Reveal in which group I'll at last be found.
I won't go on this trip with this misgiving
   And slimmest hope like all the others leaving.'
No trade will be accomplished then by you,   3090
   Because the answer's hidden far from view.
The frightened merchant with a fragile nature
   Finds neither loss nor profit in his venture.
Since he's a wretch, he'll suffer a sad plight;
   Only if you eat flames will you find light.
All things depend on hope—spirituality
   Is the best work, as through it you'll break free.
You're knocking on this door through hope's directive
   And God knows always what is most constructive.

Explanation of how the faith of an ordinary believer is based on fear and hope

Every trade's motive is the hope for gain   3095
   Even if toil should make you suffer pain.
Going down to the store to sell each morning
   Is always with the hope to make a living:
If there's no prospect, then why step outside?
   Who can feel strong with fear they'll be denied?
How can fear you'll forever be without
   Not make you hesitant to seek it out?
You say, 'Although I fear I'll be denied,
   That fear gets worse if I've not even tried:
When I strive hard, my hope feels stronger, while   3100
   In idleness I face a harsher trial.'
Why then in spiritual work, you doubting twit,
   Does fear of loss prevent you seeking it?
Have you not seen how in our marketplace
   Prophets and saints gain profit and much grace?

Huge gold-mines opened when they reached this store,
  And in this marketplace they've gained much more.
To Abraham the flames became obedient*
  And waves bore Noah safely like a servant.*
Iron obeyed, melting in David's hand;*   3105
  Wind turned to Solomon's slave at his command.*

Explanation of the Prophet's saying 'God has hidden friends'

Another group are hidden; they're not known
  To people who see outer form alone.
Though they possess all, nobody can see
  A flash of their majestic sovereignty.
They and their miracles are in this realm;
  Even Abdals don't know the names of them.
Do you not know God's bounties sent for you,
  Such as when He says, 'Come!' to that realm too.
Every dimension here is from His grace;   3110
  There's knowledge of Him every side you face.
When someone generous says, 'Enter the flame!'
  Don't say, 'But I'll get burnt.' Go all the same!

Story about how Anas threw his napkin into an oven, but it did not burn*

Concerning Anas ben Malek, they say
  That he was host to a fine guest one day.
Once they had eaten dinner, he remained,
  And Anas saw the napkin had been stained
Yellow and dirty, so he turned and said,
  'Come and put it inside the oven, maid!'
Immediately, the wise maidservant threw   3115
  It in the oven as he'd told her to.

Astonished guests could not believe their eyes—
    They thought it must then burn and smoke would rise.
After a while she took it out again—
    It was so clean and white, purged of that stain.
'Companion of the Prophet,' they then said,
    'How come it didn't burn? It's clean instead.'
'Because the Prophet after meals would clean
    His hands and lips on this cloth that you've seen.'
O heart which fire and torment fills with fear,   3120
    To such a hand and lips you must draw near.
To an inert thing it gave such great honours—
    Imagine what it shows to souls of lovers!
The Prophet made mere bricks the *qebla*,* so
    Become like dust near glorious men who know!

They then asked the maidservant, 'What's your share,
    Your own experience of this strange affair?
Why did you throw it in there at his whim
    Even if mysteries are all known by him?
How could you throw a cloth worth such a lot   3125
    Into an oven that was flaming hot?'
She said, 'I have full trust in noble saviours
    And I do not despair of their great favours.
What's a mere napkin? If he should dictate:
    "Step in the flames!" I wouldn't hesitate.
I would jump in with no anxieties;
    I have much faith in God's true devotees.
What's a napkin? I would myself dive in
    When told by knowers whom I put trust in.'
Brother, apply this powerful elixir.   3130
    A man's sincerity should be much stronger
Than such a simple woman's, otherwise
    His heart's less than a belly in our eyes.

Story about the Prophet Mohammad coming to the rescue of a caravan of Arabs, who due to thirst and drought had been stranded and had resolved to die, with both the men and the camels' tongues hanging out

Once in a valley lived some Bedouins;
   A drought had dried up all their water-skins.
Stranded inside the desert, all these men
   Seemed like a caravan towards death, when
Mohammad, helper in both worlds, appeared
   To give them help as a disaster neared.
He saw there a large caravan on sand   3135
   Which was so hot that it was hard to stand;
Their camels left their long tongues hanging out,
   And bodies of sick men were strewn about.
Moved, he told them, 'Listen! Some of you
   Run to those sandhills that I'm pointing to.
If you see a black man on camel-back
   Taking his master water, which you lack,
Bring him and his steed also back to me—
   Use force if it should turn out necessary.'
The scouts went to the sandhills without fear,   3140
   And soon they saw the following appear:
A black slave on a camel carrying
   A water-skin as present for his king.
They said to him, '*The best of humans, who
   Is best of creatures too* has summoned you.'
The man said, 'I don't know him. Who's that person?'
   They answered, 'He's most fair and the most kind one.'
They praised his qualities as so diverse.
   'He sounds like that great poet with fine verse,
Who has subdued a group through sorcery—   3145
   I won't approach such people's company.'
They therefore dragged him back against his will,
   While he, enraged, would curse and wish them ill.

Once they had reached the Prophet, he decreed:
   'Drink up the water! Share with all in need!'
That one skin sated all the people there;
   Even the camels drank with some to spare,
And from that he filled other skins up too—
   Clouds swelled with envy at what he could do.
The water from just one skin, when it poured,   3150
   Extinguished flames in hell which wildly roared.
From just one skin did any person see
   Several skins filled up so easily?
It was the waves of grace, veiled by the skins,
   Arriving from the Sea of Origins.*
Water, when boiled, endures evaporation,
   While steam, once cooled down, starts its condensation.
Rather, without cause or mere cleverness
   God makes the water out of nothingness.
As you've viewed causes since you were created,   3155
   Through ignorance on causes you're fixated
And, heedless of the Actual Causer, you
   Prefer to have such veils obstruct your view.
Once causes vanish, you will beat your head
   And cry, '*Our Lord, Our Lord!*' in utter dread.
'Go to the cause you love!' God will advise,
   'You witness My work now? What a surprise!'
'From now on I will give you full attention,
   And disregard that cause and its deception.'
God says, '*If sent back, they'd do that again*'*—   3160
   They're unrepentant, weak, and faithless men,
But I won't look at that although I know:
   My mercy's full and that's what I'll bestow.
Your broken pledges also I'll ignore
   To give you gifts now, since you call once more.'
This act raised in the caravan commotion:
   'What's this, Mohammad? You, who seem an ocean,
Turned water-skins to veils that can astound;
   You've left both Kurd and Arab fully drowned.'

How he filled the water-skin of that slave from the Unseen
with water miraculously, and also turned that black slave's
face white, with God's permission

'Slave, check your water-skin now. It is full,   3165
   So you've no reason to complain at all.'
The black slave, stunned by this proof, saw the dawn
   Of his faith from beyond, as if reborn:
He saw a fountain gushing through the air,
   His flask the veil for grace sent from up there.
He tore apart the veils that hid that vision
   To see directly the Unseen's own fountain.
This made the slave's eyes fill with tears, and he
   Forgot his home and master totally.
He lost the strength to move ahead at all;   3170
   God sent a tremor deep inside his soul.
The Prophet drew him back for his own good,
   Saying, 'Wake up! Move on to where you should.
It isn't now the time to be perplexed—
   Move quickly on. That state will greet you next.'
He pulled the Prophet's hands then to his face
   And kissed them lovingly as filled with grace.
The Prophet rubbed them on his face some more
   And this helped him gain fortune from his store:
As a result, the black slave then turned white,   3175
   Moonlike, or like the day; his night turned bright,
Handsome as Joseph, charming like him as well—
   The Prophet said, 'Go, share what you've to tell.'
Witless and drunk, he went along his route,
   Unable even to tell head from foot;
Then, with full water-skins, that transformed man
   Approached his master from the caravan.

*The master sees his slave, who is now white, and does not
recognize him, so he says, 'You've killed my slave. Blood has
incriminated you and God has put you in my hands'*

The master saw him nearing, grew perplexed,
    Then summoned all to witness what comes next:
'This is my camel and my water-skin,   3180
    But where's my black slave and what harm's he in?
A white man now draws near from far away;
    His face is so white, it lights up the day.
Where is my slave? Is he strange in the head
    Out in the desert? Have wolves left him dead?'
His slave approached and he asked, 'Who's this man?
    Are you a Yemenite or Turcoman?
What did you do to my slave? Truthfully
    Tell me if you killed him—no trickery!'
'If I'd killed him, would I have now come near   3185
    By choice to meet my own death over here?'
'Where is my slave?' 'I'm standing here! God's grace
    Transformed me, changed to white my old black face.'
'What are you saying? Where's my slave? Tell me
    The truth, for nothing else can set you free.'
He said, 'Your secrets with your slave I'll share
    One by one, so you'll see and then be fair:
Since when you bought me, all that has occurred
    Between us I'll relate till you've concurred,
So you'll know I'm the same slave actually,   3190
    Though from dark night a dawn rose suddenly.'
His colour changed, a holy spirit though
    Transcends all forms and colours from below.
Those fixed on bodies lose us due to that—
    Those who drink water miss out on the vat.
Those who know souls aren't bound by quantities;
    Immersed in seas they're free from qualities.
Become all soul! Know soul through soul's own way!
    Be vision's friend, not reasoning's child, today!

When intellect and angel share their source, 3195
    And take two forms as part of wisdom's course,
The angel having gained wings like a dove,
    While intellect's gained splendour from above—
They both become supporters of each other,
    Handsome-faced ones, each helping like a brother.
God gives to both divine intoxication,
    So each helps Man and offers a prostration.
The self and Satan were originally
    As one, Man's envier and enemy:
Those who saw Man as body turned away; 3200
    Those who saw trusted light bowed straight away.
The latter gained from this act clearest vision;
    The former saw just clay, and chose derision.
This speech is stuck just like an ass on ice.
    Who'd read to Jews the Gospels as advice?
Can one speak of Omar to Shi'ites then?*
    Or play the lute to satisfy deaf men?
But if there's someone rare who comprehends,
    This tumult I've raised will suffice him, friends.
For one fit for the teaching, brick and stone 3205
    Will speak and make the grounded truths well known.

***Explaining that whatever God has bestowed and created
of the heavens and the earth, and essences and accidents,
He created it all at the demand of a need. One must make
oneself in need of something for Him to give it, as He has
said: 'Is it not He Who answers the distressed one when he
prays?'* Distress is the proof of worthiness***

It was once Mary's need and pain that led
    Her newborn to stun men with what he said.*
Part of her spoke independently—
    All one's parts have their speech mysteriously.
Your hands and feet bear witness at the trial
    Against you—why still use them for denial?

If you're not fit for speech and information,
　The speaker leaves you for a new location.
Whatever grew did so through need, my friend,　　　3210
　As seekers find what they seek in the end.
And God has made the heavens, simply so
　He can remove all need felt down below.
Whenever there's a pain, the remedy
　Comes there; provisions come to poverty.
To where there is a problem comes the answer;
　To where the boat is docked flows gushing water.
Acquire thirst and stop searching here and there
　For water—it will then gush everywhere.
The tender-throated baby is born first,　　　3215
　Then milk flows from the breast to quench its thirst.
Go, race through highs and lows, so you can meet
　Deep thirst and be a victim of the heat—
Then, through the bee's sound in the air near you,
　You'll savour sounds of flowing streams here too.
Your need's not less than that of plants—you take
　Some water also for your own soul's sake:
You take it with your ear and draw mere drops
　To give relief to all the dried-up crops:
Kawsar's water fills clouds of kindnesses*　　　3220
　For the soul's crops and hidden essences,
So that '*Their Lord gave them to drink*'* is read—
　Be thirsty. 'God knows best what's right,' they've said.

That infidel woman comes with her baby near Mustafa, and it speaks like Jesus about the miracles of the Prophet

From that same village then an infidel
　Came near to test the Prophet once as well.
Wearing a veil, she neared him and kept hold
　Of her own baby, who was two months old.
The baby spoke, '*God grant His peace to you.*
　We've come to you, God's Prophet, since you're true.'

'Shut up!' its mother shouted angrily.   3225
   'Who put into your ears that testimony?
Who taught you this, small child who's still so young,
   Making so talkative your infant tongue?'
It answered, 'God taught me, then Gabriel:
   He utters this and I join in as well.'
She asked, 'Where is He?' 'There above your head.
   Can't you now see? Look up!' her baby said.
Gabriel now hovers over you, and he
   Serves as a guide in numerous ways for me.
'Can you see him?' 'Of course, he's over you   3230
   And radiant as the full moon in my view.
He's teaching me the Prophet's qualities,
   And through this raising me from depths like these.'
The Prophet asked it, 'Baby, now tell me
   What your name is—speak up obediently!'
'My name's "Abd al-Aziz" in God's own realm,
   But "Abd al-Ozza" with vile men like them.*
I am clean rid of "Ozza" now for good
   Through God, who gave to you your Prophethood.'
That two-month-old, bright as the full moon, said   3235
   Mature truths like those from the circle's head.*
A scent that moment wafted down from heaven;
   Mother and child both breathed that fresh scent in then,
And said, 'It is much better than to fall
   To lay before this fragrance one's own soul.'
To one whom God grants true intelligence
   Plants and inanimates give evidence;
He whom God gives protection will soon see
   Birds and fish guard his own security.

How an eagle seized the Prophet's boot and flew away with it until a black snake fell out of it

And then the Prophet heard the call to prayer   3240
   As they talked; it resounded in the air.

He sought some water for ablutions and,
    Though cold, he washed his face and then each hand.
After he'd washed his feet, he saw his boot
    Get snatched away as if it was some loot.
He reached for his boot in the usual way,
    But from his hand a bird snatched it away;
Just like the wind that eagle then flew out
    Of reach, and emptied it—a snake fell out.
When that boot was upturned, a big snake fell,   3245
    Making that eagle blessed since it meant well.
The eagle then returned with it back there,
    Saying, 'Come, take it. Then perform your prayer.
Out of necessity I dared to do
    This act, though I feel powerless next to you.
Woe to those who would trespass brazenly
    Through their desire and not necessity!'
The Prophet thanked the bird and then he said:
    'What we thought cruelty was support instead.
I felt annoyed when you snatched like a thief;   3250
    Though you took pain away, I then felt grief.
Though every unseen thing's been clarified
    For me, my heart was then preoccupied.'
The bird said, 'Negligence be far from you!
    From your reflection it came to my view;
If I see snakes in your boots from the air
    It's your reflection which casts it up there.'
The Friend of God's reflection's a bright flash;
    The dark-souled one's worse than a pile of ash.
God's slave's reflection's luminous, you'll find,   3255
    While the outsider's makes one wholly blind.
Discern each one's reflection, soul, then sit
    Next to the sort you find appropriate.

The way to learn a lesson from this story and knowing for sure
that 'with hardship there's ease'*

A lesson's in this tale, soul; its intent
    Is that with God's decree you be content,

So you'll be clever, and think positively
 Even when you face bad things suddenly.
Others turn pale with fear, but you will smile
 Like roses at both gain and loss's trial.
People tear petals off fine roses, yet   3260
 Roses don't cease to smile nor feel upset—
Each says, 'Why let a thorn make me forlorn?
 I have produced a smile due to that thorn.'
If you lose something due to fate's decree,
 It will redeem you from calamity.
What's Sufism? To find such happiness
 Inside your heart when you should feel distress.
View His chastisement like that bird, the taker
 Of that old boot from one with the best nature,
All so his foot would not endure a bite—   3265
 The intellect that's cleared of dust gains light.
God said, '*Don't grieve for what you cannot keep,**
 What you lose when the wolf devours your sheep,'
For that loss staves off a much greater sorrow,
 And this loss blocks a bigger loss tomorrow.

A man asks Moses to teach him the language of animals and birds

A young man once asked Moses, 'Will you teach
 Me languages the beasts use for their speech,
So from their howls and their hullabaloo
 I can learn lessons for my own faith too?
Since the whole point of all Man's languages   3270
 Is to gain water, bread, and cleverness,
Animals may see in a different way
 The pain of time and how life fades away.'
'Begone, abandon this wish,' Moses said,
 'For it holds danger all round up ahead.
Seek lessons and awareness from the Lord,
 Not from the speech or writings some men hoard.'

But this rebuff made that man grow more keen;
  People react this way, as you'll have seen.
He said, 'Moses, ever since your light's shone,   3275
  All things have gained much from you, every one—
Denying me what I desire this once
  Would therefore not suit your munificence.
In this you truly are God's deputy,
  So how can you cause pain depriving me?'
Moses prayed, 'Lord, it seems that Satan has
  Turned this poor simpleton into an ass.
If I teach him, it will harm him; if I
  Do not, then I'll have hurt his heart thereby.'
God said, 'Moses, teach him, for Our kind way   3280
  Is not to turn down men when they should pray.'
'But this will make that man feel so dejected
  He'll bite his own hand!' Moses then objected.
For all men power may not be suitable;
  Weakness gives godly men more capital:
Eternal pride then comes with poverty;
  The unattaining hand gains piety.
He will reject wealth and the wealthy too,
  For self-denial keeps power far from you.
Weakness and poverty give men protection   3285
  Against the greedy self's own tribulation.
Desire for more leads to anxiety;
  The ghoul's prey now feel that habitually.
Eaters of clay always desire clay sadly;
  These pitiful ones can't digest rose-candy.

*Revelation comes down from God telling Moses to teach him
    what he appeals for, or part of it at least*

God answered, 'Grant his need; release his hand,
  So he will choose once he can understand.
The salt of worship is a will that's free,
  Or else the heavens turn unwillingly:
Such turning doesn't earn a single thing,   3290
  Free will alone counts at the Reckoning.

All things in this world glorify the Lord,
  But for compulsory praise there's no reward.
Put a sword in his hand; change this weak man
  Into a warrior or a highwayman.'
Since Man's *been honoured** with free will to make
  Decisions, he's half honey-bee, half snake:
Believers all store honey in their hives;
  Infidels poison, snake-like, taking lives—
Believers ate choice herbs, so their saliva   3295
  Served bee-like for the dead as a reviver,
But infidels drank boiling water, so
  The poison in them soon began to show.
The Fount of Life is men with revelation;
  Life's poison is those prone to lust's sensation.
In this world all praise and congratulation
  Is for free will and vigilant preservation.
While they're in gaol, all rogues transform their ways,
  Becoming pious, busy with God's praise.
When will-power's gone, actions aren't valuable—   3300
  Beware lest time should seize your capital!
Will-power's your source of profit, so beware!
  Preserve your will-power's course of time with care.
Man rides the horse of '*We have honoured'** and
  Free will's reins are in his perception's hand.
Moses then kindly gave that man advice:
  'Your wish will make your face turn pale—think twice!
Be fearful of God and renounce this passion.
  The Devil has been teaching you deception.'

The seeker becomes content with being taught the language of domestic birds and dogs, and Moses complies with his request

The seeker then asked, 'Maybe just dogs' words   3305
  And what is spoken by domestic birds?'
Moses said, 'You know best. You'll have those two.
  Both of those languages now come to you.'
In order then to test them out, at dawn
  He waited by his own gate and looked on.

One of his servants shook his mealcloth clean;
   A piece of bread from this fell from between.
A cock snatched it like catching in a game.
   A dog said, 'That's not fair! We're not the same:
You can eat wheat grains, but I cannot eat   3310
   Such food, and this bread is my only treat;
You can eat wheat and other kinds of seed,
   Jubilant one! This bread's what I now need.
From dogs would you now snatch without a care
   This little crust of bread that is their share?'

The cock's reply to the dog

'Be quiet and don't grieve!' the cock replied,
   'Something else soon will come—God will provide:
The master's horse is now about to die—
   Tomorrow eat your fill and don't you cry.
The horse's death means feasts for every dog—   3315
   A day of plenty with no long, hard slog.'
On overhearing this he sold his horse;
   The cock was left embarrassed in due course.
The cock snatched bread again on the next day;
   The dog complained it acted the same way:
'O scheming cock, how many lies must we
   Endure—you're cruel and you lack honesty.
Where is the horse you claimed would die for sure?
   You lack truth like a blind astrologer.'
That knowing cock then turned to it and said: 3320
   'The horse did die, but somewhere else instead.
He sold it to avoid loss with great stealth;
   The buyers then lost much of their own wealth.
Tomorrow his old mule will die at least
   And that means for the dogs a massive feast.'
The greedy man sold it that very day,
   Avoiding loss's misery this way.
On the third day, the dog barked at the cock:
   'With drums the liars' prince just loves to mock!'

It said, 'He sold his mule all of a sudden.   3325
   His slave tomorrow will be fatally stricken,
And when he dies his family will scatter
   Bread to each dog and every single beggar.'
He sold that slave too to unwitting men;
   His face lit up, for dodging loss again.
He gave thanks and he marvelled jubilantly:
   'Three times already this has rescued me!
Since learning how the dog and cock speak, I
   Have stitched up fully *evil destiny's eye!*'
The disappointed dog said the next day: 3330
   'Where's all the food, cock? Drivel's all you say . . .

The cock is ashamed before the dog because of the falseness of those three promises

'. . . How long will you continue with your lies?
   From your nest there is nothing else that flies.'
'Far be it from me and my kind that we
   Cocks should be lying pathologically.
As truthful as muezzins are all cocks;
   We watch the sun and keep the time like clocks.
Inwardly, we stay watchmen of the sun,
   Though on our heads a basin you upturn.'
(God's Friends are its real watchmen in mankind,   3335
   Sensing the secrets to which most are blind.)
It said, 'God gave us to humanity
   For the azan* and prayer originally.
About the prayer's time if we're once mistaken,
   This will be cause for our lives to be taken:
Saying at the wrong time, "*Come to the good!*"*
   Will make it lawful then to shed our blood.'
(The one who's sinless and infallible
   Is the inspired cock, who is spiritual.)
In the home of his buyer that slave died,   3340
   Which meant his buyer's losses multiplied,
This man saved his own wealth, but this would lead
   To loss of his whole life—what use is greed?

One loss could have prevented what's more costly—
    Ransom your soul with wealth and with your body.
When kings sit to make judgments you would give
    Your wealth to flee death and be left to live—
Why now with fate are you so miserly,
    Withholding wealth from the True Judge? Tell me!

The cock foretells the death of the master of the house

The cock said, 'He will die for sure tomorrow.   3345
    His heir will slaughter then a cow in sorrow.
The owner will die finally on this day;
    Tomorrow much rich food will come your way.
Both high and low will taste some bread and meat
    And other leftovers out in the street.
They'll share the sacrificed cow and fine breads,
    Scattering it over dogs' and beggars' heads.'
The horse, the mule, and slave died, and they led
    To the doom of this man who was misled.
He had dodged loss of wealth and all its pain,   3350
    But his own death was all that he could gain.
Why then the Sufis' bodily austerities?
    The soul's made permanent by trials like these.
Unless he has gained permanence this way,
    How could he make his body waste away?
How can he toil for altruism's sake
    Unless he sees there's a reward at stake?
The one who gives without thought of reward
    Is God alone, the Needless, Holy Lord,
Or God's Friend, who has taken on His ways,   3355
    Becoming luminous through eternal rays,
For he's rich while all others feel a lack—
    Paupers can't give and not want something back.
Unless a child sees that an apple's here,
    He won't swap his vile onion out of fear;
And all the market traders, for that matter,
    Sit at their stalls just for the chance to barter:

They offer numerous fine wares, while within
　　They simply long for trading to begin.
You won't hear one '*Salaam!*', O pious fellow,   3360
　　Which won't require from you some words to follow:
I've never heard '*Salaam!*' come from another
　　Without desire to hear '*Salaam, my brother!*'
Apart from God's '*Salaam!*'—seek that rare treat
　　House to house, place to place, and street to street.
From men with special scent too I've perceived
　　The Lord's '*Salaam!*' which gratefully I've received—
Aiming for that, I savour in my heart
　　Others' salaams like they're life's sweetest part.
That saint's is God's '*Salaam!*' the ultimate aim,   3365
　　For he has set the vile self's house aflame:
Dead to his self, he now lives through the Lord;
　　God's secrets now are in his every word.
New life is gained from bodily death and suffering,
　　Because it makes the spirit everlasting.
The wretch pricked up his ears each time they'd talk
　　To harken to the words said by the cock.

How that person ran to Moses for refuge when he heard news from the cock about his own death

Once he heard these things, he began to run
　　To Moses' door—God spoke to that one.*
He rubbed his face with dust, so filled with dread: 3370
　　'Moses, Kalim,* save me from this!' he said.
Moses said, 'Sell yourself to dodge this pit,
　　Since you are so proficient now at it.
You made these buyers suffer losses and
　　At their expense watched your purse then expand.
I saw already in a brick this fate
　　That you saw in a looking-glass too late.'
(The wise foresee the outcome from the start;
　　It's seen too late by those who lack their heart.)
He kept on weeping. 'Good, kind man,' he said,   3375
　　'Don't rub it in and beat me on the head!

I got involved in what was far beyond me—
   Give me a good reward, though I'm unworthy.'
Moses said, 'Son, an arrow in the air
   Fired from a bow will not return back there.
But I'll ask God for mercy, so you can
   Leave with your faith intact, you desperate man.'
(When you take your faith with you, you're still living:
   When you die with your faith, you're everlasting.)
The man's health suffered then most suddenly;   3380
   They brought a basin close immediately.
That is death's burning, not mere indigestion.
   What use is vomiting, you raw unblest one?
Four people carried him home to recover
   And he would rub his legs against each other.
If you leave Moses' advice ignored,
   You'll dash yourself against a sharp steel sword
Which will not hesitate to take your life—
   It's your own doing; you've caused your own strife.

Moses prays for that person that he might leave the world
with his faith intact

The following dawn, Moses started to pray: 3385
   'O God, don't take this sick man faith's away.
Forgive him blunders like the King you are;
   He has been stupid and has gone too far.
I'd said, "You do not have the readiness—
   He did not heed my words with seriousness."
The one who can lay hands on snakes is he
   Whose hand transforms rods to them magically;*
To learn the Unseen's secrets one is fit
   Only if one can seal one's lips with it.
Just waterfowl are fit to join the sea.   3390
   Heed this! *God knows best what's right!* Doesn't he?
A different kind of bird dived unafraid
   And drowned—Loving One, take his hand. Give aid!'

God answers Moses' prayer

God said, 'I grant faith to him, and, if you
   Should like, this moment I'll revive him too.
I would bring back to life like a rebirth
   All of the corpses buried in the earth.'
'This is the world of dying,' Moses said,
   'Revive them in that radiant world instead.
Unlike that world of Being, this one decays;   3395
   Return of transients is not work that pays.
Scatter blessings now on them in the realm
   Of "*Present in Our Presence*".* That suits them.'
This was to teach that worldly loss gives you
   Gain for your soul, and frees it from blight too.
Austerities are what you need to purchase;
   You'll save your soul through this hard bodily service.
And if, without you choosing, it arrives,
   Bow down, and give thanks—be a man who thrives!
Give thanks He's given you austerity;   3400
   You didn't do it—He did with His '*Be!*'*

Story about that woman whose children never survived. She lamented and God replied, 'That is in place of your ascetic discipline and is for you in place of the jihad of the strugglers in God's way'

A woman would each year bear a new son,
   But none survived up to six months, not one.
After just three or four, each one would die
   And then in grief 'O God, alas!' she'd cry.
'I bore him for nine months; he lived for three—
   My blessings pass like rainbows, rapidly.'
Before the men of God she would complain
   In this way through a knowledge-bearing pain.

Twenty children went to their graves this way— 3405
  Each struck by flames that quickly burn away.
A paradise appeared to her one night,
  Verdant, eternal, lovely to her sight.
I call grace that's beyond words 'garden', though
  It's more the essence of such things below.
For *what no one's seen* 'garden' isn't right,
  But God used 'lamp' once for the Unseen's light.*
Analogy and not comparison,
  It gave a clue to that bewildered one.
In brief, she saw, then felt intoxication, 3410
  Too weak before that great manifestation.
She saw her own name on a palace wall
  And reckoned that it was hers after all.
Then she was told, 'To that one God sent bounty
  Who pledges her own soul to Him sincerely.
One must complete much service for the sake
  Of this rare meal, if wishing to partake.
In taking refuge you were lazy, so
  Instead God gave you grief and brought you woe.'
'O Lord, for a whole century or more 3415
  Give me these—shed my blood!' she'd then implore.
On entering the garden, she could see
  All of her children there alive and free.
'I lost them, but, Lord, they weren't lost to You.
  None's perfect with the Unseen lost from view.'
If you don't bleed yourself, then from your nose
  Blood flows out, lest the fever's danger grows.
A fruit's core's better than the skin; what's more
  Body's skin while the Loved One is the core.
In fact, Man has a core that is exquisite— 3420
  If you're inclined to for one moment, seek it!

How Hamza entered the battle without armour

Towards the end, when Hamza joined the fray,
  He'd fight without his armour, come what may.

His chest and torso bare, he'd head towards
   The foe's ranks, hurl himself then at their swords.
People asked, 'Uncle of the Prophet, lion
   Who breaks ranks and is known as "Monarch stallion",
Have you not heard your God's revealed instruction:
   "Don't throw yourselves towards you own destruction"?*
Why are you doing this, though that's revealed,   3425
   In such a manner on the battlefield?
When you were young, solidly built, and muscular,
   You wouldn't line up while not wearing armour—
Now you are hunchbacked, old, and frail, why now
   Behave as if you're reckless anyhow?
Recklessly you are grappling fierce foes here,
   Struggling against the sabre and the spear.
The sword has no respect for age—how can
   Arrows and swords discern an ageing man?'
Unaware sympathizers in this guise   3430
   Protectively gave counsel which seemed wise.

Hamza's reply to the people

'When I was still young,' Hamza then replied,
   'I thought that leaving this world was to die.
How should one happily go to death, walk bare
   To a snake's pit or to a dragon's lair?
But I now, through Mohammad's light and grace,
   Am not a captive of this transient place.
The King's own army camp is in my sight
   Beyond the senses—it's filled with God's light,
Tent after tent, and with each rope and stake—   3435
   Thanks be to that man who shook me awake!'
For those whose eyes see death as mere destruction
   'Don't throw yourself in harm's way!'* is instruction,
But he who sees death as an open door
   Receives the call *'Race here!'** and longs to soar.
Those who see only death had better fear!
   Those seeing Resurrection—race up here!*

Welcome, you who see grace. Rejoice, you're blest!
    Woe to those who see wrath. *Become distressed!*
For Joseph all would sacrifice their head,   3440
    The wolf makes all leave guidance, though, instead.*
Everyone's death will match him in the end—
    To foes it is a foe, to friends a friend.
To Turcomans the mirror is so fair,
    To Africans it's dark—they don't compare.
As you flee death, the thing you really fear
    Is in your self. Heed well what you now hear!
It's your vile face, not death's face, which you flee;
    Death is a leaf, but your soul is its tree
Whether it's good or bad, from you it grew;   3445
    Pleasant or ugly, each thought is from you.
If you're pricked by a thorn, who grew that one?
    If wearing silk, by whom was that silk spun?
Actions and their rewards aren't of a kind;
    Service is not like the bestowal assigned:
Rewards and deeds do not bear a resemblance,
    The latter accident, the former essence.
The latter's struggle, sweat, and servitude,
    The former silver, gold, and trays of food.
If you're accused or come under suspicion,   3450
    It's due to your own victim's prayer's petition.
You claim, 'I am immune from that concern,
    For I am not accusing anyone.'
Your sin is of a different kind—take heed!
    How should the fruit resemble your sown seed?
One fornicated and the rod was used:
    Now he protests, 'With rods who've I abused?
Wasn't this for the fornication then?
    How does a stick match it? Tell me again.'
Moses, how can a rod seem like a snake?*   3455
    Physician, how is that cure like the ache?
Instead of swinging rods, if you spurt semen
    It could grow into a most decent human:
Your semen turns into a friend or snake,
    So why is that rod's change so hard to take?

Do semen and the child look similar?
  Do sugar cubes look like the canes of sugar?
When one sows here a bow or a prostration,
  It forms in yonder world a heavenly garden;
When praise of God comes from one's mouth, each word   3460
  The Lord of Dawn* turns to a heavenly bird.
Your praises with the Lord you can't compare
  Although bird semen is a kind of air.*
When your hands give out to the others alms,
  They raise up in the next world fine date palms.
Your patience forms the water stream in heaven;
  The milk stream comes from your love and affection;
The honey stream comes through your worship's savour;
  The wine stream through your drunkenness's stupor.*
Such causes don't match their effects, do they?   3465
  Nobody knows why God fixed it this way.
Once all these causes follow your command,
  The four streams too will do what you demand.
You make them flow wherever you should please;
  They all depend on your prior qualities,
Just like your semen, all controlled by you—
  Your offspring follow your direction too:
Your son, while running where you have dictated,
  Will say, 'I'm from what you ejaculated.'
As things in this world follow your direction,   3470
  Those streams beyond too follow your instruction.
Your orders are obeyed too by the trees
  Because they bear fruit through your qualities.
Such qualities here are controlled by you,
  So your reward's in your command there too.
And when your hand deals out to victims blows,
  In hell a Zaqqum tree then quickly grows.*
In anger when you set men's hearts aflame,
  You are the source of hell's fires—you're to blame.
Since here your fire burns people, there again   3475
  What's born from it will kindle fires for men.
Other men are the targets of your flame;
  The fire produced like this sets them aflame.

Scorpion- and snake-like speeches that you make
    Bite you in hell as scorpion and as snake.
You kept the Friends of God here waiting once,
    So you must wait there for deliverance—
'Tomorrow or the next day,' you once said:
    You'll wait for God to summon you with dread:
You'll stay there waiting underneath the sun,   3480
    Which melts souls, to face up to what you've done,
Since you'd kept heaven waiting and you'd sowed
    Seeds of 'Tomorrow I'll take that good road.'
Your anger is hell-fire's original seed—
    Extinguish it! It is a trap! Take heed!
Only the Light puts out this fire, no doubt:
    *'We're grateful that your light put our fire out.'**
If you lack light, show clemency to men;
    Your flame's alive still and might grow again.
Beware too of pretence and rote! Just light   3485
    Of faith extinguishes flames of that height.
Don't feel safe till true faith's light seems quite clear,
    For later hidden fires might yet appear.
Deem the light water; hold with all your might.
    When you have water, fire can't give a fright.
It puts fire out, since fire habitually
    Burns up all of the water's progeny.
Spend time with waterfowl who'll lead you to
    Water of Life, so you can drink there to.

Land birds and waterfowl look very similar;   3490
    Like oil and water, they will fight each other;
They're opposites, each faithful to its source—
    Since they look similar, take care on this course!
Satanic whispering and God's inspiration
    Are different though they're both communication;
Both brokers in the market of the conscience,
    They advertise their merchandise, esteemed prince.
If you weigh up thoughts like a money-dealer
    Who serves the heart, discern like a slave-dealer

Between the two types; if you can't, then say   3495
  '*No to being swindled!*' and don't rush that way.

How to avoid being swindled in trade

A man said to the Prophet after meeting:
  'In trade I'm always victim of men's cheating.
All traders try dishonest trickery—
  Like sorcerers, they all bamboozle me.'
'When you are scared', the Prophet then replied,
  'Of being duped, take three days to decide.
Diligence is God's gift for feeling certain,
  While haste comes from the scheming and cursed Satan.'
If to a dog you throw a piece of bread,   3500
  It sniffs it first then eats, if it's well bred.
It uses its nose—you, wise man, should too:
  You can smell with the intellect in you.
The earth and heavens were made in creation
  By God in six days, with deliberation;
He could have simply used his order '*Be!*'*
  To raise a hundred of them instantly.
Little by little till a man is forty
  Our King makes him complete his lifetime gradually.
Although he's able in a single instant   3505
  To send forth fifty who were non-existent.
Jesus was able with one prayer he said
  Without a long delay to raise the dead.
Can Jesus' creator not raise then
  Without delay successive groups of men?
Taking His time is simply for the sake
  Of guiding you to act thus, with no break:
A little stream that flows continually
  Will not turn murky with impurity.
Deliberation's similar to eggs too   3510
  From which birds of good fortune hatch for you.
Why should the bird and egg look just the same,
  Even if from that egg this bird first came?

Wait till your limbs hatch birds on the Last Day
   Just as eggs do, exactly the same way.
Although the sparrow's egg looks like the snake's,
   They're worlds apart—avoid such big mistakes!
The quince's doesn't match the apple's seed
   Though they look so alike—discern, take heed!
We see as similar leaves on different trees,   3515
   But their fruit are diverse varieties.
Our bodies are like leaves, as in appearance
   They are alike, but each soul has a difference.
People at the bazaar appear so similar
   But one feels joy while grief consumes another.
Even in death we leave here the same way:
   Half of us lose, half of us rule the day.

The death of Belal while he was rejoicing

Like the new moon, Belal grew thin and frail;
   His African face even looked death-pale.
His wife saw him and cried, '*Oh what distress!*'   3520
   Belal said, '*No, no, it is happiness!*
I've been in grief from living until now.
   What do you know of death's joys anyhow?'
While he was saying this, his face then grew
   Narcissi, roses, and red tulips too:
The glow of his face and his shining eyes
   Were evidence that his words weren't lies.
He was black in black-hearted people's view;
   The pupil of men's eyes is pitch black too.
Blind people are in fact those black in colour,   3525
   While seeing people are the moon's own mirror.
Who sees the pupil of your inner sight
   Other than men with extraordinary light?
Since none see it except the visionary few,
   Who else has such perceptive vision? Who?
All but such men must stick to imitation—
   They can't compete with men of direct vision.

'*The parting*, husband of good constitution!'
   His wife said. 'No, dear wife, this is the union.'
'Tonight you are a stranger,' she then sighed,   3530
   'You'll leave your home and family once you've died.'
'No, no, tonight my soul departs', he said,
   'From exile back to its true home instead.'
She asked, 'Where shall we see your face again?'
   'Among God's circle of most special men.'
His special circle is now joined with you—
   From downwards to above adjust your view!
Light in that circle is now shimmering
   From God just like a bezel in a ring.
She cried, 'This home has been destroyed, my love!'   3535
   'No, watch the moon, and not the clouds above.
It's wrecked to rebuild bigger than before
   Since now my people number many more.'

The wisdom in the destruction of the body at death

Like Adam, I was trapped in misery.
   Now East and West contain my progeny.
I was a beggar in a wretched pit—
   I'm now a king for whom a castle's fit.
Castles are where the kings relax; the tomb
   Gives only to a corpse sufficient room.
For Prophets, this world is too narrow, so   3540
   They've soared beyond all space like kings we know,
While to the dead this world seems wonderful;
   Though it looks big, it really is too small.
If it's not narrow, why the groan and frown?
   Why are those who've lived long the most bent down?
At sleeping time, when it is liberated
   From this place, feel your soul become elated;
The wicked one can leave bad ways behind
   And prisoners will no longer feel confined.
This earth and sky, which look so vast and deep,   3545
   Become extremely narrow when you sleep.

This world's a blindfold that steals sense of space;
    Its smile is weeping and its pride disgrace.

*A comparison involving this world, which is wide in appearance
and narrow in reality, and a comparison involving sleep, which
is release from this narrowness*

Like steam-baths, where, due to the heat, you felt
    Uncomfortable, as if about to melt.
Although the steam-baths might be broad and long,
    You don't feel well there, as the heat's too strong.
Your heart won't feel good till you exit it,
    So that room's space gives you no benefit;
Like wearing tight shoes in the desert when   3550
    You wander there, misguided wretch, for then
The desert's vastness will feel so restrictive
    Just like a prison when you are a captive—
Whoever sees you from afar might say:
    'He's in the desert like a flower today,'
Not knowing you seem flower-like outwardly
    But groan like wicked people inwardly.
Sleep is like kicking off your shoes—your soul
    Breaks free in sleep from body's tight control.
Sleep is a kingdom to God's Friends, and so   3555
    They're like the Seven Sleepers long ago.
Without sleep they can dream, and they can soar
    To Non-existence and not need a door.

'A narrow house that cramps the soul He's wrecked,'
    Belal said. 'Now huge castles He'll erect.
Stuck in a womb just like an embryo,
    I've reached nine months and now it's time to go.
Unless my mother now feels childbirth's pain,
    Amid the flames in this gaol I'll remain.
Death's pain compels my nature's mother to   3560
    Give way, so that the lamb can leave the ewe,

Then graze on lush, green pastures, so take heed!
   Open the womb wide—this lamb's huge indeed.'
In childbirth every mother suffers aches;
   The baby pushes till the gaol's lock breaks.
The mother weeps, '*Where is the refuge?* Near?'
   The baby laughs, 'Deliverance is here!'
Under the sky all mothers possible,
   Mineral, animal, or vegetable,
None of them know the other ones' affliction   3565
   Except those mystics who have reached perfection.
A modest man sees more of men's affairs
   Than they themselves do with long beards and airs—
The things the man of heart knows of your state,
   My brother, you yourself can't estimate.

Explanation of how heedlessness, grief, laziness, and darkness all originate from the body, which is of the earth and lower world

Heedlessness comes from bodies; spirits see
   All of the mysteries with full certainty.
When earth leaves the celestial atmosphere,
   Then night and day completely disappear:
The earth brings darkness and blocks out the light;   3570
   The heavens and the moon don't bring the night.
Smoke rises from the firewood through the air,
   Not from the flaming stars up over there.
Mere fancies lead to error; intellect
   That's true leads always to what is correct.
All heaviness and laziness's source
   Is body; souls can even fly of course.
A rush of blood makes your face blush red, while
   A face turns yellow due to too much bile;
Phlegm is the reason why a face turns white;   3575
   Black bile will make it turn as dark as night.
He is the Maker of effects, that's true,
   But look beyond, don't take the simple view!

The kernels cannot choose while trapped in shells,
　　Still under doctors' and diseases' spells.
When someone's born a second time, he'll tread
　　Upon all causes, stepping on their head;
This Man's faith isn't for the first cause, friend,
　　Nor do particulars hate him or offend.
In the horizon, like the sun, he'll sail;   3580
　　Sincerity's his bride, while form's the veil.
Beyond horizons and beyond the heavens
　　Like intellects and souls, beyond locations.
Our intellects are shadows of That One:
　　They trail His feet like shadows in the sun.
When jurists know of a revealed law, then
　　They won't apply analogy for men,
But if there's no revealed law, then you'll see
　　Them have to count on an analogy.

Comparison of a revealed text with analogy

The Holy Spirit's words of revelation   3585
　　Surpass analogy by means of reason.
Spirit enables intellect to see—
　　It can't be under its authority!
Rather it shapes the lower intellect
　　And that controls things due to its effect.
If, as with Noah, spirit aided you,
　　Where is the sea and ark? Where's the flood too?
Intellect reckons an effect's the spirit,
　　The sun's light and its orb, though, are quite separate.
A wayfarer's content with bread—one bite   3590
　　Might send him near the sun's orb through its light.
This light which we can see here as a ray
　　Does not endure when night succeeds the day—
The ones who're at the sun's orb permanently
　　Are deluged in the light perpetually;
Sunsets and clouds do not disturb their station,
　　As they've been freed from painful separation.

And from the heavens they originated,
  Or, if from earth, they must have transmutated,
Because terrestrials can't bear that light's rays   3595
  To shine directly down on them always:
For if the sun shines on your soil non-stop,
  It burns it, and you cannot grow your crop.
Fish must remain in water, not a snake—
  How can it join the fish inside a lake?
But there are skilful snakes up in the mountain
  Who act the way that fish act in an ocean;
Their trickery makes men crazy and brings awe,
  Their fear of water though remains a flaw.
And there are skilful fish in this sea, who   3600
  Transform snakes into fish through magic too.
The fish deep in the Sea of Majesty*
  Have been taught lawful magic by that sea.
And, through their radiance, the impossible
  Is managed, bad luck turns to good as well.
If till the end of time I talk this way,
  Many times over there'd be more to say.

The proper etiquette of listeners and disciples at the emanation of wisdom from the tongue of the master

To weary people this is repetition;
  To me it is the cause of Resurrection.
The candle flares up if we should repeat   3605
  Lighting it; earth forms gold through constant heat.
Among seekers, if there's one weary soul,
  The messenger won't pass on news at all;
Clairvoyant messengers would like an audience
  With Esrafil's zealous manner and obedience.
They have a monarch's pride and attitude;
  From this world's men they seek some servitude.
Unless you should observe their stated rules,
  Do not expect to gain from them, you fools.

How should they now pass on to you the trust,   3610
   If you won't bow down in submission first?
How should they deem nice any old behaviour
   When they've come from high castles as your saviour?
They are not beggars to feel now obliged
   For service from you who have schemed and lied.
Though you lack spirit and are not yet bold,
   Spend gold for such a king. Do not withhold.
Messenger, please ignore each weary one,
   And let your marvellous horse still gallop on.
Happy the Turcoman who shuns debating,   3615
   Whose horse leaps into flames, not hesitating;
This makes the horse so hot that it will try
   To race up to the summit of the sky.
The one who keeps this world far from his eye
   Can burn, like fire, wet things as well as dry.
And if repentance finds fault and gives blame,
   Fire first will set repentance all aflame.
Repentance can't spring up from nothingness
   To face the mystic's ardent powerfulness.

***How every animal knows the smell of its enemy and
takes precaution, and the folly and baseness of that
person who is the enemy of that person against whom
one cannot take precaution, nor flee from, nor resist***

Although they're beasts, most horses know the smell   3620
   Of a fierce lion, and its roar as well.
Indeed, each animal can tell its foe
   By a clear sign or mark that they all know.
By day the little bat won't flap about—
   Like thieves, at night it flies to seek food out.
The bat is the most base and wretched one,
   Because it is the foe of the bright sun;
It cannot bear the wounds earned in their fray,
   Nor, through its curses, ever drive away

The sun, which looks away from all of that 3625
    Rage and anxiety of a mere bat.
That sun's the height of kindness and perfection;
    That bat's defenceless, lacking real protection.
If you should pick a foe, pick one your size
    So you can capture it, if you are wise.
If a drop picks a fight now with the sea,
    It will just show itself up stupidly.
Its cleverness can't pass beyond its nose—
    How then can that one reach where no one goes?
Here's the rebuke for the sun's enemy: 3630
    You're foes with its source too, though you can't see.
Foe of That Other Sun whose glories make
    Each single star in our sky start to shake,
You're not His foe, but your own foe! Why should
    The fire care that you've turned to burning wood?
Should it feel loss because it's burning you?
    And sorrow for the pain it's causing too?
His mercy's not like human mercy, where
    Sorrow is mixed in—it's beyond compare.
The mercy shown by men comes from their stress; 3635
    God's mercy's free of sorrow and distress.
Know that God's mercy, which you have received,
    Differs—just its effect can be conceived.

The difference between knowing something by comparison and blind acceptance and knowing the essential nature of that thing

The fruit and influence of His mercy's clear,
    But who knows its essential nature here?
None knows the actual nature of perfection
    Except through its effects and by comparison:
A child can't know what sex is like you do,
    Even if he says, 'It's like sweets to you.'
How can delight in sex be really similar 3640
    To what you feel while eating sweets and sugar?

A clever man compared them once through pleasure
    They both give, since you're childlike by his measure.
Thus, through comparison a child might know—
    It can't sense it's essential nature though.
You say, 'I know'—that's not inaccurate,
    But 'I don't know' is just as accurate:
When someone asks, 'Do you know Noah, who
    Is God's own Messenger and pure light too?'
If you say, 'How should I not know that one   3645
    When he's more famous than the moon and sun,
When children say his name in recitations
    Like leaders of the prayer for congregations,
All using the Qur'an as source, to tell
    His legends from past glorious days so well.'
That would be right as far as his description,
    Even though his essential nature's hidden.
'How can I know him?' if instead you ask,
    'Only one like him can fulfil that task:
I'm a lame ant, how can I know for real   3650
    Elephants' natures or pure Esrafil?'
This is right too, since you can't comprehend
    Him in his own essential nature, friend.
We can't know the essential nature then—
    That's the condition of all common men,
But eyes of perfect mystics still can view
    Essential natures and deep secrets too.
What then is harder to see in existence
    And then to understand well than God's essence?
When that's not hidden from those who are near   3655
    To Him, what essence can stay hidden here?
The scholar's brain says, 'That's deep and obscure;
    Ignore such nonsense, as it's not secure.'
'Weak one!' the Sufi master will then state.
    'It seems like that since it's beyond your state:
Didn't the knowledge now revealed to you
    At first seem like the craziest nonsense too?
From ten gaols through God's kindness you've been freed;
    Don't turn expanses to a cage—take heed!

The agreement and concord of the negation and affirmation of the same thing owing to the relativity of different perspectives

One can affirm things, then deny them too: 3660
  Both can apply from different points of view.
'*You did not throw when you threw*'* gives direction—
  It proves both affirmation and negation:
You threw it—it flew from your hand that hour;
  You didn't throw it, for God used His power.
A human's strength is limited—how then
  Can sand defeat vast armies full of men?*
'That handful's yours, but it was I Who threw'—
  Here's affirmation and negation too.
Prophets are recognized by foes among men,   3665
  *Just as those foes know theirs from others' children:**
All their own children they can always tell
  With numerous proofs and many signs as well,
But, out of envy, they instead will hide,
  Claiming, 'I can't tell!', but these foes have lied.
God says, '*He knows*', so why elsewhere does He
  Say, '*None knows them at all apart from Me*'?*
'*They're hidden under my domed tents*'* and no one
  But God can recognize those ones for certain,
So see this as a relative thing too,   3670
  For Noah's known and isn't known by you.

The annihilation and subsistence of the dervish

'There is no dervish in the world,' one said
  'And he'd be non-existent, if instead
There were one here: subsisting in God's essence,
  His attributes would be effaced in God's ones.'
Candlelight in the sun is non-existent,
  Yet it is still considered an existent—

Its essence still exists, for if you poke
   Cotton into it, that will burn with smoke;
It's non-existent—naught's illuminated   3675
   By it; in sunlight it's annihilated:
To jars of honey if you add *one cup*
   Of vinegar, the honey soaks it up,
And yet the vinegar will leave no taste,
   Although on weighing scales the cupful's traced.
Before a lion deer will fall unconscious;
   That lion's being swamps their own. It's obvious.
Analogies that show our work's deficient
   Next to God's come from love—they're not impertinent.
The lover's pulse without restraint will race   3680
   Towards the king and claim an equal place;
In this world no one seems so impolite,
   Yet none is so well-mannered far from sight.
These are two poles—polite and impolite—
   Which relativity can still unite:
He is ill-mannered from what you can see,
   Since his love-claim suggests some parity,
But look in him then tell me what's to blame—
   The Sultan has effaced him and his claim.
If Zayd's the subject of these words: '*Zayd died*',*   3685
   When he's no more, how is that justified?
Zayd is the subject from the view of grammar,
   Though he's the object, death is here the killer.
What kind of subject can he be like this—
   Effaced, he's lost all of his 'subjectness'.

Story about the deputy of the Sadr-e Jahan who left Bukhara in fear of his life, only for his love to draw him back there, because a matter of life and death is not major for lovers

Bukhara's *sadr* once had a slave who hid
   When he was blamed for what another did.

Confused, for ten long years he roamed and ran
   In deserts, mountains, and through Khorasan.
After ten years his yearning meant that he   3690
   Could not bear separation endlessly.
He thought, 'I cannot take more banishment.
   Nothing heals feelings of abandonment.'
These lands are barren now from separation;
   Dirt gives the water its discoloration.
The life-increasing wind gets filled with sickness
   And fire turns ground beneath us into ashes.
Even heavenly gardens face disease:
   Leaves yellow, rot, then drop off from the trees.
Separate from friends the intellect feels low,   3695
   Just like an archer with a broken bow.
This separation made hell-fire so scorching,
   And it makes old men's limbs continue shaking.
If I talk of this spark-like separation
   Until the end I'll have said just a fraction.
Don't breathe a word about its burning then—
   Just say, '*Lord, save me!*' and say it again.
Imagine what it's like to be apart
   From things here that bring joy inside your heart:
Others enjoyed what you enjoy here, friend,   3700
   But it still fled them wind-like in the end—
Don't love that thing. It will soon leave you too.
   Escape from it before it flees from you!

The appearance of the Holy Spirit in human form to Mary when she was naked and bathing, and her taking refuge in God

Before the passing of your prized possession
   Like Mary say: '*I pray the Merciful One*
Saves me from you!'* She'd seen a form she found
   Exhilarating, which made her heart pound:
Like sun and moon, the spirit all can trust
   Rose up before her eyes from the ground's dust;
Beauty unveiled and rose up in this way   3705
   Just as the sun appears each single day.

Mary's limbs shook at this strange interruption,
    For she was naked and feared some corruption.
If Joseph had seen what then Mary saw,
    Like women he'd have cut his hands in awe.*
Just like a rose in soil it magically
    Came up as if the heart's own fantasy.
She lost her wits as though she had just dreamed;
    'I flee now to God's refuge!' she then screamed,
For that pure-bosomed woman then had been   3710
    Accustomed to escape to the Unseen;
And, since she'd seen this world's impermanence,
    She'd made a fortress from God's presence once,
So, after death, she'd have a sanctuary
    Beyond the reach of every enemy.
She saw none better than God's own protection,
    So chose her resting place in that direction.
She'd seen some amorous glances which could start
    Fires to burn intellects and pierce men's hearts.
God placed both king and army into slavery;   3715
    He made wise rulers fall unconscious easily.
He owns such kings as slaves who do His will
    And He's made full moons look so thin and ill.
Venus won't dare to breathe a word at all
    And Universal Intellect feels small.
What can I say when I don't have the choice,
    When His strong furnace has burned out my voice?
I'm that fire's smoke; I'm its proof from the King—
    Keep far *the nonsense they're interpreting*!
Sunshine has no proof other than its light,   3720
    Which shines out from itself and gives us sight.
How can mere shadows be His evidence?
    They're fit to show just His pre-eminence.
His glory tells the truth to you instead;
    Perceptions lag behind, while He's ahead.
They're for lame donkeys, and if you compare
    He rides the wind like arrows in the air.
None even reaches His dust if He flees;
    If they try to, He blocks their way with ease.

All sense-perceptions lack tranquillity—
    It's time for war, not for festivity:
Just like a falcon one of them will fly;
    Another, arrow-like, tears through the sky;
Another's like a ship with sails at sea;
    Another is retreating constantly.
On seeing in the distance some new prey
    All those birds launch an ambush straight away.
They're left perplexed, though, when it vanishes;
    Like owls, they head towards the wilderness.
They wait with one eye open, in this way
    Hoping for reappearance of the prey,
But after a long wait, so wearily
    They question, 'Was the prey there actually?'
It would be better if for just one hour
    They'd rest, regaining all their strength and power.

If there were no night, greed could make a nation
    Consume themselves with all their agitation.
The greed for profit would make men consume
    Their bodies long before they reach the tomb.
The night descends on them like mercy's treasure,
    So they can flee their greed for a short measure.
And if contraction ever comes to you,
    That's good—don't tear your heart out as some do,
For you are spending when you feel expansion*
    And that needs income from a prior transaction:
If it were always summer, then the sun
    Would scorch the orchard, and would quickly burn
All flower-beds down to their roots inside,
    And dried-up plants would not then be revived.
December's sour-faced, but it's kind, while summer
    Will laugh with all, then burn them to a cinder,
So, in contraction, feel joy anyhow.
    Be youthful and don't heavily crease your brow!
Children will laugh while learned men feel bitter;
    Joy fills the lungs, but grief blocks up the liver.

3730

3735

3740

The child looks to the stable like an ass,
   The wise to the Last Day, not things that pass;
The child deems stable-straw food that can nurture,
   The sage sees he'll be slaughtered by a butcher—
Straw given by the butcher will taste hideous;   3745
   He's set his scales up as he wants to weigh us.
Eat wisdom's fodder, which God gave without
   His own desire. Shame you can't work it out!
It seems that all you understand is bread,
   Even though '*Eat what He provides!*'* God said!
God feeds you wisdom in degrees, my friend,
   So it won't choke you at the very end.
You've closed your mouth and that's produced another
   That eats the morsels of the secret, brother.
If you've cut off your body from the Devil   3750
   And his milk, you'll be blessed to a new level.

Mine's like the Turcoman's own half-cooked meat,
   But Hakim Sana'i's words are complete;
In his *Divine Book* it is clarified
   By 'the Unseen's Sage' and 'the Mystics' Pride':
'Eat grief, not bread, from those who make grief bigger.
   While sages take grief, children eat up sugar.'*
Sugar of joy is picked from fields of grief;
   Joy is a wound, while grief brings it relief.
When you see grief embrace it lovingly,   3755
   Then with perspective view reality!
The wise see wine in grapes, though it seems distant;
   Lovers see things that are still non-existent.
Two porters quarrelled just the other day:
   'Don't take it, let me in a manful way!'
Since they saw profit in their toil and bother,
   Each tried to take the load back from the other.
One sees in God's reward such a huge difference:
   God gives you gold, while men give you a pittance.
God's golden treasure is a special kind,   3760
   For, when you die, it isn't left behind:

It races past your funeral procession
   To stay in exile's grave as your companion.
Be dead now, to prepare for when you'll die.
   You'll join eternal love like this on high.
Patience shows you that through your toil today
   Your love's fair face and curls will come your way.
Grief is a mirror that's placed opposite
   The striver who sees opposites in it—
After toil's turn the opposite appears: 3765
   Expansive joy and glory to raise cheers.
Your own hand shows how opposites will function:
   After it's closed, it opens up for certain.
If someone's hand is always closed or open,
   This means that person's hand must have been broken.
One's deeds are regulated by these two;
   They're vital, like a bird's two wings, for you.
When Mary suddenly grew agitated,
   Like fish on land who had been relocated . . .

The Holy Spirit tells Mary: 'I am a messenger from God to you. Don't be agitated or hide from me, for this is God's command!'

. . . Generous God's representative then said: 3770
   'I come from Him. Trust me and don't feel dread.
Don't turn your gaze from God's exalted ones.
   Don't draw back from His special confidants.'
As he said this, a ray of purest light
   Rose out of his lips up to the stars' height.
'To nothingness would you flee my existence?
   I'm like a king beyond in Non-existence.
My origin and home are in Non-being;
   My form in front of Mary's all you're seeing.
I am a difficult form now to view—   3775
   I'm the new moon and the heart's image too.
You cannot flee an image in your heart;
   It goes with you wherever you depart.
But not the worthless transient fancies—they,
   Just like a false dawn, quickly fade away.

I'm like the true dawn, made out of God's light,
    Whose day will never be replaced by night.
Mary, don't cry out "*God's strength!*" out of fear,
    Since from *God's strength* I have descended here
And it's my sustenance and origin: 3780
    God's strength's* light shone before speech could begin.
You seek out refuge now in God from me,
    But I've been there since Pre-eternity.
I am that refuge. I've saved you so often
    Now you seek refuge and must have forgotten.'
Failure to recognize is the worst thing:
    In her arms, but unskilled in love-making.
You think your friend's the stranger, and you want
    To name joy 'grief'; you're truly ignorant.
Such a date palm is Our Beloved's grace;   3785
    We're thieves and His palm is our gibbet's place.
Musk wafts from our commander's locks. No brain
    Remains with us, and so this forms our chain.
His grace flows like the Nile, and now that we
    Are Pharaohs it becomes blood instantly.
The blood says, 'I am water none must spill;
    I'm Joseph, but a wolf to foes who'd kill.
Don't you see that a stalwart friend can be
    Snake-like when you become his enemy?
His substance hasn't changed from what you knew;   3790
    He's only turned bad from your point of view.

The vakil resolves through love to return to Bukhara without worrying about his own welfare

Leave Mary's candle lit, because that lover
    Whose heart's aflame is going to Bukhara
Impatiently and in a blazing furnace—
    Read in the tale of the great *sadr* to learn this.
Bukhara stands for knowledge's true source;
    All who possess it are Bukharans of course.
When near the shaikh you're in Bukhara too,
    So don't look down on that place seen by few.

Its ebb and flow forms such a major hurdle   3795
  That none reach this Bukhara but the humble.
Happy the man whose *self is brought down low!*
  Stubbornness ruins others. It's your foe.
The exile from the *sadr* had torn apart
  The lover's soul's foundation part by part.
He said, 'I will return to faith once more
  Although I was an infidel before.
I'll go back there and fall down at the feet
  Of that great *sadr* whose thoughts are always sweet.
"I've flung my soul before you!" I will say,   3800
  "Revive me or chop off my head today!"'
Being dead and slain near you, O moon of graces,
  Is better than being king in other places.
More than a hundred times I've tried this out—
  Without you my life won't taste sweet, no doubt.
My wish, sing me the tune of Resurrection!
  Kneel, she-camel! My joy has reached perfection.
Earth, swallow up my tears. They will suffice.
  Soul, drink the pure draught straight from paradise.
Welcome, my Eid! You've come back like last year.   3805
  O breeze, how sweet is what has wafted here.
'Farewell, my friends! I've headed out,' he said,
  'To that *sadr* whose commands are all obeyed.
Each moment I'm more roasted in the heat,
  But, come what may, I'll go and not retreat.
And though he makes himself so stony-hearted,
  Towards Bukhara my soul has departed,
That is the seat of my beloved king—
  "*Love of one's homeland*" means no other thing.'

A lover asked her estranged lover, 'Which city did you find the
finest, the largest, the most magnificent, the most bountiful,
and the most heart-expanding?'

His sweetheart asked her lover, 'My young man,   3810
  You've seen fine towns while travelling, so can

You tell me which is the most fair around?'
  'The town where the beloved can be found.
Wherever her royal carpet's spread in size
  Is a huge plain, even small *needles' eyes*;
And any place where moon-like Josephs dwell
  Is heaven, even deep inside a well.'

His friends prevent him from returning to Bukhara and make threats. He responds, 'I don't care!'

'You clueless one!' a counsellor then said,
  'If you can, think about what lies ahead:
Ponder your past and future rationally!   3815
  Only moths burn themselves so passionately.
How will you reach Bukhara? You're insane
  And should be bound in prison with a chain.
The angry *sadr* champs iron as he tries
  To find your whereabouts with twenty eyes.
He's sharpening a knife for you alone—
  He's like a starving dog and you're the bone!
You have escaped him once when God let you,
  So why head back to gaol? What's wrong with you?
If you had gaolers chasing now, we'd say   3820
  You'll need to use your wits to get away,
But nobody is chasing you at all,
  So why yourself create an obstacle?'
A secret love had kept him prisoner;
  But this was not seen by that counsellor.
A hidden gaoler chases gaolers too—
  If not, why do these curs act like they do?
Into their souls the king of love's rage came,
  Forcing them to a thuggish life of shame:
His rage strikes, saying, 'Beat him!' On account   3825
  Of hidden thugs I've wept a huge amount.
Whomever you see in decline, though he
  Appears alone, a thug's his company.
If he knew of God's presence, he would moan
  And rush to the Most Powerful Sultan's throne,

Scattering dust on his own face in shame,
　　For refuge from the frightening demon's aim.
You're less than ants, but you thought you might be
　　A prince; that's why, blind fool, you couldn't see.
These false wings filled you up with self-deception　　3830
　　And drew you to a harmful self-destruction.
You can fly high if you keep your wings light,
　　But if they're muddied there's no hope for flight.

Due to love, the lover says, 'I don't care!' to his adviser
and scolder.

'How long will you advise me? Please refrain,
　　For I've been tied up with a heavy chain
That's harder to endure than your advice.
　　Your expert didn't know love and its price:
The jurists have no teaching they can offer
　　About how love increases pain we suffer.
Don't threaten me with death, for desperately　　3835
　　I thirst for my own blood. What's death to me?'
Each moment a new death is found by lovers;
　　Their deaths are not one kind; they've many others,
For Guidance's Soul gave lives by the score:
　　Each moment he will sacrifice some more,
Since for each he gets ten in compensation:
　　'*Ten of their like*'*—recite this revelation.
'If that Beloved sheds my blood, I'll throw
　　My life before home, dancing as I go.
I've tested it. Death is this life for me—　　3840
　　When I leave life it's for eternity.'
Murder me, murder me, my trusty friends!
　　In being killed there's life that never ends.
Eternal Soul, you who make all cheeks glow,
　　Draw up my soul to union You bestow!
Love for my lover roasts my bowels, but still
　　If He wants to walk on my eyes, He will.*
Speak Persian although Arabic thrills more;
　　Love has a hundred languages in store.

But all those languages are dumbstruck when   3845
   That Pure Beloved's scent wafts here again.
I'll stop, for the Beloved will speak now—
   Be all ear! *God knows what's best anyhow.*
If lovers should repent, beware, for they
   Will teach drunk on the gallows come what may.
This lover may be going to Bukhara,
   But teachings aren't what he is chasing after—
The Loved One's beauty is the lover's teacher,
   His face their notebook, lesson, and class lecture.
They're silent, but their inner repetition   3850
   Rises up to His throne and seat in heaven.
Their lesson is to whirl in ecstasy,
   Not to read texts or spout philosophy.
The 'chain' of this group is His musky tress,
   Their 'circle case' concerns His curls no less.
If someone asks about 'the purse's case',*
   Then say: 'God's treasure's not found in that place.'
If there's talk of types of divorce, don't you
   Find fault, as this evokes Bukhara too.
Mention of things has special influences,   3855
   As attributes have their own substances.
You prosper in Bukhara with your virtues,
   But being truly humble is what frees you:
Mere knowledge couldn't burden this Bukharan
   Who'd concentrated on the Sun of Vision.
Whoever's found true vision through seclusion
   Shuns knowledge gained through theory and tuition;
If someone's seen the beauty of the soul,
   He won't be moved by sciences at all;
Vision is knowledge's superior, so   3860
   Most men succumb to this world down below—
They see this world as theirs and so immediate,
   But think the other world is bought on credit.

The lover-bondsman turns towards Bukhara

That lover's heart throbbed as he wept blood tears,
   Heading fast to Bukhara with no fears.
Scorching sands felt to him like silk, so cool,
   And the great Oxus seemed a little pool;
Wilderness seemed a rose garden—he'd fall
   From laughter like a rose that's grown too tall.
Candy's from Samarkand, but his lips found   3865
   It in Bukhara, and to it felt bound.
Bukhara, you who'd boost intelligence,
   Removed my faith and knowledge all at once.
I'm crescent-like, for I seek the full moon;
   In this world's waiting line, I want him soon.
Bukhara's skyline came within his sight
   And passion made that black form brilliant white.
He fell flat out unconscious suddenly,
   His mind flown to the source of mystery.
Men dabbed his head and face then with rosewater,   3870
   Not knowing the rosewater of his lover.
He'd seen a hidden rose garden; love had
   Cut him off from himself like one gone mad.
You're not fit for such breath, your heart is stone;
   Though cane, you have no sugar of your own.
You follow just the brain that you still bear;
   Of *armies you can't see** you're unaware.

The reckless lover enters Bukhara and his friends warn him against showing himself

He entered in Bukhara happily,
   Near his beloved and tranquillity,
Like drunken mystics who all gladly race   3875
   To heaven, telling the moon: 'Let's embrace!'
All the Bukharans told him, 'Get away!
   Don't let a soul see you. You cannot stay.

That angry ruler's looking for you here
   To take his vengeance for each passing year.
Don't walk towards your own blood—don't rely
   On clever words and spells: you're going to die.
You were the great *sadr*'s deputy before,
   His master engineer—not any more.
After committing treachery, you fled,   3880
   So having got free why come back instead?
You fled grief using so much trickery—
   Has fate returned you or stupidity?
Your intellect scorns Mercury, but fate
   Makes fools of learned intellects—just wait!
Hares who hunt lions have no luck—where is
   Your cunning and unrivalled cleverness?
Destiny's spells are numerous times as great;
   Fate makes the open field a narrow strait.
There are a hundred paths and sanctuaries,   3885
   But they are blocked by dragon-fate with ease.'

The lover answers those who reproach and threaten him

'I suffer now from dropsy,' he then said.
   'Water draws me, though I know I'll be dead.
None suffering dropsy can flee water still,
   Though they know from experience it will kill;
My hands and belly swell, but can't abate
   My love for water. It's a sorry fate.
When asked about my inner state, I'll say:
   "Would that the sea still flowed in me today!"
Belly, get burst by water! Now if I   3890
   Die from this, it is a good way to die.
I envy water I see in the stream.
   "I wish I were in its place now," I dream.
With body swollen, drum-shaped, I compose
   Rhythms for love of water as a rose.
If Gabriel sheds my blood, like soil below
   Gulp after gulp I'd swallow what would flow.

I drink blood like the earth and embryo;
  While I'm in love, this is all that I know.
I boil above the flame like pots of stew   3895
  And drink blood all the time as dry sands do.
I now repent that I tried trickery
  To flee what his rage wished to do with me.
Let him spur on his rage at my drunk soul;
  He's Eid; the slaughtered beast is my small role.*
Whether the buffalo should sleep or feed,
  We nurture it before we make it bleed.
Moses' cow's tail once resuscitated—
  Likewise my parts revive the liberated.*
Moses' cow was sacrificed; God willed   3900
  Its small tail to revive one who'd been killed:
He sprang up from the spot where he lay dead;
  "Strike him with part of her!" the Lord had said.*
Slaughter this cow, my friends, if your decision
  Is to revive the souls that have true vision.
On death, I left being mineral then grew
  And changed from plant to animal form too,
Then died to that, to be a human here—
  When did death make me less? What should I fear?
I'll die to humanness at the next battle,   3905
  Then spread my wings and soar above each angel:
I must transcend the angels' status too—
  *All perishes except God's face** proves true.
Sacrificed, I'll die to the angel then
  And go beyond imaginings of men.
I'll then be Non-existent, and I'll hear
  *"To Him we are returning"** sound so clear.
Death is one thing agreed on by mankind;
  Water of life is very hard to find.
Leave this side of the stream just like a lily,   3910
  Like dropsy sufferers, seek out death greedily.
Water they seek means death, yet they won't rest
  Till they can drink it. *God knows what is best.*
Cold one who loves material comforts, you
  Flee the Beloved scared for your life too.

Even girls think you're shameful—look above
　　As spirits celebrate the sword of love.
You've seen the stream—empty your jug inside!
　　How can that water now escape outside?
When the jug's water enters, it's effaced;　　　　3915
　　Once in the stream and merged, it can't be traced.
Its essence stays; its attributes have gone—
　　It won't be less or ugly from now on.
I've hung myself like this on his palm tree,
　　Because I'd fled—it's my apology.'

That lover reaches his beloved once he has washed his hands of himself

He touched his head and face then to the floor
　　Before the *sadr*, with eyes about to pour.
Expectantly, all people looked ahead—
　　Would he burn him or hang him there instead?
'He'll show this wretched man who's desperate　　3920
　　What time shows men who are unfortunate.'
Like moths, he saw the flames as light, then he
　　Gave up life by approaching foolishly.
Love's candle has a very major difference,
　　It's radiance in more radiance in more radiance;
The opposite of candles with flames' heat,
　　It looks like fire, but is completely sweet.

Description of that mosque that kills lovers and of the death-seeking, reckless lover who became a guest there

Listen, good fellow, to this tale today:
　　There was a mosque close to the town of Rayy.*
The children of those who had spent one night　　3925
　　In there were orphaned by the dawn's first light;
Strangers with few clothes even to put on
　　Were in their graves like stars when it was dawn.
Pay close attention! Dawn has come—awake!
　　Cut short your sleep. Don't make that same mistake.

'Some evil spirits haunt it!' people said.
    'They use blunt swords to leave the guests there dead.'
'It's talismanic magic,' some would say,
    'That is the foe that takes their lives away.'
Another said, 'Put a sign on the door   3930
    That clearly warns: "Don't stay here any more!"
If you like life, don't stay a single night
    Or death will come, though it's now out of sight.'
Another said, 'Lock it at night! If men
    Come heedlessly, they'll be locked outside then.'

A guest comes to that mosque

One night, a guest came there who'd heard about
    Its stunning reputation, to find out
The truth by trying an experiment,
    For he was very brave and confident.
'I care so little for my head and belly,   3935
    Or one grain being lost from this life's treasury,
So tell the body's form right now: "Begone!"
    The husk's worth little when I will live on.
I was breathed into* from God's grace. Take heed!
    I'm God's breath, separate from the body's reed.
I hope to see the pearl escape its shell
    And that His breath survives this place as well.
"*Sincere one, long for death!*"* the Lord has said.
    I'll give my soul sincerely, unafraid.'

The people of the mosque blame that lover guest for wanting to sleep there and warn him of its dangers

They said, 'Beware, don't sleep here or remain.   3940
    Your own life's foe will pound you just like grain.
Stranger, you do not realize that men
    Who sleep here die in consequence, so then
It's not by chance or a coincidence;
    It's known by all who have intelligence,

A cruel death in the middle of the night
   Awaits those who should stay here overnight.
A hundred times we've seen this, not just once;
   It isn't blind belief through ignorance.
The Prophet said, "Religion's consultation,"   3945
   And that's the opposite of self-deception.
"Be true in friendship" is the wisest counsel.
   Man's treacherous and dog-like when deceitful.
We urge you out of love, as we're not treacherous—
   Don't turn away from reason and from justice!'

The lover's answer to those who scold him

He said, 'O counsellors, is it not clear
   I've had enough already of life here?
I am a vagrant seeking to be hit—
   Don't hope for tramps' minds to be sound and fit.
I'm not a tramp who seeks out food, but one   3950
   Who seeks out his own death without concern,
Not one who steals your money, but one who
   Crosses that bridge more quickly than most do;
Not one who hangs around near stores, for instance,
   But one who runs away from his existence.
Death and departure are all that I love:
   The caged bird longs to flee and soar above;
Its cage is in the garden, where it sees
   Beyond the rosebush and the lovely trees.
A flock of birds come to the cage and sing   3955
   Their happy songs of freedom on the wing.
The caged bird, due to that scene, now no longer
   Seeks food, nor has much patience or composure.
Through every gap it sticks its head out now,
   And tries to shake the fetter off somehow;
Its heart and soul are in this sense outside—
   Imagine when the cage is opened wide!
It's not the caged bird with depression that's
   Surrounded by a circle of fierce cats:

Can that possess amid the grief and fear   3960
    Any desire to leave the cage down here?
It wants more cages built around its own
    To ward off harm from cats, as it feels prone.

The love of Galen* is for the life in this world, for his skill is useful here, and he does not profess any skill that is useful in that other marketplace. He sees himself in the same position over there as ordinary people

The scholar Galen said once, people claim,
    Due to desire for this world and his aim:
'Half of my soul's intact—I'm satisfied
    I see the world through a mule's fat backside.'
He sees a file of cats around him there;
    His bird fears it can't fly up in the air.
Only this world exists to his perception,   3965
    Since he can't see the hidden Resurrection.
God's kindness draws the baby gently out,
    But it retreats because it's filled with doubt:
Though it is being led out by God's grace,
    It stays inside the womb in any case,
Saying: 'If I fall out of this great city,
    I can't come back and that would be a pity.
Out in that dirty town is there a door
    Through which I can gaze at this womb once more?
Is there a path, even one needle-wide,   3970
    Through which to see the womb while I'm outside?'
Of other worlds this baby's also blind,
    Uninitiated, like Galen's kind.
It doesn't know the juices found inside
    Arrived as aid from that 'bad' world outside,
Just like the world's four elements, no less,
    Which gain a hundred aids from Placelessness.
Water is in the bird's cage and some grain,
    But they came from the garden and the plain.

The Prophets see the garden at the stage   3975
    When they're released and transferred from the cage.
Freed from both Galen and the world, they'll soon
    Appear up in the heavens like the moon.
And if those words weren't Galen's actually,
    My answer's not for him specifically,
But for the one who did make that remark,
    And, far from light-filled hearts, lives in the dark.
Because it heard the cats stay '*Stop!*' its soul
    Has turned into a mouse that seeks a hole.
That's why his soul perceived, just like a mouse,   3980
    This world as a fit place to build a house.
It started building down here with the goal
    Of gaining knowledge fit for such a hole.
It chose the skills that would give benefit
    And would prove here the most appropriate.
Since it held back its heart from trying to flee,
    That road closed to its body fatefully.
Spiders aren't of the phoenix's great ilk,
    Or else they wouldn't live on flimsy silk.
The cat has pushed its paws inside the cage;   3985
    They're called 'cramp' and 'delirium', good sage.
The cat is death and its claws are disease—
    It strikes the bird and rips its wings with ease.
Running to find the cure is one with sickness;
    Death is the judge, this sick man is the witness.
This witness comes like the official who
    Summons you to the court-house, forcing you
To beg respite with hope you'll get away—
    Will he accede, or order, 'Come today!'?
Seeking respite means remedies you can   3990
    Use on your body's tattered cloak, good man.
He'll come back angry once much time has passed:
    'How long you've had! You should feel shame at last.'
Jealous one, beg forgiveness, use your head
    Before the day comes which you deeply dread.
The one who rides into the dark this way
    Pulls back his heart from that light straight away—

He's fleeing from the witness and his aim,
  But will be called to judgment all the same.

The people of the mosque blame the visitor again for wanting to sleep in the mosque

Leave this behind—head to that man from earlier   3995
  Who came at night to that mosque as a visitor.
'Don't be a fool! Begone!' the people said,
  'Or do you wish to pawn your soul instead?
From distance it looks easy, but it's worse;
  This path is such a hard one to traverse.
Men hanged themselves as their necks broke and tried
  To grasp support, but all too late. They died.
Before the war starts, people's hearts can see
  Evil distinct from good so easily,
But once inside the battlefield how can   4000
  That not be difficult for any man?
You're not a lion, so take heed and keep
  Your distance; doom's the wolf, your soul the sheep.
If you're an Abdal and your sheep's become
  A lion, then don't fret! Your death won't come.
Who's an Abdal? One who's been substituted;
  To vinegar his wine has been transmuted.
But you are drunk, foolhardy, and now dare
  To dream you are a lion. Halt! Beware!
God said about foes with hypocrisy: 4005
  'Among themselves they act courageously!'*
Among themselves they're brave, but in the fray
  They're scared like women who should keep away.
The Prophet, King of the Unseen, said: 'Son,
  Bravery's no use before the war's begun.'
Mouths foam when drunk on talk of the next battle,
  But in that actual fight what use is spittle?
One draws his sword out, ready at war's mention,
  But in the fray it's wrapped up like an onion.
His heart seeks wounds when war's anticipated,   4010
  But with one needle his bag is deflated.

I'm stunned by those who're seeking purity,
　But, at the time of scrubbing, choose to flee.
Love's just a claim; pain is your proof, my friend.
　If you've no proof, your claim's void in the end.
When this judge asks for proof, don't feel distressed,
　But kiss the snake to find the treasure-chest!*

That harshness is not aimed at you, but at
　Bad qualities in you. Remember that!
When a man beats his carpet clean, we trust   4015
　His target's not the carpet, but the dust.
If a harsh man should lash his horse, don't grumble—
　His aim is to make sure that it won't stumble,
So it will start to trot in a straight line;
　Fermenting grapes are sealed to turn to wine.
'You struck the orphan many times!' one said,
　'Didn't God's vengeance hold you back with dread?'
'When did I ever strike him?' he replied.
　'I struck the demons that he had inside.'
If your own mother screams, 'May you die!' she   4020
　Means that bad nature and iniquity.
People who flee from their own reformation
　Forsake their dignity and reputation.
They flee the battleground because of scolders,
　And turn to sodomites instead of soldiers.
Don't listen to the babbler's boasts again.
　Don't line up at the battle with such men.
'*They would have just increased confusion.*' Run
　As far as you can from each feeble one,
For if they go with you to war today,   4025
　Your army will feel empty soon like hay;
They'll join your side, then flee and break apart,
　Making your battle-line weak at its heart.
Without such men a smaller army's better
　Than one which, through such hypocrites, grows bigger:
Pick almonds that taste sweet, though they be few,
　Not huge piles that contain the bitter too.

For rattling, sweet and bitter are the same;
   The defect is inside and that's your aim.
The infidel has theorized about   4030
   The next world sceptically, and now his doubt
Scares him: he roams but doesn't know way stations—
   The blind at heart walk with such trepidations.
How does he walk and not know the right way?
   With anguished heart and dithering all day.
If someone tells him, 'This route isn't right.'
   He stops there in his tracks because of fright.
But if his heart had learnt the right direction
   How then could their words make him suffer tension?
Don't go with camel-like men, who sink down   4035
   When they feel stress, and lie there with a frown.
They'll run away and leave you with no one
   After they boast of power like Babylon.
Do not expect fair-looking men to fight;
   Peacocks are not the right birds to invite—
Don't give your carnal soul an invitation
   To tempt you with sweet talk from your high station.

How Satan told the Qoraysh: 'Go to war with Mohammad and I will help you and call my tribe for support and how he fled when the two battle-lines faced each other'*

Satan became the army's chief this way:
   He said: '*I'll be your helper from today!*'*
When the Qoraysh then made their preparation   4040
   Before the armies came in confrontation,
Satan saw angels lined up on the flanks
   Prepared to fight with the believers' ranks.
Those troops you couldn't see* lined up so near
   That they set Satan's soul on fire with fear.
He turned around and started to withdraw,
   Saying: 'What an amazing troop I saw!
I fear God and against Him I've no aid.
   Begone! I see what you can't—*be afraid!*'

Hareth said, 'You are in Soraqa's guise,   4045
   So why did you not forewarn of demise?'
'It's only now that I have seen destruction.'
   'Just feeblest Arabs entered in your vision;
You see just them, but you're base anyhow
   For time to talk has passed—the war starts now.
You promised yesterday, "I swear success
   Will be yours through my help and won't grow less."
Then, you were the whole army's surety;
   Now you are useless, vile, and cowardly.
After we've swallowed your words on each duel,   4050
   You flee to hot baths and use us as fuel.'
When Hareth said this, that cursed enemy
   Grew angry at his chiding, and then he
Drew back his hand and turned round to depart,
   Because these words had brought pain to his heart.
Then, suddenly, he struck him on his chest,
   Slaying the helpless one as he knows best.
When he had ruined worlds of men, he spoke:
   '*I now am quit of you!*'* This is no joke.
He struck him on his chest and made him fall;   4055
   Fear of God made him run then from it all.

The self and Satan are one body; they
   Make themselves look like two in their own way.
And angel and true knowledge are united,
   Although for wisdom's sake they seem divided.
You have a foe in your most hidden part
   Which fights with your own faith, your brain, and heart.
Lizard-like it will launch attacks, and then
   It scampers quickly down a hole again.
It has so many holes inside men's hearts   4060
   From which to stick its head out as it darts.
It's called '*the one who slinks back*':* from men's souls
   The Devil slips inside its secret holes.
It shrinks back in the way that hedgehogs do,
   Popping their heads back out when they want to.

God called that Devil '*he who shrinks back*'* for
   The hedgehog's action is so similar:
It hides its head for periods due to fear
   A savage hunter might then hurry near,
Until it's safe to stick its head back out;   4065
   It can foil snakes with such tricks—have no doubt!
If his self hadn't robbed you from inside,
   How could the robbers touch you from outside?
Because of that thug, lust, your heart will bleed,
   Captive to covetousness and petty greed.
That inner hired thug has made you depraved,
   So when the others come you'll not be saved.
Heed what the Prophet counselled long ago:
   '*Between your two sides is your fiercest foe.*'
Don't pay attention to its pomp, but flee,   4070
   For, Satan-like, it quarrels endlessly.
For this world and for fighting others too
   It's made eternal pain seem light to you.
If it makes death seem light, don't be astonished—
   There's so much more its magic has accomplished.
Magic can turn straw to a mountain, or
   Transform a massive mountain to mere straw.
It makes the ugly pretty in men's view,
   And pretty things seem ugly then to you.
Magic's work is to breathe and then transform   4075
   Realities far from their previous norm.
It shows a man to be an ass, and can
   Transform an ass into a marvellous man.
A sorcerer who does that is in you:
   Temptation's mystery's hidden from your view.
In that world where there are such sorceries,
   Resisters have great powers as strong as these.
In that plain where the poison grows, my son,
   The antidote grows too for everyone.
The antidote says, 'Seek a shield from me.   4080
   I'm closer than the poison, if you see.
Its words are magic, but they cause destruction;
   My words are magic, yet they give protection.'

The scolders repeat their advice to that visitor to the mosque that kills guests

'The Prophet said, "*Clear talk has sorcery*,"
    And that great hero spoke so truthfully.
Don't be so dumb! Go back the way you came!
    Don't make us and the mosque receive more blame,
For foes speak out of enmity, and they
    Will set fire to us on the following day,
Claiming: "A cruel man strangled him. No noose.   4085
    The murderer's safe due to that mosque excuse:
He easily can give the mosque the blame,
    And leave scot-free due to that mosque's bad name."
Brave man, don't lay suspicion on us. We
    Are far from safe from our foes' trickery.
Don't be so stupid! Don't be a mad fool!
    You cannot measure Saturn with a rule.
Men tried their luck as you wish to in vain,
    Then tore their beards out, clump by clump, with pain.
Cut short this talk. It's time for you to go.   4090
    Don't cast yourself and us in much more woe.'

The visitor answers them and tells the parable of the guard of the cultivated land who, by beating a mere tambour, fended off a camel on whose back they were playing Shah Mahmud's* kettledrum

He said, 'I'm not a devil, honestly!
    And so "*God give me strength!*"* won't stifle me.'
A boy who used to guard a field would beat
    His kettledrum to make the birds retreat,
Scattering away because of that drum's sound,
    To leave the field safe with no birds around.
When the great Shah Mahmud passed by that way
    He pitched a huge tent near it, for he'd stay
With a huge army like a galaxy,   4095
    All-conquering brave-hearts who fought valiantly.

The army's kettledrum was on a camel,
    A Bactrian which strutted like a cockerel.
That kettledrum was banged each night and day
    When they returned or set out for the fray.
The camel entered that field for the wheat;
    The boy took out his drum, began to beat.
'Don't bang your little drum!' a wise man said,
    'For it is used to drums and won't feel dread.
What good's your small drum? Don't you realize   4100
    It carries one that's twenty times its size?'

I am a lover, sacrificed for '*No!*'*
    My soul's the bandstand for the drum of woe.
These threats are like that little drum next to
    What my eyes have already had to view.
I'm not one of those frail ones who would end
    His wayfaring due to imaginings, friend.
I'm like the Ismailis: I lack dread;*
    Or like Ishmael, with no care for my head.*
From pomp and ostentation I am free—   4105
    Say '*Come!*'* He told my soul 'Come!' didn't he?
The Prophet said, '*When sure of recompense*
    The generous one will meet all the expense.'
Whoever sees a hundredfold return
    Will rush to pay first, since he wants to earn.
For this men join the marketplace to trade:
    To spend when profit can be easily made;
With gold inside their purses they will sit
    Waiting for more to come, for spending it.
When one sees goods more valuable than his,   4110
    His love for his own then diminishes.
He had stayed keen, because he hadn't known
    Any more valuable gifts than his own.
With knowledge, skills, and art it's similar
    Once one sees something that's superior.
When there's none better, life is loved by all;
    When something better comes though, it seems small.

To small girls lifeless dolls have much more worth
　　Than life, until they grow up and give birth.
Your dolls are fancies and imaginings—　　　　　　　　　　4115
　　If you remain a child, you need such things.
But when your soul leaves that for unification,
　　It needs no senses and imagination.
No confidant's here to speak openly,
　　So I'll stop. *God knows best our harmony.*
Like snow, wealth and the body melt to naught;
　　God is their buyer, for *The Lord has bought.**
The snow seems better than the price for you,
　　Because, uncertain, you doubt what is true.
And your conjecture is so strange that it　　　　　　　　　4120
　　Does not seek certainty's fine realm one bit.
O son, conjecture thirsts for certainty,
　　And, bird-like, flaps its wings incessantly.
On gaining knowledge, wings then turn to feet;
　　Certainty's scent makes knowledge then complete.
On this inspired path, knowledge is inferior
　　To certainty, though it excels conjecture.
I tell you knowledge seeks out certainty
　　And that seeks vision gained immediately.
Seek this—'*Alhaykom's*' chapter's where to go,　　　　　4125
　　After '*Kalla*' and after '*If you know.**
Knowledge takes you to vision; you can see
　　Hell for yourself once you have certainty.
Vision is born of that without delay.
　　A thought comes from a fancy the same way.
In '*alhaykom*' it's said transparently—
　　Knowledge of it to *vision of certainty.**
But knowledge and conjecture fail the same;
　　My head does not turn to react to blame.
Once I ate halva from him, the first bite　　　　　　　　　4130
　　Made my eyes see him and become so bright.
I tread with boldness, since I'm going home,
　　Unlike blind men who tremble as they roam.
The thing God said to raise smiles from the rose
　　He told my heart, which now continually grows,

And that touch that made cypresses stand straight,
   And that which wild rose and narcissus ate,
And that which sweetened each cane's heart and soul,
   And that which made a Turk so beautiful,
And that which made the eyebrows like love's magnet,   4135
   And cheeks to blush just like a pomegranate,
And gave the tongue spells that must be divine,
   And Ja'far's pure gold* to the lowly mine.
The day the armoury's doors were opened, glances
   Which tease came from the archers: from their stances
They aimed at me, driving me thus insane—
   They made me love both thanks and sugar-cane.
I am in love with that one to whom all
   Belong. His coral's guards are mind and soul.
I don't boast normally, but when I do   4140
   Like water I quench fires without ado.
How should I steal from treasuries that He
   Protects? His aid makes me act brazenly:
Whoever's back the sun warms acts the same—
   He'll be hard-nosed and not feel fear or shame.
His face is like the face of the bright sun:
   Veils are for it to rend, and foes to burn.
Each Prophet sent was hard-nosed similarly,
   Defeating armies single-handedly;
And never turning round with grief or fear,   4145
   He took the whole world on while present here.
The rock is hard-nosed and its eyes are bold;
   Among brickbats it won't let fear take hold—
Brickbats were made hard by a mere brickmaker;
   The rock though was made hard by the Creator.
Even if sheep are numerous in the pastures,
   How can the butcher ever fear their numbers?
'*Each is a shepherd*': with the Prophet being
   A shepherd, men are flocks he's overseeing.*
The shepherd isn't scared when they're rebellious—   4150
   He shields them from both heat and cold regardless.
If he yells at them, this is actually done
   Out of the love he has for everyone.

New Fortune whispers constantly: 'I will
   Give you much suffering, but don't you grieve still!
I'll send you so much sorrow that you'll cry,
   To shield you from the evil people's eye—
I'll make you bitter with these sorrows, to
   Compel the evil eye to move from you.
Aren't you a hunter seeking me, a minion   4155
   Flung down prostrate in front of my opinion.
You dream up schemes to reach me, but you are
   Helpless when kept apart so very far.—
Your pain looks for a way to reach me—I
   Could hear last night from you each aching sigh.
Without requiring you to wait, tomorrow
   I could give access and show tracks to follow
To flee time's dangerous whirlpool finally
   And reach the treasure of My unity.'
When you arrive the sweet taste you will gain   4160
   Is in proportion to the journey's pain—
You'll reach your final home and destination
   Only once you've borne trials of separation.

Comparison of the believer's fleeing and impatience during affliction with the agitation and resistance of chick-peas and other such vegetables in the boiling-pot, and their rushing up to jump out

Look at the chick-pea in the pot and how
   It leaps when heated by the stove right now.
While being boiled it rises constantly
   Up to the top. Listen to the chick-pea:
'Why are you boiling me now, after you
   Have paid for me? Why treat me as you do?'
The cook then hits it with her spoon to say: 4165
   'Boil properly! Don't try to jump away!
I'm not doing this because I'm harming you,
   But so you'll taste good and be wholesome too.
As food, you'll blend in with the soul, and so
   I'm not doing this to make you suffer woe.
You drank in watered fields while fresh and green—
   That drinking was for this fire.' This must mean

His mercy's prior to His wrath*—that's best
  For it means mercy is what sets your test.
His mercy comes before His wrath*—this way   4170
  Being's capital can be acquired today:
Through food our skin and flesh can grow then serve
  As objects to be melted by His love.
If all this boiling causes harm at all
  Such that you give up all your capital,
Grace will come to excuse it straight away:
  'You've washed and stepped from that stream,' it will say.
The cook says, 'Chick-pea, you fed in the spring—
  Pain is your guest now; treat it well. Its king
Might witness it come back with praise for you   4175
  When it goes home and shares its point of view.'
Then, the Bestower might be much more generous
  And come Himself, making all bounties envious.
I'm Abraham; you're my son—lay your head.
  '*I see I'll sacrifice you*'* we've all read.
Lay it before wrath with calm heart, because
  I want to cut your throat as Ishmael's was.*
I'll chop your head off, but it's an exception,
  Immune to death and to decapitation.
Your aim's been to submit yourself for ever—   4180
  Muslim, you always have to seek surrender.

Chick-pea, keep boiling painfully with persistence
  Until you have no self nor self-existence.
Though you laugh gaily now inside earth's garden,
  You're really flowers of the soul and vision.
If you should leave this place for one perfected,
  You'll be a morsel and then resurrected.
Become food, nourishment, and thought—don't struggle!
  Then milk, be now a lion of the jungle.*
You grew out of His attributes initially—   4185
  Return to them now eagerly and nimbly.
You came down from the clouds, the sun, and sky,
  Became His attributes, went back on high.

As rain and heat you came down, and you should
   Return with attributes deemed very good.
Once with the sun, the clouds, and stars, your lot
   Was to become soul, action, words, and thought.
Animal being comes from plant's death: recite
   *'Kill me my trusty friends!'** It now sounds right.
After checkmate comes victory: you have heard   4190
   *'There's life in my death'**—vouch then for each word!
Action, sincerity, and speech became
   The angels' food, and went up to its aim.
That morsel turned to food for Man, and he
   Rose from inanimateness magically.
I'll give a more extensive explanation
   Of this point in a subsequent location.
From heaven continually a caravan
   Arrives, trades, then returns all to a plan.
Proceed too by your own choice, happily,   4195
   Not like a thief with loathing, bitterly.
If I say bitter words to you, this is
   Only to clean you of all bitterness.
Frozen grapes by cold water can be thawed;
   They won't stay frozen once cold water's poured—
When your heart fills with blood through anguishes
   You'll be released this way from bitterness.

*A comparison exemplifying the way a believer becomes patient once
he understands whether tribulation is for better or for worse*

A dog that's not for hunting has no collar,
   Just as uncooked food lacks a hint of flavour.
'Dear cook, since it's this way,' the chick-pea said,   4200
   'I'll happily boil, if you give me your aid,
For when I boil you are the engineer—
   Hit me now sweetly with your ladle, dear!
I'm elephant-like—beat me, brand me too!
   I'll then not dream of India thanks to you,
But just submit to boiling, to discover
   A way to the embrace of my true lover.'

Once they're too self-sufficient, men rebel;
  A dreaming elephant does this as well—
When such an elephant should dream of India,   4205
  It will turn nasty and not hear its keeper.

How the lady cook apologized to the chick-pea, and the wisdom in her boiling the chick-pea

The lady cook told it, 'For what it's worth,
  I was before, like you, a piece of earth.
Once I drank ardent struggle down, I grew
  Acceptable and most deserving too.'
In time's world, I boiled till I grew so hot,
  And then boiled more inside the body's pot.
These boilings helped me make the senses richer;
  I turned to spirit, then I was your teacher.
Though when inanimate, I'd say, 'Now hurry   4210
  To knowledge and the soul's traits and don't worry.'
I've been endowed with soul, so now let me
  Get boiled, to pass from animality.
Appeal to God that you won't stumble, friend,
  On these fine points, and that you'll reach the end.
By the Qur'an many were led astray;
  That rope made some fall in the well. I say:
'Stubborn man, you can't claim the rope's to blame.
  You lack the zeal to rise up to your aim.'

The remainder of that story about the visitor to that guest-killing mosque and his resolve and sincerity

The mosque's ambitious guest who knew no fear   4215
  Declared, 'Tonight I will sleep over here.
O mosque, if I find Kerbala in you
  You'll be the Kaaba that fulfils me too.
Tonight permit me, chosen house, to play
  With rope just as Hallaj did on that day.
And, though you counsel now in Gabriel's ways,
  Abraham won't seek help from any blaze.*

Gabriel, begone, for once I'm lit I'm better
   Than any aloes wood or burning amber!
Gabriel, though you protect and help me now,   4220
   Treating me like a brother, anyhow,
Brother, I'm racing to the flames with savour,
   For I am not a soul who's known to waver.'
Through fodder that base animal soul grew;
   It was a fire and burns like firewood too.
It would have borne fruit if it didn't burn,
   Thriving and causing gain for men in turn.
This fire's a scorching wind—it is one ray
   And not its essence burning in this way.
Fire's essence is beyond this world we men know;   4225
   On earth there's just the ray and its own shadow.
When the ray flickers it won't last the course
   And hurriedly returns back to its source.
Your solid form is stable, but your shadow
   Will vary, short this evening, long tomorrow.
One can't find permanence in just one ray—
   Reflections go back to their source one day.
Sedition wants to speak, so press lips tight.
   Finish now! *God alone knows what is right.*

Mention of the conception of evil thoughts by those who lack understanding

Before this story can reach its conclusion   4230
   An envious man's stench has made an intrusion,
And, though this doesn't bother me one bit,
   Men's simple minds may be tripped up by it.
Ghazni's Hakim explained the point so well
   By aiding veiled men with a parable:
'If those who've lost their way, with their own eyes
   See naught in the Qur'an, that's no surprise.
Since only heat is sensed by a blind eye
   From rays of the bright sun up in the sky.'
An idiot, like a nasty, foul-mouthed crone,   4235
   Peeped out of the ass stable's door to moan:

He said, '*The Masnavi* is poor; it's shallow:
 Only the Prophet's life and how to follow,
Naught on research in lofty mysteries
 To which God's Friends' steeds race—there's none of these,
Nor stations from the first renunciation
 Step by step to Him through annihilation,
No definition of the stages where
 Mystics gain wings to fly with through the air.'
When God's Qur'an came down, each infidel   4240
 Dismissed and criticized that text as well,
Saying, 'Legends and old wives' tales abound
 In here, not what is lofty and profound.
Children can understand it and are moved;
 It tells just what's approved or disapproved,
The Prophet Joseph and his curly hair,
 Zulaikha's love for him and her despair*—
It is so obvious all read it with ease;
 Nothing beyond one's mind: no mysteries.'
'If this seems simple now to you,' God said,   4245
 'Produce one simple chapter—go ahead!
Tell the Jinn and the most skilled in mankind:
 "Produce one verse of this 'too simple' kind!"'

Explanation of the saying of the Prophet: 'The Qur'an has an outer and an inner dimension, and its inner dimension has seven inner layers'

There is an outer form to the Qur'an,
 Its inner is more powerful though, good man,
And inside that there's even a third layer—
 All intellects would lose themselves in there.
The fourth layer inside none have seen at all
 But God, Who's peerless and incomparable,
So don't look at its outer form that way—   4250
 The Devil saw in Adam naught but clay.*
The outer form is just like Adam's person,
 That's visible although his spirit's hidden:

During your life your uncle may stay near
  But still, to you, his inner state's not clear.

*Explanation of how the retreat of Prophets and Friends of God to
mountains and caves is not in order to hide themselves, nor out of
fear of distraction by people, but instead in order to guide people and
to urge them to sever links with the lower world as much as possible*

'God's Friends are in the mountains,' people claim,
  'Because to hide from men's eyes is their aim.'
Next to such men they're higher than a mountain,
  And they can step above the seventh heaven,
So why should they seek mountains now to hide,   4255
  When they're beyond all mountains far and wide?
They have no need for mountains, nor to flee;
  Colt-like the sky pursues them desperately,
And fails to see dust leave shoes of their souls—
  That's why the sky is dressed for funerals.
Fairies, they claim, are hidden outwardly,
  But Man is much more hidden, isn't he?
The wise think humans hidden from our eyes
  Much more than fairies. Wise men recognize
All human beings as hidden, all of them—   4260
  Imagine Adam's pure rank in that realm.

*Comparison of the appearance of the Friends of God and their
speech with the appearance of Moses' rod and Jesus' incantations*

A human is like Jesus' best spell
  And just like Moses' famed rod as well.
*Between two fingers** is the faithful's heart,
  In God's hand, so it's just and fine. To start
It seems mere wood, but the whole world would fit
  Inside its throat when opened just a bit.
Don't think of Jesus' spells as mere sounds—
  Notice how death flees him. They know no bounds.
Don't notice just the sounds of his spells—see   4265
  The corpses come to life miraculously.

Don't view the rod as something commonplace—
    It combed the Nile's waves somehow from their place.
You noticed a black canopy, then you
    Stepped closer and the army came to view.
When you are distant, dust is all you notice—
    Approach to see a man there you can witness.
His dust restores sound vision to your eye
    And he can uproot mountains that tower high.
Remember how, when Prophet Moses came,   4270
    Mount Sinai danced, as if with heart aflame.*

The exegesis of the Qur'anic verse 'O hills and birds, repeat his praise!'*

Glory made David's face appear so bright;
    Hills in devotion wept at such a sight.
The hills joined Prophet David when he'd sing,
    All minstrels, drunk with deep love for their king;
When the command '*Repeat his praise!*' first came,
    They all became one voice, their song the same.
God told him, 'Separation you have known,
    Cut off from good friends for my sake alone,
A stranger with no close associate,   4275
    In whose heart flames of longing have been lit;
You seek companions, minstrels, singers too—
    Eternal God presents these hills to you.'
He makes them singers who can sing so well;
    He makes these hills fall drunken in a spell,
So you'll know God lets hills without mouths sing
    And God's Friends too experience such a thing—
The particles of that pure-bodied man
    Send melodies to his ears—yes, they can,
Though not heard by those in proximity—   4280
    He who has faith in him lives joyfully.
Inside his soul he finds inspired words too,
    Although those sitting near him have no clue.
Questions and answers at a rapid pace
    Enter your heart from realms beyond all space;

Though you can hear them, others cannot hear,
  Even if they should bring their own ears near.
Deaf man, I know your ears do not perceive;
  You've seen the outward signs—why not believe?

The answer to the one who criticized The Masnavi owing to deficient understanding

Deriding dog! You're barking. Sense you lack!   4285
  You're mocking the Qur'an behind its back.
This is no lion from which you can flee
  And save your faith from its ferocity.
Till Resurrection the Qur'an declares:
  'You slaves of ignorance once had such airs,
Reckoning me a fable none should heed,
  Sowing your unbelief and mocking's seed—
What you were scoffing at you now can view:
  The transient, worthless fairy tale is you!
I am God's speech, subsisting through His essence,*   4290
  The purest gem, food for the soul's transcendence.
I am the sun's light shining on you now,
  Though I've not parted from it anyhow.'
The Water of Life's spring is here, behold!
  I free the mystic lovers from death's hold.
If your vile greed had not caused such a smell,
  God would have poured drops on your grave as well.
No, I'll heed the advice from Sana'i—
  I won't let critics' comments bother me.

Parable about the foal that refused to drink water because of the clamour by the grooms and trainers

Sana'i told of a foal next to its mother   4295
  Which once were trying to drink up some water.
Some men yelled at the horses constantly:
  'Hurry up! Drink your water rapidly!'
When the foal heard the clamour, it instead
  Refused to drink by lifting up its head.

The mother asked, 'Foal, why is it you shun
   Drinking the water now, before you're done?'
The foal replied, 'This group are yelling here
   And all their clamour stiffens me with fear,
So my heart trembles and leaves my control—   4300
   The yelling brings dread which consumes your foal.'
Its mother said, 'Since this world was created,
   Such people have lived who've just irritated.'
Do your own work, good man! Each one you've feared
   Will soon be witnessed tearing out his beard.
Time is short and the waters are in motion—
   Hurry! Don't fall apart in separation.
The Water of Life's stream is one all know—
   Draw some, so in you mystic plants will grow.
We drink Khezr's water from the streams, where you   4305
   Find God's Friends' speech—all thirsty should come too.
If you can't see this water, like the blind
   Dip your jug in the stream and never mind!
You've heard there's water in this riverbed
   And blind men have to imitate instead.
Now take along your thought-filled water-skin,
   Feel it gain weight as water's flowing in.
When yours is heavy, you'll learn true cognition,
   And then your heart will shun blind imitation.
Although the blind man can't see water there,   4310
   He can tell his jug's weight to be aware,
And say, 'Stream water's entered my jug now—
   Before light, it's grown heavier somehow.
Since every breeze would sweep me off before,
   But, now I'm heavier, they can't any more.'
Any old gust sweeps wretched men away,
   For they've no faculties that we can weigh:
The wicked man's an anchorless ship, so
   He has no guard against the winds that blow.
Intellect's anchor gives security   4315
   For wise men—beg for one now desperately,
Since he's grabbed wisdom's graces from the treasury
   Of pearls inside the Ocean of God's bounty.

Such grace fills hearts with virtues that then fly
   From the heart to illuminate the eye:
The heart's light settles in the eye, which turns
   To heart itself, then by itself discerns.
Hearts come in contact with true wisdom's rays,
   And give a share to eyes through hidden ways.
Regard the blessed water poured from heaven,   4320
   Their inspiration and true exposition.
Let's drink stream water like the foal, and then
   Disregard bad suggestions from those men.
If you're a follower of the Prophets, then
   Take this path and ignore those scolding men.
Why should the lords who have completed it
   Listen to barking from mere dogs one bit?

Remainder of the mention of that visitor at the mosque that killed its guests

Divulge now what appeared in that mosque to
   That lion-heart gambler! What then did he do?
He slept there, though that's just how it would seem,   4325
   For how can drowned men sleep in a mere stream?
Immersed in whirlpools of their grief, such lovers
   Sleep lightly, bird-like, underneath the covers.
A very frightening voice at midnight said:
   'I'm coming for you! All you'll gain is dread!'
Five times this powerful voice rose up and tore
   His heart apart each time he heard it roar.

Exegesis of the verse 'And use your horses and footsoldiers in an assault against them!'*

Whenever you strive in religion's way
   The Devil shouts at you within, to say:
'Don't take that path! Think, stray one, or you'll be   4330
   A captive soon to pain and poverty.
Cut off from friends, you'll have no food and you
   Will be debased, humiliated too.'

The Devil's shouts will fill you with such terror
   That you'll flee certainty and head to error,
Saying: 'Tomorrow or next year I will
   Follow religion's path; there is time still.'
You will see death again, which everywhere
   Is killing friends, whose cries now fill the air.
You'll then turn to religion's path again   4335
   From mortal fear and be a man, so then
You'll put on knowledge and true wisdom's armour,
   Vowing: 'I won't retreat again in horror.'
That voice will try again its trickery:
   'Be scared! Give up the sword of poverty!'
You'll flee enlightenment's straight path once more,
   Shedding knowledge's armour as before.
For years you'll be his slave due to one shout
   And settle in a place that's dark throughout.
Men are enslaved through fear of such a yell   4340
   From that cursed Devil who grabs throats as well,
To make their souls lose hope of light, as slaves
   To his dark ways, like infidels in graves.
If that cursed one's yell spreads such terror, then
   Imagine what God's yell will spread to men.
The partridge dreads the falcon, but the fly
   Does not feel dread—here is the reason why:
The falcon doesn't hunt them: realize
   That only spiders ever hunt for flies.
The spiderish Devil lords it over you,   4345
   Not over partridges. This is not new.
The Devil's yell acts as the damned men's herder,
   That of the Great King is His Friends' protector.
Since these two are as different as can be;
   None of the sweet sea joins the salty sea.*

The talismanic roar reaches the guest in the mosque at midnight

Heed now the tale about that roar that proved
   Too weak for that man, as he wasn't moved.

'Why should I fear the drums of Eid?' he said,
    'Let all those beaten drums feel fear instead!'
Lacking hearts, empty drums, your only share   4350
    Of spirit's Eid is being struck—beware!
Resurrection's Eid, infidels the drums:
    We laugh and celebrate the day Eid comes.
Hear how he cooked good fortune's broth: he made
    It in a pot while drums were being played.
That man with vision heard the drum and said:
    'Why should Eid's drum fill up my heart with dread?
Don't tremble, heart, for souls that are too prone
    To doubting die from that, and them alone.
The time has come for me to act like Ali: 4355
    To seize the kingdom and give up my body.'
He leapt up, shouting, 'Prince of this loud drum,
    I'm ready; if you are a real man, come!'
At his voice that drum's talisman broke, while
    Nuggets of gold rained down, pile after pile.
So much gold rained down that he was left shocked
    And feared the doorway even might get blocked.
Then that strong lion rose up and went on
    Dragging the gold all out until the dawn.
He buried one huge pile and then went back   4360
    To get some more with a huge, empty sack.
That one who'd gambled his own life was fearless,
    Piling treasures, leaving fear for retreaters.
The thought that it's gold of the earthly kind
    Comes to each blind gold-worshipper's stray mind:
Children break earthenware and then they name
    It 'gold' and pocket it in their own game;
During that game, if you say 'gold' you'll find
    Only this unreal 'gold' comes to their mind.
Real gold displays God's hallmark, so it never   4365
    Loses its value, and it lasts for ever.
From that gold this world's gold acquired its lustre,
    Brilliance, splendour, and its fine hue and colour.
That gold makes hearts rich and it can outshine
    The moon at its most radiant—it's divine.

He was the moth while that mosque was his candle;
 With his own self this moth desired to gamble.
His wings were singed, but he liked this the best
 Because, from diving in, he'd be so blest;
That fortunate man was just like Moses, who   4370
 Saw the bush burn, then heard words that were true.
Since so much grace rained down, what in his sight
 Had seemed to be fire was in fact pure light.
You see a Friend of God from the outside
 And think he has a human's fire inside,
Because you have that and it shapes your vision;
 Our low realm hosts the fire of vain opinion.
He's Moses' bush and is filled with light—
 Call him 'light'. Don't say 'fire'. Get this fact right!
Severance from here seemed fire to your own eyes, 4375
 But turned out to be light to your surprise.
Faith's candle always rises just the same;
 It doesn't melt like those that have a flame
And seem like light but burn those who come near—
 This looks like fire, but roses greet you here.
That one seems friendly, but burns body parts;
 This one at union gives pure light to hearts.
The flame of pure light's form to those who're present
 Is light, but it seems fire to those who're distant.

The meeting of that lover with the Sadr-e Jahan

That brave Bukharan threw himself in too;   4380
 His deep love meant the pains he felt were few.
His burning sigh rose to the heavens and
 Softened the *sadr*'s heart, although unplanned.
The *sadr* said to himself at the next dawn:
 'How is our wandering friend, Pure, Holy One?
We saw him sinning, but he didn't know
 About the mercy we like to bestow.
The sinner's conscience fears us, but it's clear
 A hundred hopes are found too in his fear.

I frighten impudent men who have strayed,   4385
  But how can I scare one who's not afraid?
The flame is for the cold pan, not the other
  One which is so hot that it's boiling over.
With knowledge I scare those who don't fear me,
  While calming those who do with clemency.
I'm one who stitches patches where they fit;
  I serve men drinks that are appropriate.'
A human's heart is like the tree's roots, friend:
  Leaves grow from solid branches in the end;
Leaves grow to match the hidden roots of trees,   4390
  And souls and minds act just the same as these.
Loyalty's trees grow wings that reach on high:
  Its root is firm, its branches in the sky.*
Wings that can take you up to heaven grew
  From love, so love can fill the *sadr*'s heart too.
Forgiveness's wave surged inside his heart;
  A window joins each heart that is apart.
Since there's a window that links hearts together,
  They aren't, like bodies, separate from each other.
Though two parts of a lamp aren't joined, you've seen   4395
  How still their light will mix there in between.

There is no lover seeking union who
  Is not being sought by his beloved too.
The lover's love will waste away his body,
  But the Beloved's love makes Him so lovely.
When love for Him makes lightning enter in,
  It's clear that heart contains His love within.
When love for truth is doubled in there too,
  You'll know without doubt God has love for you:
One hand can't make a clapping sound, can it?   4400
  It needs another hand that it can hit.
The thirsty man yearns, 'Wholesome water, help me!'
  The same time water yearns, 'Those thirsty, drink me!'
Thirst in our souls is water's strong attraction;
  As we belong to it, it's our possession:

God's wisdom has in destiny and fate
  Made us each other's lover and true mate.
And all the world's parts due to destiny
  Are paired with mates whom they love equally.
Each particle in this world seeks its partner   4405
  Exactly the same way as straw and amber.
The heavens tell the ground, 'Greetings to you!
  I can attract you just as magnets do.'
The earth is female, heavens male—the latter
  Casts down things which the former then will nurture.
When earth lacks heat, they send some down below;
  When it lacks moisture, this too they'll bestow.
The zodiac's earth signs help all dry ground,
  While water signs spread moisture all around.
The air signs will dispatch some clouds earth's way,   4410
  So they can drag unhealthy fumes away.
The fire signs heat the sun up to the limit,
  The way one makes red hot a cooking skillet.
Time makes the heavens turn round dizzily
  Like men who for their wives' sake busily
Seek wages, while the greatest housewife's earth,
  For it will nurture after it gives birth.
Heavens and earth are both intelligent:
  They act like those who are—that's what I meant.
And if they aren't in truth a pair of lovers,   4415
  Why do they move in harmony like partners?
Without the earth how could a flower grow?
  What then would heat and water raise below?
The female is inclined towards the male,
  So each one's work is finished without fail.
God put this inclination deep inside,
  So, through this union, our world would abide.
He put it in each particle pair too,
  So something's born from union of the two:
Night is thus in embrace with day—they're different   4420
  In looks, but really they're in full agreement.
Night and day look like opposites and foes,
  But they attest to one truth, and it shows.

Just like itself each one desires the other
    In order to make its own actions better.
Men would lack God's infusions without night,
    So what could they accomplish when it's light?

How each element attracts its own kind that has been trapped in human form by a different element

Clay tells the body's clay, 'Return and be
    Quit of the soul. Just like dust, rush to me!
You're my kind, so to be with me is better—   4425
    It's best to flee that body and its moisture.'
'Yes, but my feet are bound,' says body's clay.
    'I'm sick though of being kept apart this way.'
The waters seek the body's moisture too:
    'Come back from exile that you've been put through!'
The ether calls the body's heat, 'You are
    Of fire—come back to your source from afar!'
Seventy-two pains keep the body full
    Of pain, due to the elements' strong pull.
Shattering the body is the ailment's aim,   4430
    So elements can leave the way they came.
The elements are bound birds—injury,
    Disease, and death are what can set them free,
Untying their feet from each other, so
    Each element's bird will be free to go.
These sources' and derivatives' attractions
    Each moment gives our bodies new afflictions,
To tear apart compounded forms by force,
    So each part's bird can fly back to its source.
What stops this quickly happening is God's power,   4435
    Which keeps them joined until the Final Hour.
God says, 'It's not time yet, you parts, so wait!
    It's pointless to fly off before your fate.'
Since every part seeks union, how much more
    The exiled soul seeks what it had before.

*How the soul is attracted, too, to the world of spirits and appeals for
its own residence there, and how it is severed from body parts that
are a fetter on the spiritual falcon*

'O my base bodily parts,' the soul will moan,
    'Exile pains me—I should be near the Throne.'
Body loves fields and water as its realm,
    Because the body's origin's from them;
Soul loves life and the Living One no less—   4440
    Its origin's That Soul in Placelessness.
Soul heads to wisdom, body heads to orchards
    And pleasure gardens, not to mention vineyards.
The soul inclines towards ascent and honour,
    The body, acquisition and mere fodder.
That honour's love and passion also leans
    To it—that's what '*He loves and they love*'* means.
The upshot's that, if one seeks something out,
    Its soul desires one also without doubt.
If I try to explain, there'd be no end—   4445
    The Masnavi would stretch too long, my friend!
Man, animal, plant, and inanimates
    Are loved and love their lovers, as is fit;
The latter join their objects of desire
    Which have attracted them and pull them higher.
The lovers' love makes them thin like a hair,
    While the beloved's makes them plump and fair,
Giving their cheeks more colour in this way,
    While that of lovers makes them burn away.
Amber's a lover that appears desireless;   4450
    Straw makes the journey to it and is tireless.
Leave this aside! Love for that thirsty one
    Shone in the breast of the Sadr-e Jahan:
Smoke from his love and fire-temple of passion
    Entered this master and turned to compassion,
But, due to his own pride and dignity,
    He was ashamed to seek him openly.

His mercy yearned for that one who was helpless,
But his nobility obstructed kindness.
The intellect is stunned and left to wonder: 4455
Did this one draw that one first or the other?
Don't be presumptuous! It's beyond you—close
Your lips, *What's hidden no one but God knows.*
I'll bury this talk now for ever more,
For the Attractor pulls—can I add more?
Who is now drawing you close, anxious one?
He Who won't let you now tell anyone.
For your trip you make countless preparations,
Then He draws you instead to new locations,
Because in all directions He can turn   4460
The bridle, so the untrained horse might learn
About its rider—even if he's hidden;
It moves well when it knows that it's being ridden.
He made you fix your heart on things, just to
Deny you them and break your heart in two.
When He broke your first thought's wing, in that instance
How could you doubt that Wing-breaker's existence?
When His decree snapped your control's cord too,
How could That One's ordainment not be true?

The ruining of resolutions is in order to inform Man that He is
the Ruler and Conqueror, and that His occasional non-annulment
of Man's resolution and His putting it into effect is in order that
desire may lead him to make a resolution, so that next time he can
ruin it, and thus warnings can be repeated

Sometimes things that you have resolved and willed   4465
Just as you want them all become fulfilled.
This is to make your heart attempt once more,
So He can make that fail unlike before,
For if he always should deny you, then
Your heart would lose hope and not try again;
And, lacking hope's seed, how would it then see
Its fruitlessness and that it's His decree—

Through being unsuccessful like this, lovers
    Become acquainted with their lords and masters.
Your unfulfilment is the guide you need: 4470
    *Paradise is surrounded,** so take heed!
Since all your wishes' legs get broken, there
    Must be winners with whom you will compare:
Sincere ones have been broken, but you'll find
    Breaking of lovers is a different kind.
The learned ones are broken by compulsion,
    But lovers seek themselves their own destruction.
To Him the scholars are just slaves who're bound,
    Lovers the sweetest candy that is found.
'*Against your will come!*' speaks to just the former.   4475
    '*Come willingly!*'* gives lover's hearts spring's ardour.

*How the Prophet looked at captives and smiled, saying:
'I marvel at people who have to be dragged to paradise with
chains and shackles!'*

The Prophet saw a group of captives being
    Taken somewhere while all of them were screaming.
That lion who perceived their situation
    Saw them glance furtively in his direction,
Each angry with him to such an extent
    They'd gnash their teeth and bite as they would vent.
Despite being angry they did not dare say
    A word, since they were bound in chains that day.
Then their custodians brought these captives down   4480
    With force from infidel realms to their town.
'He won't accept a ransom,' they'd protest,
    'And none will intercede at our behest.
Thy call him "Mercy to the World", yet he
    Chops off the necks of people mercilessly.'
They went along with thousands of objections,
    Railing beneath their breath at this king's actions:
'We've solved so many problems on our own,
    But not this one—his heart's as hard as stone.

We're thousands of brave men and yet we dread   4485
  These few weak, naked men who look half-dead—
Why are we helpless? Due to straying far
  Or magic, or an inauspicious star?
His fortune tore up ours, and then his throne
  Overturned our throne; Now we're so alone.
If he prevailed through sorcery, then why
  Did it not work when we gave it a try?'

Exegesis of the Qur'anic verse 'If you ask for a decision, the decision
has come:* O railers, you were saying, "Give the decision and
victory to us or Mohammad whoever is correct."' You were saying
that in order that it might be thought that you were seeking the
truth without personal interest; now that we have given
Mohammad the victory, you can see who is correct

'We'd told God and the idols, "Tear us up
  If we are not correct, as we'll give up.
Grant victory to him or us, the side   4490
  Who's in the right and who has never lied."
We said the prayer and bowed our heads to Lat
  And fellow idols Ozza and Manat,*
And said, "If he's correct, then make it clear,
  And if not make him subject to us here."
When we saw clearly that he'd been victorious,
  That he's the light while we are drowned in darkness,
We heard this: "What you asked for all day long
  Has been made manifest—you're in the wrong."'
They hid the truth then from themselves again,   4495
  And banished that thought's memory from the brain,
Saying: 'It was our own unlucky plight
  That made our hearts believe that he was right.
So what if he prevails now and again:
  Success eventually comes to all men,
And it has made us fortunate previously,
  When over him we'd tasted victory.
When we defeated him a while ago
  It wasn't like this: now we're being dragged low.'

This is because good fortune secretly   4500
    Gave him much joy from losing—can't you see
He didn't look at all like one just vanquished?
    No stress or misery could be distinguished.
Defeat is not a truth-revealing sign,
    But only the believers still feel fine:
If you crush musk or ambergris, you'll send
    Sweet perfume through the whole world, end to end,
But if you crush a donkey's turd, you'll fill
    Houses with its vile stench and make men ill.
He came from Hodaybiyya, and all the same   4505
    Drums rolled '*We gave you victory!*' to his name.*

*The secret reason why God called the Prophet's return unfulfilled
from Hodaybiyya a 'victory', saying: 'We have opened to you
a victory.'* In form it was being locked in defeat, but in reality
it was an opening up to victory, just as crushing musk appears
to be a defeat, but is in fact causing its musky scent to emerge
and perfecting its virtues*

Good fortune told him, 'Go forth and do not
    Be saddened. We withheld what you had sought,
For, through abasement, you'll earn victory—
    That fort and town will be your property.
Remember well when you retreat from here
    What happened with Qurayza and Nadir:*
The forts at those two towns fell to your hands
    And you gained booty from their conquered lands.
Look at this group! If this is not the case   4510
    Why do they smile despite the grief they face?
They eat debasement's poison up as though
    It's sweet: like camels they chew thorns of woe.
That's all for grief's sake and not for relief:
    Defeat's a ladder up in their belief.
They're happy at the bottom of the pit
    And dread the crown and thrones on which kings sit.
With the Beloved there, that place's worth
    Transcends the sky and can't be under earth.

Exegesis of the saying of Mohammad: 'Don't say I am superior to Noah!'

Mohammad once said, 'Don't claim my ascension   4515
    Transcends how Jonah once rose up to heaven:
My route was up, while his was down below,
    Nearness to God is not geographical though—
It doesn't mean going up or down from here,
    But fleeing from existence. Is that clear?'
Non-being has no link to trivial factors
    Like near or far, early or late—none matters.
God's workshop's in Non-being, but when you
    Are dazzled still by being, you have no clue.

In short, defeat for them does not resemble   4520
    Our own defeat, not even just a little.
They are as glad with losses and demotions
    As we are with good fortune and promotions.
He's happy with what Non-being should provide;
    Poverty and abasement give him pride.
One of the captives said, 'If he's that way,
    Why did he laugh when we were bound today?
If he has changed and does not feel delight
    At his own freedom and our sorry plight,
Why does he feel joy when his enemy   4525
    Becomes subdued, and bask in victory?
His soul felt joy because he gained with ease
    God's aid in bringing us all to our knees,
And that's how we know he's not liberated
    And that mere worldly gains leave him elated.
If not, why did he laugh? Holy men should
    Be kind towards bad men as well as good.'
Under their breath these captives muttered this
    Among themselves as their analysis,
Adding, 'Make sure the guard won't overhear   4530
    And take what we say to his ruler's ear!'

The Prophet becomes aware of their criticizing him
for Schadenfreude

Although the guard did not hear what they said,
  Through God directly it reached him instead:
To Joseph's keeper his shirt gave no clue,
  But Jacob smelt it from afar and knew;*
Even if they reach heaven sneakily,
  Those devils wouldn't hear Truth's mystery.
Mohammad was reclining on the ground
  And sleeping when the secret circled round.
The one whose share it is will eat the halva,   4535
  Not the one who can boast the longest finger.
A shooting star became a guard and said
  To those men, 'Learn from Ahmad truth instead
Of stealing.' You who stare at shops from dawn,
  Go to the mosque for sustenance you're set on!
The Prophet learned of their talk, then he said:
  'My smiles were not from enmity. They're dead
And have begun already to decay—
  Killing a corpse is not the brave man's way.
In truth, who are they when compared with me—   4540
  I who can make the moon split suddenly.*
When you were free and had a rank so high,
  You were then chained just as now to my eye:
You who love wealth and what belongs to you,
  You're vain and worthless in a wise man's view.
Your bodies fell down from the roof like plates;
  My eyes see all things and their future fates.
In the unripe grape I see wine already;
  In nothingness I see a thing so clearly—
I see a hidden world that lies within;   4545
  Adam and Eve's time there's yet to begin.
I'd seen you at Alast too, you should know—
  Then you were all felled, tied up, and brought low.
That knowledge did not need to be updated
  After the pillarless heavens were created.

I saw you falling upside down before
  I grew from clay and water, and what's more
I've seen naught new to bring me happiness.
  I saw this when you once were prosperous
And bound by hidden wrath which was so great—   4550
  Candy containing poison you then ate.
If one sees poison eaten by those men
  One counts as foes, who would feel jealous then?
You used to eat that poison with such glee
  When death had blocked your ears up secretly.
I didn't wage war just for conquest, and
  I don't seek the whole world within my hand,
For this world is a corpse that is so worthless—
  How should I covet such a rotten carcass?
I'm not a dog that pulls a corpse's hair—   4555
  I'm Jesus who revives it. Now compare!
I broke through battle ranks with the intention
  Of rescuing you from complete destruction,
But I do not slit men's throats needlessly,
  Hoping that power and glory come to me—
I will slit some throats, if that is the way
  To save a whole world as the price to pay,
For you, in ignorance, like moths, will make
  Throwing yourselves at flames the path to take—
With my own hands I stop you falling in   4560
  The fire like drunkards with your mind in spin.
What you took for your victories were the seed
  Of your misfortune, but you paid no heed.
You called each other earnestly, then rode
  Straight to the dragon's mouth—that's what you sowed.
You vanquished men, but at the same time you
  Were conquered by time's fearless lion too.'

Explanation of how the tyrant is overwhelmed while overpowering
and is made a captive when he gains victory

A thief held down a merchant and stole gold;
  A magistrate saw all of this unfold.

If he instead had fled the merchant, then   4565
   The magistrate could not have sent his men.
His overpowering caused him loss instead
   Because this act robbed him of his own head;
It turned into his snare—the magistrate
   Had time to come and then retaliate.
You who have conquered many people and
   Are steeped in conquest all across the land,
God made your victims lose to you, so He
   Could draw you into His net gradually.
Beware, draw rein! Don't chase that victim or   4570
   You will be stabbed soon in a greater war.
Once he has drawn you like this to the snare,
   You'll see men surge at you from everywhere.
Intellects can't rejoice in victory
   When that should lead to sheer depravity.
Wisdom's sharp-sighted and clairvoyant too,
   For God's applied His kohl for wisdom's view.
The Prophet said, 'People of paradise
   Are poor debaters, for this is the price
For their self-criticism and sheer firmness;   4575
   It's not deficiency or inner weakness.'
While giving deference they would listen to
   '*If there were no believers*'* though none knew.
From striking infidels they were held back
   So all believers stayed free from attack:
Read Hodaybiyya's pact, and understand
   From that what's meant by '*He restrained your hands.*'*
He saw himself, though he'd gained victory,
   As overpowered by God's majesty:
'I am not laughing at your chains,' he said,   4580
   'Or due to seizing you last night. Instead
I laugh because I now must force you to
   Come to the garden with chains tied on you.'
How strange that we must drag you now with chains
   From hell-fire to such lovely, verdant plains.
I'm dragging you with heavy chains from hell
   To lasting paradise, but you rebel.'

God drags each man who follows what He says
   Up to His presence bound in similar ways.
All *travel this path bound in chains of fear*   4585
   And trial apart from God's Friends who live near;
By force the rest are dragged in that direction,
   With those who've gained the secrets the exception.
Strive hard so that your light will shine bright too
   And service will seem easy then to do.
You drag a child to school against his will,
   For he can't tell the benefits there still;
The child will run there once he is aware,
   His soul smile at the thought of going there.
The child who still resents attending it   4590
   Has failed to see tuition's benefit,
But when he gains a coin that he can keep,
   Just like a thief he'll even give up sleep.
Wait till you see obedience's good wages—
   You'll envy those who've been that way for ages.
'*Against your will come!*' rallies imitators,
   '*Come willingly!*'* invites God's instigators.
The former love God for another factor,
   But God's the only motive for the latter:
The former love the nurse for milk she gives,   4595
   The latter's love for her makes their hearts live.
The former only love her milk, for they
   Can't see her beauty—milk gets in the way.
The latter love the nurse herself, without
   Ulterior motives—their love's pure throughout.
Those who love God with hope and fear just read
   The notebook of religious men's *taqlid*,*
While those who love for God's sake stand apart—
   Self-interest can't fit into such a heart;
Such men seek God no matter the condition   4600
   They're in—they're drawn to God by His attraction.
Whether one loves God for some other ends,
   Partaking in the goodness that He sends,
Or for His own sake in pure isolation,
   Fearing only the trial of separation,

You'll find that both of these two searches starts
From up beyond, since He traps all men's hearts.

*The beloved's attraction of the lover works in such a way that
the lover neither knows it nor hopes for it, nor has the occurrence
in his mind of it, nor has a trace of that attraction appear inside,
except the fear that is mixed with despair and combined with
the continuation of seeking*

We've realized now that if the attraction
   By his beloved *sadr* had not been hidden,
The lover wouldn't have been dying to   4605
   Run back to the sole home he really knew.
While the beloved's loves are under cover,
   Trumpets and drums announce those of the lover.
There is a story that can illustrate
   This point, but the Bukharan cannot wait—
He's longing now to see with his own eyes
   His own beloved's face before he dies,
To flee death and in this way be delivered:
   Water of Life is seeing one's beloved.
If seeing someone won't cause death to flee,   4610
   That's not your real beloved obviously.
O ardent drunkard, this is a rare matter—
   If death comes during it, then it tastes better;
It is the proof of true faith that death should
   Be made by it to taste and feel so good—
If your faith isn't like this, soul, then it
   Still needs work to become immaculate.
Whoever loves his own death just for you
   Is your beloved, since his heart is true.
It isn't death when he feels no aversion;   4615
   It looks like death, but really is migration.
When there is no aversion, death must be
   Bringing gain—it is blocked then fittingly.
God is the true beloved and those few
   To whom God said, 'You're mine and I'm for you.'

Listen, the lover's reaching near: love tied
    Him up in *a palm-fibre cord** inside.
On seeing that *sadr*'s form which won his love,
    His soul flew from his body high above;
His body fell down like dry wood below,   4620
    Felt cold to touch from his head to his toe;
No matter how much incense and rose water
    They used, he didn't stir or even mutter.
Once the king saw his saffron-coloured face,
    He stopped, dismounted, and approached his place,
Then said, 'Lovers seek their beloved keenly,
    And when he comes they disappear completely.'
You are God's lover; He is the One Who
    By His arrival here effaces you.
His gaze does this to hundreds of your kind;   4625
    Maybe it's such effacement you've in mind?
You are the shade that loves the sun, despite
    The fact that you're effaced by that sun's light.

The flea appeals for justice against the wind in the presence of Solomon

A flea came from the garden's grassy field
    To seek out Solomon and then appealed:
'Solomon, justice is dealt out by you
    To demons, humans, and the fairies too;
Birds and fish feel protected by your justice—
    Has anyone escaped your grace's notice?
Grant justice to us, for we are downtrodden   4630
    Without shares in the orchard or rose garden.
You solve the problems of all who are feeble
    And "flea" is used for them by many people.
We're known for weakness and being frail of wing;
    You're known for kindness and for nurturing.
The top degree of power is your high station;
    We've reached the peak of lack and destitution.
Grant justice and relieve us of this grief—
    Your hand is as God's hand in our belief.'

Solomon said, 'Seeker of justice, say   4635
   Some more about the justice sought today.
Who is the tyrant? Who is so conceited
   That he's made you feel trapped and badly treated?
I'm curious where the tyrant of our age
   Can be if he's not chained or in a cage?
When we were born, oppressors died, so who
   In our great age is being cruel to you?
When light dawned, it removed all trace of darkness;
   Darkness is cruelty's origin and buttress.
Some demons take on much activity   4640
   While other ones are chained restrictively.
The Devil is the source of cruelty here,
   So while he's chained how can that still appear?
"*Be! And it was*"* bestowed on us dominion,
   So people wouldn't need to cry to heaven,
So smoke would not rise there from people's sighs,
   So none would bother stars in heaven's skies,
So that the orphan's wails would not alarm
   The Throne and shake it, nor souls suffer harm.
Inside our kingdoms we've established laws   4645
   So to cry out "O Lord!" there'd be no cause.
Victim, don't look up to the heavens when
   A heavenly king is here among the men.'
The flea said, 'I complain of the wind's hand,
   Which it used to mistreat us. In this land
We all are suffering inside from its cruelty
   With closed lips, though we feel such pain acutely.'

Solomon commands the plaintiff flea to bring its adversary to court

Solomon said, 'Sweet-voiced flea, understand
   You must hear with your soul the Lord's command:
God has told me, "Judge, you must take great care   4650
   Not to hear one side when their foe's not there—
Until both sides of the dispute appear
   To judges still the truth remains unclear.

Though plaintiffs raise a hundred cries, still bide
    Your time till you have heard the other side."
I dare not disobey the Lord's command—
    Bring your adversary here! Understand?'
The flea said, 'What you say is very true
    And my adversary is here with you.'
Solomon shouted, 'East wind, do you hear   4655
    The flea's complaint about your rage? Come here
To see the plaintiff face to face—that moment
    You can give your response to your opponent.'
On hearing this, the wind rushed straight away
    And that flea tried to fly the other way.
Then Solomon said, 'Flea, now where are you?
    Stay here, so I may judge between you two.'
'O king, its being here will leave me dead.
    Its smoke has blackened my whole day,' it said.
'When it arrives I've no security;   4660
    It squeezes out all of the breath in me.'

In the same way the seeker of God's court,
    Once God arrives, becomes reduced to naught.
Although that union's an abiding station,
    It first appears through self-annihilation.
When shadows seek the light, they disappear
    As soon as that sought-out light should appear;
Once the head's given up, mind has no place,
    For *everything will perish but His face.**
Before His face, both Being and Non-being die;   4665
    Being in Non-being! This fact can stupefy;
Inside this presence minds leave your control—
    The pen breaks when it nears this lofty goal.

The beloved caresses the stupefied lover, so he returns to consciousness

The *sadr* then drew him out at gentle pace
    From his unconscious state with generous grace.

'O beggar!' he screamed in his ear, 'I've brought
    Some gold to throw—you can keep what you've caught.
Your soul would tremble when in separation—
    How come it fled once I brought it protection?
In exile from me you've experienced all   4670
    Nature of things, but wake up now I call!'

A hen brings home a camel stupidly
    As guest to show its hospitality,
But once the camel takes one step within
    The hen-house falls down and its roof caves in.
The hen-house is our intellect and sense;
    God's camel's sought by sound intelligence,
And when that camel enters into clay
    That clay can't stay; the soul too fades away.
Man has turned greedy. Once pre-eminent,   4675
    Seeking excess he's cruel and ignorant.
He's ignorant while on an arduous chase
    Like hares that drag lions—they don't know their place:
How would it drag a lion otherwise
    If it could see the lion's actual size?
Man is unjust as well to his soul—witness
    Injustice that surpasses all injustice.
His ignorance can teach all of the sciences
    And his injustice guides all kinds of justice.
The *sadr*, taking his hand, said, 'This man's death   4680
    Requires me to bestow life through my breath.
When this corpse is brought back to life through me,
    It will be my own soul that faces me.
I will be honouring him then with this soul
    That I'll give, which will witness my bestowal.
Outsiders can't see the Beloved's face;
    That's for those who come from no other place.
I'll breathe on him like butchers—in my mind
    I'll hope his marrow leaves his skin behind.
O soul that has fled agony, don't fear!   4685
    We've opened up our union's door—come here!

O you whose selflessness and drunkenness
　　And being constantly emerge from us,
Without lips I'll convey to you today
　　Ancient mysteries—listen to what I say!
Beware that this breath makes lips run away,
　　So banks of hidden streams tell it their way.
Open up now, pure earlessness's ear!
　　"*God does what He should will*"* you'll clearly hear.'
This invitation to a union then　　　　　　　　　　　4690
　　Induced his corpse to slowly stir again.
He isn't less than soil that you have seen
　　Rising due to the breeze, and turning green,
Nor semen, through which due to God's Speech one
　　Brings forth a Joseph radiant as the sun,
Nor wind, which, when God's word '*Be!*'* has been heard,
　　Brings forth a peacock or a sweet-voiced bird;
He's not less than that rocky mountain either
　　That bore a camel that then bore another.*
Leave this behind! Did not what's non-existent　　　4695
　　Bring forth a whole world and more every instant.
The man sprang up, trembled, then happily
　　Whirled round and fell prostrate for all to see.

The unconscious lover comes to his wits again and starts to praise and give thanks to the beloved

He said, 'Phoenix of God, each soul will turn
　　Around you—thanks for making a return
From Qaf.* Esrafil of love's resurrection,
　　You who are love's love and love's yearning passion!
As the first gift of honour you give me,
　　Please bring your ear to hear what none can see.
Although, through purity, you know my state,　　　4700
　　My nurturer, please hear what I relate!
Unique *sadr*, countless times I fell aswoon,
　　Yearning for your ear—it can't come too soon.
That hearing of yours with your understanding
　　And smiles from your lips which are soul-expanding,

That bearing of my big and small affairs
    As well as my soul's flirting with such airs—
My false coins by which you weren't taken in,
    Yet you accepted them as genuine:
You saw my haughty mischief, but could spare   4705
    Clemency next to which ours can't compare.
When I had strayed far from the net you cast
    I lost it all from first until the last.
The next thing, loving *sadr*, which you must hear
    Is how I searched because you have no peer.
Thirdly, since leaving you, it feels like I
    Have been a Trinitarian. Who knows why?
Fourth, since my field has been burned, though I strive
    I cannot tell apart still four from five.
Wherever you find blood drops, realize   4710
    By looking closely that they're from my eyes.
My speech is thunder, and its booming sound
    Wants all the clouds to rain down on the ground.
Speaking or weeping—I'm torn by these two:
    Should I now speak or weep? Which should I do?
If I speak now, I can't keep weeping too;
    If I don't speak then how can I praise you?
My eyes weep blood from my heart, king—behold
    What has poured out of my eyes; don't be cold.'

He said this then began to weep with dread,   4715
    While all and sundry wept at what he'd said.
His heart let out such screams that at their sound
    The People of Bukhara gathered round.
As he spoke, wept, and laughed there, mesmerized,
    All of those watching him felt paralysed:
The whole town now shed tears in the same way,
    As if assembled there for Judgment Day.
The sky that moment told the earth, 'If you
    Have not seen Resurrection, there's a view.'
'What love, what stupor!' intellect then said,   4720
    'Is union stranger or being far instead?'

The heavens read out words for Judgment Day,
  Then tore their clothes up to the Milky Way.
Love is a stranger to both worlds; in it
  Are diverse madnesses and more can fit.
It's hidden with a dazed manifestation;
  The King of Souls seeks it in separation.
Beyond all of the sects one finds love's school;
  It sees no worth in thrones of men who rule.
During *sama'** love's minstrel's new refrain   4725
  Is 'Slavery chains; lordship gives your head pain.'
What is our love then for Non-being's sea,
  When reason's foot breaks in proximity?
Slavery and lordship are both known—behind
  These two veils love is what you're going to find.
If only Being had a tongue, it then
  Could lift the veil that hangs before all men.
Breath of existence, anything you tell
  Places another veil in front. Heed well!
Your speaking is itself perception's bane: 4730
  Washing blood up with more blood is in vain.
Since I'm familiar with the drunkard's way,
  I murmur in this cage both night and day.
You're drunken, witless, with a frenzied head—
  Did you get out the wrong side of the bed?
Take heed, don't breathe a single word—beware!
  Catch up with one who's close enough to share.
You are a drunken lover with loose lips—
  By God, you're near the brink—avoid more slips!
My tongue tells of his mystery and his flirting,   4735
  Then heaven recites: '*You who are good at hiding!*'

How can one hide it? Flames are spreading here;
  The more you try, the more he will appear.
If I conceal his secrets, then he'll raise
  His head flag-like—'I am right here,' he says.
Try as I might, he grabs me by the ear,
  Saying, 'Fool, you can't make him disappear!'

'Begone, you have boiled over!' I protest,
  'You're like the soul: hidden yet manifest.'
He says, 'My body's trapped inside the vat   4740
  Like at wine banquets—I rejoice at that.'
I answer, 'Go away before you're pawned
  And drunkenness's bane has finally dawned.'
He says, 'With my fine wine-cup I'll rest there
  Throughout the day until the evening prayer.
When evening should attempt to steal my cup,
  I'll say, "Return it, for my time's not up."'
The Arabs have named wine 'continual'*
  Because the drinker never feels he's full.
Love boils the wine of realization, so   4745
  Love is God's *saqi* for His Friends below.
When you seek properly, then wine transforms
  To your souls' water in your jar-like forms.
When He increases wine of guidance, that
  Extra force makes it burst right through the vat;
Water becomes the *saqi*, and it too
  Becomes so drunk! *God knows best what is true.*
The *saqi*'s glow shines on the wine's must and
  That must boils, starts to dance and then expand.
Ask that bewildered one, 'Where have you seen   4750
  Wine must behaving as this must has been?'
Those in the know need not think hard then later
  Explain each stirred thing needs an agitator.

Story about being in love, lengthy separation, and substantial trial

A young man was love-crazed due to a woman,
  But stayed deprived of the good fate of union;
Love gave him so much torture while apart—
  Why does love act with spite right from the start?
Why does love shed blood so relentlessly?
  To make outsiders to love's truths all flee.

When he dispatched to her a messenger,   4755
    That man, through envy, would try stealing her.
And what was written by his secretary,
    On his behalf, was read out differently.
If he made wind his messenger to trust,
    That would become polluted by the dust.
If he sewed on a bird's wing his love note,
    It would get burned by heat from what he wrote.
God's jealous guarding blocked paths to solution
    And snapped the flags of troops of his cognition.
Expectation was his consoling friend   4760
    At first, but this destroyed him in the end.
'This anguish has no cure,' at times he'd say,
    'No, it's life for my soul,' another day.
Sometimes he'd re-emerge in self-existence;
    He'd then eat of the fruit of non-existence.
Once he'd grown cold towards his constitution,
    He'd then see boil the hot springs of his union.
Once he got used to exile's state of lack,
    Provisions from Non-being then hurried back.
Chaff from the wheat-ears of his thought was shed;   4765
    Just like the moon, night travellers he led.

Many a parrot talks though it stays mute;
    Many a kind soul looks a bitter brute.
In silence sit inside the graveyard, then
    You'll clearly witness talking silent men.
Their soil has the same colour, but inside
    Their state is not the same once they've all died.
Though living flesh is uniform, within
    Some sadly frown while others happily grin—
Until you hear their words what can you tell,   4770
    Seeing as their state's veiled from you as well?
You might perceive them holler, yell, and shout,
    But what about their state can you find out?
Our forms are one, but made of differing parts;
    Their clay is one, with vastly different hearts.

Voices are likewise uniform, but pain
  Fills one, while other voices sound so vain.
On battlefields you'll hear a horse's sound,
  And squawks of birds when you should walk around.
One comes from hate, the other comes from friendship;   4775
  One comes from joy, the other comes from hardship.
Whoever doesn't know his state at all
  Hears all their voices as identical.
An axe's blow can cause the sway of trees;
  Others sway simply due to dawn's soft breeze.
The worthless pot caused me a serious error,
  Because its contents boiled beneath its cover.
'Come here!' a stranger's fervour now might yell—
  He could be true, he could be false as well;
If you've no clue from that higher soul that knows,   4780
  Acquire a proper, clue-detecting nose!
The rose in the rose garden's company
  Can even, through its scent, make Jacob see.*
Tell more about that sad love-stricken one,
  For we have strayed from that Bukharan, son!

*How the lover found his beloved, and the explanation of
how the seeker becomes a finder, for 'Whoever does an atom's
weight of good work will see it'**

For seven years that youth searched ceaselessly,
  Becoming ghost-like for his fantasy;
God's shade was over this devotee's head;
  Seekers transform to finders up ahead.
The Prophet said, 'When you knock on a door   4785
  Someone will come out if you wait some more';
If you wait at a man's address, you'll see
  That person's face appear eventually;
Dig deeper each day in a muddy pit
  And you'll find water there by doing it.
Even if you do not believe, please know
  That you will reap one day what you now sow.

You struck a stone on iron and yet there
  Was no spark—this can happen, though it's rare.
The intellect of one who doesn't gain   4790
  Fortune one time will claim that all's in vain,
Saying: 'One sowed, but didn't reap as well;
  Another found no pearl inside his shell.
Balaam and Satan didn't gain a smidgen
  From all their acts of worship and religion.'
A hundred thousand Prophets and great mystics
  Do not come to the notice of such sceptics;
He cites two who spread darkness, so how should
  His fate bring to his heart things that are good?
There are so many who eat bread with glee,   4795
  Then die when one bite chokes them suddenly—
Ill-fortuned one, don't eat bread as they do
  Lest you fall into tribulation too!
Millions of men eat bread and strengthen from it;
  They find bread nourishes as well their spirit—
So why are you in the minority
  Unless deprived due to stupidity?
Dismissing this world that is brightly lit
  By sun and moon, he looks into a pit,
And says, 'Where is the light if all that's true?'   4800
  'Lift your head from the pit—look where we do!
That light has shone down all across the land,
  But won't reach your head buried in the sand.'
Leave that pit—enter palaces instead.
  Don't squabble! *Squabble brings bad luck you dread.*
Don't tell me, 'So-and-so sowed seeds right here,
  But locusts ate up all his crops that year—
When there's a risk why should I till this land
  And scatter seeds around with my own hand?'
Despite your trusted reasoning, others still   4805
  Sowed seeds and now their barns receive their fill.
Whoever knocks upon doors patiently
  One day gains entry and finds intimacy;
Fearing gaolers, he hid in fields at night—
  He found the one he loves there, shining bright,

Torch-like. He then asked God, 'Who made this happen?
　　O God, have mercy on this poor nightwatchman!
You made the means, though I knew not my fate;
　　You took me up from hell to heaven's gate.
You made the means for this act for this reason: 4810
　　So I won't think ill even of a tree's thorn.'
When legs break, God gives wings, which are worth more;
　　Likewise in pits he opens up a door.
God says, 'Don't think about being on a tree
　　Or in the pit—look at Me; I'm the Key!'
Dear reader, if you want to read some more,
　　You'll find the rest by looking in Book Four.

EXPLANATORY NOTES

PROSE INTRODUCTION
[written in Persian prose; numbered by page and line]

4:10   *You used to be . . . God was generous to you*: Qur'an 4: 94, where this represents God's reminder to believers lest they judge their foes dismissively by forgetting that they were once in their position before God saved them.

4:20   *desire to . . . even if the infidels hate it*: Qur'an 61: 8, in reference to disbelievers in God.

4:21   *We have sent down the reminder and We are its guards*: Qur'an 15: 9, which is usually understood as referring to the Qur'an.

4:22   *Whoever alters it . . . God is Hearing, Knowing*: Qur'an 2: 181, where it refers to wills.

TEXT
[numbered by verse, or couplet]

1   *the Prophet would do things in threes*: this refers to reports that the Prophet Mohammad preferred to do repetitive actions an odd rather than even number of times, especially three times.

10   *coolness and comfort too*: Qur'an 21: 69, where God commands fire to become cool and comfortable miraculously for Abraham's sake.

16   *The mountain split . . . it began to dance*: an allusion to Qur'an 7: 143, where Moses asks God to reveal Himself, and, in response, God reveals Himself to a mountain, flattening it. On witnessing this, Moses himself collapses and faints.

37   *He gave a throat . . . the other rods then thrown*: a reference to the Qur'anic story (20: 65–72) about the help given by God to Moses, so that he could meet the challenge of Pharaoh to perform a miracle greater than the sorcery of his magicians. By magic they make their rods move about, while through God's help the transformation of Moses' rod into a snake is more astonishing.

50   *A foetus feeds on blood, which is unclean*: blood is an unclean contaminant in Islamic legal discourse.

85   *Moses stun Pharaoh with a piece of wood?*: an allusion to Moses' wooden rod. See further note to v. 37.

86   *Or Noah . . . Submerge the East and West so easily*: an allusion to the story of Noah's ark, which is repeatedly mentioned in the Qur'an (e.g. 11: 25–49).

87   *If not, could Lot have razed . . . settlements around?*: an allusion to the story
       of Lot and his people, which is mentioned in the Qur'an (e.g. 29: 26–35).

102   *God said, 'He is an ear'*: Qur'an 9: 61, where in response to the use of this
       as a dismissive insult to Mohammad by his enemies, the notion of being
       an ear that hears good tidings and serves as a mercy to people is positively
       embraced.

109   *Later, inside their graves . . . by Monker and Nakir*: in Islamic eschatology
       Monker and Nakir are the two angels who fulfil the role of testing one's
       faith after one's death and before the Resurrection.

122   *Such birds which sing too early or too late*: a Persian expression for bad
       timing.

127   *bow down, approach!*: Qur'an 96: 19, where it is given as an instruction
       combined with ignoring those who would try to dissuade one from
       worship.

161–2 *One who smells scent from Yemen . . . far away*: an allusion to divine
       communication with Ovays al-Qarani, who became a follower of
       Mohammad in Yemen without ever having met him.

172   *Come here!*: part of the Muslim call to prayer.

175   *Come to the good!*: part of the Muslim call to prayer.

194   *Here I am!*: an exclamation made during the pilgrimage to Mecca, imply-
       ing that one is ready to be of service.

208–9 *The dog of Sleepers . . . mystic grace*: this alludes to the tradition that
       the dog of the Seven Sleepers in the Cave (see Glossary), who is also
       mentioned in the Qur'an (18: 9–26), will go to heaven in the form of
       a human.

218   *Joseph, don't head towards the wolf today!*: an allusion to Qur'an 12: 13–17,
       where Jacob fears letting Joseph venture out with his brothers in case a
       wolf should harm him. Later the brothers return weeping and claim that
       a wolf has devoured Joseph.

228   *If you're Ramin, Vis is your sole desire*: Vis and Ramin are the lovers in a
       famous epic composed by the poet Gorgani in the eleventh century and
       recently translated into rhyming couplets by Dick Davis: Gorgani,
       Vis and Ramin, tr. Dick Davis (Harmondsworth, 2009).

263   *Sebawayh . . . be harming you!*: Amr ibn Othman Sebawayh (d. *c.*797),
       though himself of Persian origin, was the most famous early linguist of
       the Arabic language and is considered highly influential for the forma-
       tive development of Arabic grammar. The reference to him here is some-
       what obscure, but it is appropriate for a father to refer to his son using a
       diminutive form as the name Sebawayh appears; moreover, the towns-
       man's son has just argued a case to him eloquently, as the famous gram-
       marian Sebawayh might have done.

282   Heading   *the People of Sheba*: see 'Sheba' in the Glossary.

314 *that dog in the cave*: see note to vv. 208–9, and 'Seven Sleepers in the Cave' in the Glossary.

323 *Who is more true than me to promises?*: Qur'an 9: 111, after mentioning the promise of heaven.

345 *like Jesus used to soar, Nor, like Korah . . . earth's deep core*: according to the Muslim tradition, Jesus was not crucified, but instead ascended to heaven. See 'Korah' in Glossary.

349 *Contraction*: contraction here is being used as a technical term for one of the spiritual states experienced on the Sufi path.

354 *If you block Our Remembrance . . . We'll make you blind!*: Qur'an 20: 125, where it is a warning from God in the story of Adam's fall.

363 *expansion*: expansion here is being used as a technical term for one of the spiritual states experienced on the Sufi path, usually paired with 'contraction'.

373 *Ingratitude! May he be killed today!*: Qur'an 80: 17, where it refers to mankind's ingratitude. The remainder of these lines in Arabic are similar to poetry attributed to the most celebrated pre-Islamic Arab poet, Emr ol-Qays (d. 540).

374 *Kill yourself!*: Qur'an 2: 54, where it is part of Moses' response to his community after they worshipped the golden calf.

406 *I'm Ahmad, left as captive . . . Saleh in Thamud's gaol, due to their ruse*: an allusion to the rejection of Mohammad by the Jewish tribes of Medina and their plots against him, followed by an allusion to the Qur'anic story about Saleh (e.g. 7: 73–9), who was sent to the Thamud (see Glossary), who hamstrung his she-camel mercilessly.

408 *Would that I'd been mere dust!*: Qur'an 78: 40, where it represents what men will say on Judgment Day when regretting their past deeds.

416 *Let us play!*: Qur'an 12: 12, where it represents what Joseph's brothers ask their father, Jacob, to permit them to do together with their brother, though at the time they planned to harm him.

417 *Let's play!*: see previous note.

454 *We made you from mere dust*: Qur'an 22: 5, where it represents an example God gives of His power to convince mankind that he can resurrect humanity in the afterlife too.

464 *We're returning to Him*: Qur'an 2: 156, where it represents the words of people who maintain faith in God through tribulations.

465 *zekr*: the Arabic name, sometimes transcribed alternatively as dhikr, is the central practice of Sufis, namely the remembrance of God through repetition of His Names or formulas about Him.

471 *And Harut back to Babylon again*: see 'Harut and Marut' in the Glossary.

474 Heading *the People of Zarwan*: in Qur'anic exegesis the Zarwan are presented as a nation who became disobedient to God in ceasing to care

for the poor and needy by picking their crops before they could approach them, and consequently suffered His wrath.

479 *'Does not Your Maker know your wish?' God said*: a paraphrase of Qur'an 67: 14, where it is asked rhetorically in relation to knowledge about what humans hide within.

494–5 *Do not fear!*: Qur'an 20: 68, where it represents God's advice to Moses in the story about his encounter with Pharaoh's magicians.

534 *The moon becomes, through travelling, Kaykhosrow*: the meaning intended here seems to be that the moon through phases becomes full and complete, like the legendary Persian ruler Kaykhosrow of Ferdowsi's *Book of Kings*.

535 *And bring to Joseph outcomes he'd foreseen*: Joseph foresees future events through his dreams in the Qur'anic rendering of the story, which forms the bulk of its twelfth chapter.

567 Heading *How Majnun petted that dog which lived in Layli's neighbourhood*: Majnun and Layli (also known as Layla) are the archetypal pair of lovers in the Arabic and Persian literary traditions.

575 *It is the blest dog of the cave to me*: see note to vv. 208–9 and 'Seven Sleepers in the Cave' in the Glossary.

580 *Like Ali, you'll dislodge those Khaybar gates*: the Prophet Mohammad's cousin and son-in-law Ali is said to have pulled down one of the gates of the settlement of Khaybar and used it as a shield, while he fought as the standard-bearer in a battle on behalf of the Prophet Mohammad's followers.

593 *Kind God taught the Qur'an*: Qur'an 55: 1–2, as the first example of God's beneficence to mankind.

594 *He taught with pen*: Qur'an 96: 4, as part of the famous verses traditionally believed to have been the first revealed to Mohammad in the cave of Mount Hira.

604 *We'll drag him by the forelock!*: Qur'an 96: 15, where it describes what God will do to those who deny His existence and dissuade others from worship.

671 *Men who drink date-wine or eat carrion . . . despite the ban*: this alludes to flexibility in traditional Islamic jurisprudence which can allow the drinking of alcohol that does not contain fermented grapes or the consumption of things considered forbidden when nothing else is available to eat, under certain interpretations or circumstances, respectively.

676 *For blind men there's no blame*: Qur'an 48: 17, from a passage exhorting the Arabs to fight in the cause of the truth. The blind, the lame, and the sick are not to be blamed if they turn away.

688 *the Last Day's blast's sake*: an allusion to the blast of the trumpet that will signal the Resurrection at the end of time in Islamic eschatology.

690 *Jonayd or Bayazid you claim to be*: see 'Jonayd' and 'Bayazid' in the
     Glossary.

692 *Mansur Hallaj . . . the cotton of the friends you get*: see 'Hallaj' in the
     Glossary. Hallaj means cotton-wool carder, the profession of the father
     of the famous [al-Hosayn ebn] Mansur Hallaj (d. 922).

693 *I can't tell Omar and Bu Lahab apart*: Omar and Bu Lahab were contem-
     poraries of the Prophet Mohammad, the former being one of his close
     companions and the latter being one of his mortal enemies, and therefore
     easily distinguishable in normal circumstances. See also 'Bu Lahab' in
     the Glossary.

703 *David turned iron to wax*: an allusion to Qur'an 21: 80 and 34: 10–11,
     where it is said that God taught David how to make garments of chain-
     mail and gave him the power to make iron soften for this purpose.

740 *The truthfulness of truthful men prevails*: Qur'an 5: 119, where it is a state-
     ment from God about how being truthful in your life will lead to gains in
     the afterlife.

741 *Be steadfast and be straight!*: Qur'an 11: 112, where it represents God's
     instruction to the Prophet Mohammad.

745 *Each one of them is tested twice a year*: Qur'an 9: 126, where it refers to
     those who do not believe that the Qur'an is from God.

769 *"Pride of the world", "Pillar of faith"—they suit me*: 'Pride of the world'
     and 'Pillar of faith' are titles of honour commonly used in medieval
     Islamic societies.

770 *The Tablet where divinity's shown too*: in Muslim theology, the Preserved
     Tablet is where all knowledge is recorded and the source of all revelation,
     of which the Qur'an is one part.

775 *To reach Mena, there's a long way to go*: in the Muslim Hajj pilgrimage
     itinerary, the town of Mena is the final destination.

790 Heading   *You will know them through the corruption of their speech*:
     Qur'an 47: 30, where it refers to the 'hypocrites', those people in Medina
     who pretended to follow the Prophet Mohammad but opposed him
     in reality.

791 *hypocrite*: see preceding note.

797 *I've shared a little of this tale before*: this refers back to Book One of the
     Masnavi, vv. 3334–68.

954 *fire be cool! . . . will not be hot and wild!*: an allusion to Qur'an 21: 69, where
     God commands fire to become cool and comfortable miraculously for
     Abraham's sake.

966 *It was a snake . . . through God's aid*: a reference to the Qur'anic story
     (20: 62–76) about the help given by God to Moses, so that he could meet
     the challenge of Pharaoh to perform a miracle greater than the sorcery of
     his magicians. By magic they make their rods move about, while through

God's help the transformation of Moses' rod is even greater (according to tradition, it changes into a snake).

967   *The end is to Him*: Qur'an 53: 42, where it represents one of the things that those who deny God are ignorant about.

969   *'None but God' is in truth worth naught*: a play on the Muslim testimony of faith 'There is no God but God.'

984   *Of God's pure spirit you must not despair!*: Qur'an 12: 87, where it appears in the same context in the Qur'anic story about Joseph.

989   *Tuba tree*: the tree of paradise, which is called 'Tuba' in the Islamic tradition.

1010 *Moses' rod had here a transformation*: see note to v. 966.

1014 *Mountains sang David's Psalms . . . like wax in David's hand*: an allusion to Qur'an 34: 10, where mountains and birds repeat David's Psalms at God's command, followed by an allusion to Qur'an 34: 10–11, where it is said that God taught David how to make garments of chain-mail and gave him the power to make iron soften for this purpose.

1015 *The wind would bring what Solomon conveyed*: this miracle of Solomon features in a memorable story in Book One (vv. 960–74).

1015 *The sea would understand what Moses said*: an allusion to the parting of the waves for Moses and his followers.

1016 *The moon saw Ahmad point*: an allusion to the Prophet Mohammad's miraculous splitting of the moon in two.

1016 *wild flames would turn . . . to roses and not burn*: an allusion to God's rescue of Abraham from Nimrod's fire. Abraham was miraculously protected by God, who turned the fire into a comfortable rose garden for his sake.

1017 *Just like a snake, the earth gulped Korah down*: a biblical figure (Num. 16) who is also mentioned in the Qur'an (28: 76–82, 29: 39, and 40: 24). As a punishment for behaving arrogantly towards Moses and hoarding his wealth, he was swallowed up by the earth.

1017 *The pillar learnt to moan and earned renown*: an allusion to the story about the moaning pillar in the Prophet Mohammad's biography, which is also retold by Rumi in Book One (vv. 2124–30).

1018 *Stones gave Mohammad a salute one day*: an allusion to the story about the gravel testifying to Mohammad's Prophethood, which is also retold by Rumi in Book One (vv. 2165–71).

1018–19 *To John the Baptist . . . with the uninitiated*: this alludes to a tradition among the 'Stories of the Prophets' which relates that a mountain opened up to protect John the Baptist from his pursuers.

1027 *This is the view of the Mu'tazilite*: a member of the first school of Sunnite systematic theology, which established the methodology adopted by the later schools. The Mu'tazilite school itself grew out of favour by the tenth century among Sunnites. They were criticized by traditionalist Sunnites for overstressing the value of reason and giving it precedence over revelation, including by interpreting scripture analogically.

1037   *Resurrection Day*: see 'Resurrection' in the Glossary.

1051   *like Hajjaj, are cruel!*: Hajjaj ebn Yusuf al-Thaqafi (d. 714) was a notoriously tyrannical governor of Iraq for the Umayyad dynasty.

1066   *By his snake-like rod doing what God willed*: see note to v. 37.

1080   *Adam and Satan's duel shows I'm right*: an allusion to the Qur'anic story (2: 30–4) where God instructs the angels to prostrate before Adam, His vicegerent on earth. All of them obey except Satan (known also as Eblis).

1086   *Tammuz*: the name of a mid-summer month in various ancient calendars.

1118   *You are returning*: see note to v. 464.

1125   *Divine Truths take you to His company*: this involves wordplay centred around the term *ladunni*, which came to be used to designate the divinely communicated knowledge of mystics, but originates from the Qur'anic story (18: 65–82) about Moses and Khezr, where it specifies that Khezr's knowledge came from God's presence.

1130   *'We've no knowledge!' you should say Until 'You taught us'*: Qur'an 2: 32, where it represents the angels' response to God after He informs them that He is establishing Man as His vicegerent.

1138   *not from East nor West*: Qur'an 24: 35, where it forms part of the famous and enigmatic description of the Light of God.

1148   *the people in prostration*: Qur'an 26: 219, where it refers to devout worshippers of God.

1149   *the state Bu Bakr gained in his presence*: this alludes to the story about the Prophet Mohammad's escape from Mecca. He hides in a cave with his friend Abu Bakr to evade pursuants, and in later tradition Abu Bakr's presence in his company is regarded as a means by which this friend of his gained spiritual benefit.

1150   *Mere tales of past folk*: Qur'an 6: 25, where it represents a dismissive opinion about the Qur'an expressed by those who deny its divine origins.

1153   *A roof is under Zayd yet over Amr*: Zayd and Amr are the names used in Arabic grammatical constructions, similar to X and Y in English.

1207   *from fish to moon*: this expression involves wordplay because in Persian moon is *mah* while fish is *mahi*.

1216   *souls of your father*: this is simply a term of endearment for one's children and has no mystical connotations.

1252   *Not those tales again!*: this is a Persian translation of Qur'an 6: 25, concerning which, see note to v. 1150.

1304   *The Red Sea in which lower selves are drowned*: an allusion to the drowning
       of Pharaoh's army during their pursuit of Moses and his followers, for
       whom the waves had parted.

1320   *Neither born nor begetting*: Qur'an 112: 3, part of a famous monotheistic
       declaration in a short chapter of the Qur'an that is often interpreted as
       being polemically aimed at Christians.

1427   *Each Sufi is 'the moment's son'*: a very frequent epithet for Sufis, 'the
       moment's son' is usually interpreted as meaning the Sufi has surren-
       dered to the dictates of each moment's divine command that is inwardly
       inspired in him.

1430–1   *That sets . . . 'The ones that set aren't loved by me!'*: Qur'an 6: 76, in
       the account of Abraham's search for a god truly worthy of worship—he
       worships in turn a star, the moon, and the sun, until he witnesses
       that each one of these is transient, at which point he declares, 'I don't love
       the ones that set.' This search leads him ultimately to worship none
       but the Eternal Creator.

1436   *never born . . . does not beget nor was begotten*: Qur'an 112: 3; see note
       to 1320.

1467   *enter their homes through the gate!*: Qur'an 2: 189, a verse that is often cited
       as a proverb to mean that one should do things in the proper way.

1499   *seventy-two sects*: a motif that is found in various hadiths (see Glossary)
       referring not only to Muslims but also to Jews and Christians, it invari-
       ably serves to underline divisions and disputes.

1515   *it will travel straight . . . or hobbling feebly*: this is a play on Qur'an 67: 22,
       which poses the question 'Is one who walks with his face hung down
       better guided or one who walks erect on a straight path?'

1523   Heading   *Parable about a man becoming ill . . . and the story about the
       teacher*: this heading is inappropriate because it is followed only by the
       story about the teacher, so it suggests a complicated relationship between
       section headings and their content.

1607–8   *Like the Egyptian women . . . cannot see what's there*: an allusion to the
       Qur'anic story about Joseph. His beauty causes Egyptian women to
       become so mesmerized that they cut their own hands with knives (12: 31).

1622   *Homa*: see 'Homa' in the Glossary.

1642   *Each dawn I have a new activity*: an allusion to Qur'an 55: 29, which also
       describes how God is always involved in activity.

1665–6   *a palm-fibre cord*: Qur'an 111: 4–5, where it describes the wife of Abu
       Lahab (see 'Bu Lahab' in the Glossary), who is interpreted in tradition as
       a mortal enemy of the Prophet Mohammad in Mecca.

1666   *the carrier of fuel*: see previous note.

1757   *Are blind and seeing men the same to you*: Qur'an 6: 50, where it is part of
       what Mohammad is instructed to say to sceptical contemporaries.

1796   *I am a master, though not yet a youth!*: this alludes to the presentation of Jesus in the Qur'an as a Prophet from birth through its report of him confirming his status while still a newborn (Qur'an 19: 30).

1806   *a mercy to the world of men*: Qur'an 21: 107, where it appears to refer to the Prophet Mohammad because it is part of an address to the recipient of the Qur'an in the second person ('We have not sent you except as a mercy to the worlds'). This is not an inherently exclusive statement, and Rumi applies it here to the Friends of God.

1855   *By the time*: this is a common way of referring to the 103rd chapter of the Qur'an, which begins with this phrase. That short chapter indeed pairs patience and truth with each other in its third verse.

1925   *Daquqi*: this does not appear to be a historical figure. In view of the miraculous, visionary content that is relayed in autobiographical form here, it is perhaps Rumi's way of sharing his own experiences. 'Daquqi' appropriately means 'seller of eye salve'.

1970   *where the two seas merge*: Qur'an 18: 61, where it also identifies the location where Moses found Khezr.

1992   *He guides whom He pleases*: Qur'an 74: 31 in a theological statement about God and his relationship with His creation.

1998   *I can't find praises fit for You to send*: this is based on a saying of the Prophet Mohammad.

2007   *the lote tree's place*: Qur'an 53: 14–16, where, in a passage about the Prophet Mohammad's ascension to heaven, it refers to a lote tree marking the utmost reach of heaven and the limits of human understanding.

2008   *Beyond the ox and fish and then some more*: in medieval Islamic accounts about the process by which God created the world, an ox and fish commonly feature, with the former lifting up the earth and the latter serving as its foothold.

2018   *Would that my people now could see!*: Qur'an 36: 26, where it refers specifically to the ability to see how God has shown generosity to His Prophets.

2020   *We've sealed their eyes. There are no sanctuaries*: the first part of this hemistich alludes to Qur'an 2: 7, which refers to unbelievers.

2035   *Read 'Not until the Prophets . . . they'd been denied'*: Qur'an 12: 110, where it similarly describes the point at which aid came to the Prophets.

2036   *tashdid*: this is the doubling of a consonant in the Arabic language, which causes a significant change in the meaning of verbs.

2053   *He told the stars and trees to all prostrate*: Qur'an 55: 6, where this miracle is presented among a list of the evidences for God.

2089   *A congregation-leader who is blind*: it is classified as disapproved, though not forbidden, for a blind person to lead the congregation for the Islamic prayer.

2098   *from Syria to Rayy!*: Rayy is south of modern Tehran. This expression therefore means a long distance apart.

2144   *the takbir*: the statement 'God is great!' (*Allah akbar*) with which the call to prayer begins.

2146   *While making sacrifices they exclaim 'God's Great!'*: this alludes to the fact that the same statement, 'Allah akbar', is used when making sacrifices in the Islamic tradition at the culmination of the Hajj pilgrimage.

2147   *Ishmael's the body . . . the takbir in the slayer's role*: Rumi here makes use of the story of Abraham's willingness to sacrifice his son (identified as Ishmael in the Islamic tradition) to represent the soul's discarding of the body.

2148   *Bismillah*: an abbreviation of the Arabic phrase meaning 'In the name of God, the Merciful, the Compassionate', with which the Qur'an begins and which is used by pious Muslims to start any important activity.

2167   *He turns his head right for the salutation*: this action is performed at the end of the Muslim ritual prayer.

2282   *pir*: this Persian word means both 'old man' and Sufi master.

2301   *When he said, 'I'm of fire, while he's of clay'*: Satan's protest at Man's elevation by God above the angels in Qur'an 7: 12.

2305   *Where?*: in Persian *koo* means 'where?' as well as representing the cooing of a dove.

2306   *'I'll answer'*: an allusion to Qur'an 40: 60 where, using the same construction, God says he will answer the petitioner's prayer.

2345   *Abraham's fire changed just like this as well*: see note to v. 954.

2358   *Did we not expand?*: Qur'an 94: 1, at the start of a chapter of the Qur'an that is traditionally interpreted as God's reassurance and encouragement to the Prophet Mohammad on the basis of the support He had already provided for him.

2403   *My joy's in ritual prayer*: a saying of the Prophet Mohammad.

2409   *So how then was Man honoured?*: an allusion to Qur'an 17: 70, which mentions how God has honoured mankind using the same verbal construction.

2467   *I'm part of fire . . . Not light, which goes to God like a pure soul*: this alludes to the understanding in the Islamic tradition that Satan and the jinn are made from fire, in contrast to angels, which are made from light.

2497–9   *Take me with you . . . slaying there a foe*: this refers to the episode about David's famous fight with Goliath that is mentioned in Qur'an 2: 249–51.

2500   *Iron became wax . . . Made chain-mail you'd been specially taught to do*: see note to v. 703.

2501   *Mountains were Prophets . . . in their recitation*: an allusion to Qur'an 34: 10, which is commented on further by Rumi in vv. 4271–84 of this book.

2524   *The stones of those birds . . . that poor beast bore the brunt*: an allusion to the story referred to in Qur'an 105 about God's miraculous intervention by means of birds throwing down stones to destroy enemies of the Prophet's tribe who boasted an elephant with their huge army.

2525   *Strike the slain man with that cow's tail!*: reference to a Qur'anic version (2: 67–73) of the Old Testament story of the red heifer. The animal is referred to simply as 'Moses' cow' in the text (and it is yellow rather than red in colour according to the Qur'anic version). God commands through Moses that such an animal be sacrificed and its tail used to whip a dead body, in order to make it come to life again.

2535   *Night of Power's*: this is the most auspicious night of the Muslim calendar, when there is intense communication between the divine and earthly realms, on the basis of the short 97th chapter of the Qur'an's description of it.

2538   *would He Have said that infidels are dead?*: this refers to Qur'an 39: 30, where God describes infidels as being dead, using the same Arabic term.

2541   *The Torah, Psalms and Bible . . . the truth inside*: this alludes to the Muslim belief that all the Abrahamic books of Revelation come from the same source and confirm each other.

2550   *The self's a snake . . . the emerald that blinds*: an allusion to the belief that emeralds can blind snakes.

2645   *They do not know*: in numerous verses of the Qur'an, sceptics are described as those who 'do not know' using the same verbal construction.

2670   *Be firm and constant!*: Qur'an 11: 112, where it represents a command from God to the Prophet Mohammad.

2695   *Simoom-self's effect*: the Simoom is a devastatingly strong desert wind.

2702   *was parted*: Qur'an 26: 63, which describes Moses' parting of the waves.

2728   *Be silent!*: Qur'an 7: 204, where the command is given to be silent when the Qur'an is recited.

2740   Heading   *Kalila and Dimna*: a collection of fables originating from South Asia in the third century CE, which was available to Rumi in Arabic and Persian translations.

2761   *Satan's eye could perceive no more than clay*: see note to v. 2301.

2779   *Between two fingers*: this alludes to a saying of the Prophet Mohammad about the hearts of all men being held 'between two fingers of the Merciful God'.

2781   *pair of fingers*: see previous note.

2789   *What do you know . . . that cheeks and tresses you should mention?*: this alludes to the symbolic use of the parts of a human head in Persian poetry.

2790   *Moses thought it a rod . . . showed it was a snake*: this alludes to the story about Moses and the magicians which is referred to many times in the Qur'an. See note to v. 37.

2794　*Cursed Satan used analogies . . . till Judgment Day*: see note to v. 2301.

2819　*Unembalmed corpses . . . reached Lot's community!*: see note to v. 87.

2820–1　*What's a mere elephant . . . could not stand up again!*: see note to v. 2524.

2821　*ababil*: is the Arabic word for the birds mentioned in the Qur'anic account of God's intervention against the foes of Mecca who had an elephant with their army.

2822　*Who hasn't heard of Noah's flood . . . the troops of Pharaoh were undone?*: see notes to vv. 86 and 2702.

2824　*Who hasn't heard of Thamud's fate . . . the Aad away?*: see 'Aad' and 'Thamud' in the Glossary.

2833　*The soul remaining wolf-like . . . Joseph's face assuredly*: see note to v. 218.

2834　*David's Psalms reached . . . men still couldn't hear*: see note to v. 1014.

2849–55　*O children of God's deputy . . . Adam would weep for years, disconsolate*: God's deputy refers here to Adam as seen in the Islamic tradition, the forefather of all mankind, whom the Devil caused to fall.

2858　*God give me strength!*: an abbreviated form of 'There is no strength or power except through God', which is an invocation recommended in many of the sayings of the Prophet Mohammad, especially when one is faced with extreme difficulties.

2874　*Return like this and we will too . . . with rewards ahead*: this seems to allude to Qur'an 17: 8, where God warns that misdeeds will receive an appropriate response.

2941　*For those men in the cave . . . sorrow, harm, and tears*: see 'Seven Sleepers in the Cave' in the Glossary.

2985　Heading　*Come either obediently, or disliking it!*: Qur'an 41: 10, where it refers to God's power to bring created things into being.

2990　*I made Mankind and jinn for just one thing*: Qur'an 51: 56, where God states that he created them only for the purpose of worshipping Him.

3000　Heading　*Enter the gate . . . 'God lighten our burden!'*: Qur'an 2: 58, where God is addressing Moses about His past support.

3016　Heading　*mealcloth*: the cloth put on the floor to use instead of a dining table when you sit on the floor to eat meals.

3030–1　*Egyptians viewed the Nile . . . would not be saved*: see note to v. 1304.

3035　*No prayer unless you've washed*: a saying of the Prophet Mohammad that alludes to the necessary ablution before the Islamic ritual prayer.

3079　Heading　*Until when the messengers lose hope*: Qur'an 12: 110, where God explains how, when His Prophets despair and give up hope, He has always come to their aid.

3082   *The First Soul brought the Second Soul forth*: this alludes to Neoplatonic theories of emanation that had already come to have a significant influence on Sufi theosophy before Rumi's time. Here it is used to point out that a specific order is followed sequentially in many aspects of the creation.

3083   *Deliver!*: Qur'an 5: 67, where God tells Mohammad to deliver the message he has been given for the people or else he will not have completed his duties.

3104   *To Abraham the flames became obedient*: see note to v. 10.

3104   *And waves bore Noah safely like a servant*: see note to v. 86.

3105   *Iron obeyed, melting in David's hand*: see note to v. 1014.

3105   *Wind turned to Solomon's slave at his command*: see note to v. 1015.

3112   Heading   *The Story about how Anas threw ... but it did not burn*: the story instead describes Anas's maid throwing the handkerchief in the oven on his instruction.

3122   *The Prophet made mere bricks the qebla*: this is the direction of the Kaaba (see Glossary) in Mecca towards which Mohammad instructed Muslims to pray. It is a roughly cube-shaped brick structure, and is the destination of the Muslim pilgrimage.

3152   *Sea of Origins*: an epithet used by Rumi for God.

3160   *If sent back, they'd do that again*: Qur'an 6: 28, where it refers to the inhabitants of hell, who would return to their misdeeds if brought back to the world.

3203   *Can one speak of Omar to Shi'ites then?*: the second caliph Omar ebn al-Khattab (r. 634–44) is considered an illegitimate usurper by Shi'ites.

3206   Heading   *Is it not He ... when he prays?*: Qur'an 27: 62.

3206   *It was once Mary's need ... with what he said*: see note to v. 1796.

3220   *Kawsar's water fills clouds of kindnesses*: Kawsar is the heavenly fount of divine grace mentioned in Qur'an 108: 1.

3221   *Their Lord gave them to drink*: Qur'an 76: 21, where the inhabitants of paradise are the ones to whom God gives a drink.

3233   *My name's 'Abd al-Aziz' ... But 'Abd al-Ozza' with vile men like them*: this wordplay alludes to the fact that Abd al-Ozza was a pre-Islamic name meaning 'slave of the idol called Ozza', while Abd al-Aziz is a Muslim personal name meaning 'slave of God'.

3235   *the circle's head*: this refers to the position of a teacher in a teaching circle, as the focus of the students sitting facing him in a circle.

3257   Heading   *with hardship there's ease*: Qur'an 94: 5.

3266   *Don't grieve for what you cannot keep*: Qur'an 57: 23, where it is mentioned in the context of stressing that everything has been ordained by God.

3293 *Man's been honoured*: Qur'an 17: 70, where it is clarified that all of 'the progeny of Adam' have been honoured by God through His protection and nurturing.

3302 *We have honoured*: see note to v. 3293.

3336 *azan*: the Muslim call to prayer recited by a muezzin.

3338 *Come to the good!*: see note to v. 175.

3369 *God spoke to that one*: see note to v. 1964.

3370 *Moses, Kalim*: see note to v. 1964.

3388 *The one who can … transforms rods to them magically*: see note to v. 37.

3396 *Present in Our Presence*: Qur'an 36: 32, where God's ability to raise the dead is referred to.

3400 *Be!*: the divine fiat; the way in which God is repeatedly described as granting created things existence, before which they are described as non-existents in a storehouse. See Qur'an 16: 40, 15: 21.

3408 *For what no one's seen … 'lamp' once for the Unseen's Light*: the first hemistich refers to a saying of the Prophet Mohammad where it describes what God bestows on His slaves. The second hemistich refers to the well-known enigmatic verse in the Qur'an (24: 35) about God's Light.

3424 *Don't throw yourselves towards you own destruction*: Qur'an 2: 195, among a list of general commandments to Muslims.

3436 *Don't throw yourself in harm's way!*: see note to v. 3424.

3437 *Race here!*: Qur'an 3: 133, where people are urged to strive for God's forgiveness and entry to paradise.

3438 *Those seeing Resurrection—race up here!*: see previous note.

3440 *For Joseph … The wolf makes all leave guidance, though, instead*: see note to v. 218.

3455 *Moses, how can a rod seem like a snake?*: see note to v. 37.

3460 *The Lord of Dawn*: a title used for God in Qur'an 113: 1.

3461 *Although bird semen is a kind of air*: this refers to a common belief in Rumi's time regarding how birds reproduce.

3463–4 *the water stream … your drunkenness's stupor*: a reference to the four streams in paradise, which the inhabitants will drink from (Qur'an 76: 17–18).

3473 *In hell a Zaqqum tree then quickly grows*: the Qur'anic (37: 62) tree in hell that grows out of fire.

3483 *We're grateful that your light put our fire out*: according to a saying of the Prophet Mohammad, when believers walk across the bridge over hell, hellfire expresses gratitude like this for their light's ability to extinguish its flames.

3503 *Be!*: see note to v. 3400.

3601   *Sea of Majesty*: this expression is used by Rumi to refer to the divine realm.

3661   *You did not throw when you threw*: Qur'an 8: 17, in a passage interpreted as describing the Prophet Mohammad's action of throwing sand in the direction of enemy troops as being in reality God's actions. This is one of the most frequently cited Qur'anic verses in Sufi discussions of annihilation in God.

3663   *Can sand defeat vast armies full of men?*: see note to v. 3661.

3665   *Prophets are recognized . . . from others' children*: this alludes to Qur'an 2: 146, which similarly refers to Prophets being recognized by people as they recognize their sons.

3668   *God says, 'He knows' . . . 'None knows them at all apart from Me'*: part of a Sacred Tradition, or saying of the Prophet in which he presents a message from God in his own words, about the hidden nature of Friends of God.

3669   *They're hidden under my domed tents*: see previous note.

3685   *If Zayd's the subject of these words: 'Zayd died'*: see note to v. 1153.

3702–3   *Like Mary say: 'I pray . . . Saves me from you!'*: Qur'an 19: 18, where Mary says the same prayer on first seeing the Angel Gabriel.

3707   *If Joseph had seen . . . cut his hands in awe*: a reference to Qur'an 12: 31, where women cut their own hands by mistake owing to the awesome handsomeness of Joseph.

3736–7   *And if contraction . . . you feel expansion*: see notes to vv. 349 and 363.

3747   *Eat what He provides!*: Qur'an 67: 15, where it is emphasized that God is the Provider to Mankind.

3753   *Eat grief, not bread . . . children eat up sugar*: this is a couplet from Hakim Sana'i's *Garden of Truth*, which is the book Rumi refers to as 'The Divine Book'.

3779–80   *'God's strength' . . . God's strength*: see note to v. 2858.

3838   *Ten of their like*: Qur'an 6: 160, where mankind is promised that for every good deed ten times its reward will be given on Judgment Day.

3841–3   *Murder me, murder me . . . He will*: these verses in Arabic are from a famous poem attributed to the Sufi al-Hallaj (d. 922).

3852–3   *The 'chain' . . . Their 'circle case' . . . 'the purse's case'*: these all refer to intellectual puzzles that interest philosophers and theologians as opposed to mystics, who are focused on God exclusively.

3873   *armies you can't see*: Qur'an 9: 26, where it refers to invisible soldiers sent by God to aid the Prophet Mohammad and his followers in battle.

3897   *He's Eid; the slaughtered beast is my small role*: this alludes to the ritual slaughter during the Eid after the Hajj pilgrimage.

3899   *Moses' cow's tail . . . revive the liberated!*: see note to v. 2525.

3901   *'Strike him with part of her!' the Lord had said*: Qur'an 2: 73. See note to v. 2525.

3906   *All perishes except God's face*: Qur'an 28: 88, where it is emphasized that there is no deity except Him.

3908   *To Him we are returning*: Qur'an 28: 88. See previous note about the first part of the same Qur'anic verse.

3924   *Rayy*: see note to v. 2098.

3937   *I was breathed into*: Qur'an 15: 29, where God describes how He breathed His spirit into Man, as a sign of his superiority in creation, and commands the angels to prostrate before Adam.

3939   *Sincere one, long for death!*: Qur'an 62: 6, where Jews are told that if they believe they are favoured by God then they should long for death and the return to Him.

3962   Heading   *Galen*: Greek physician and authority on medicine of the second century CE, whose works came to symbolize Greek medicine and ethics in the medieval Middle East.

4005   *Among themselves they act courageously*: Qur'an 59: 14, where 'hypocrites', those who pretend to follow Mohammad but oppose him in reality, are described.

4013   *But kiss the snake to find the treasure-chest!*: in Persian literature, snakes are invariably found with treasure, which is usually hidden in ruins.

4039   Heading   *Qoraysh*: Qoraysh is the name of the tribe into which the Prophet Mohammad was born in Mecca about 570. The leaders of the tribe rejected Mohammad and forced him out of Mecca, after which they waged war against him and his followers in Medina.

4039   *I'll be your helper from today!*: Qur'an 8: 48, where Satan makes the same promise of support to an army of enemies of the Prophet.

4042   *Those troops you couldn't see*: Qur'an 9: 26, where a reminder is given to the Prophet of help previously given by God, including such invisible troops.

4054   *I now am quit of you!*: Qur'an 8: 48, where Satan turns back on the promise of support he had given to an army of enemies of the Prophet.

4061   *the one who slinks back*: a name given to the Devil, which is found in Qur'an 114: 4.

4063   *he who shrinks back*: see previous note.

4091   Heading   *Shah Mahmud's*: Shah Mahmud was the ruler of the Ghaznavid dynasty between 971 and 1030, and is celebrated by Iranians and Afghans as a heroic king who achieved much success on the battlefield.

4091   *God give me strength!*: see note to v. 2858.

4101   *I am a lover, sacrificed for 'No!'*: 'No' here is the Arabic 'La' used in the statement 'There is no deity but God', so Rumi's point is that he has sacrificed himself in the process of denying everything other than God through self-annihilating love.

4104   *I'm like the Ismailis: I lack dread*: this seems to be a reference to the Nizari Ismailis, who were perceived in Rumi's time as fearless assassins of their oppressors.

4104   *Or like Ishmael, with no care for my head*: see note to v. 2147.

4105   *Say 'Come!'*: Qur'an 3: 61 and 6: 151, where it means 'Come and worship God!'

4118   *The Lord has bought*: Qur'an 9: 111, where it is used to mean 'bought' in the sense that the faithful serve God and He rewards them with paradise.

4125   *'Alhaykom's' chapter's . . . If you know*: Qur'an 102, which is about the eventual realization of material possessions once one has acquired better knowledge, knowledge of certainty followed ultimately by immediate vision of certainty.

4128   *In 'alhaykom' . . . vision of certainty*: see previous note.

4136   *And Ja'far's pure gold*: it is unclear whether this refers to the coinage of an Abbasid vizier called Ja'far, or to Ja'far al-Sadeq, the sixth Shi'ite Imam and important Sufi authority, who is attributed with works on alchemy.

4149   *'Each is a shepherd' . . . he's overseeing*: a saying of the Prophet Mohammad.

4169   *His mercy's prior to His wrath*: a Sacred Tradition, or saying of the Prophet in which he presents a message from God in his own words.

4170   *His mercy comes before His wrath*: see previous note.

4177   *I see I'll sacrifice you*: Qur'an 37: 102. See note to v. 2147.

4178   *cut your throat as Ishmael's was*: see previous note.

4184   *Then milk, be now a lion of the jungle!*: this is a play on the fact that the word for milk and the word for lion are written the same in Persian.

4189   *Kill me my trusty friends!*: see note to v. 3841.

4190   *There's life in my death*: see note to v. 3841.

4218   *Abraham won't seek help from any blaze*: see note to v. 10.

4243   *The Prophet Joseph . . . Zulaikha's love for him and her despair*: a reference to the life story of Joseph in the twelfth chapter of the Qur'an, which is introduced as 'the most beautiful of stories'.

4250   *The Devil saw in Adam naught but clay*: see note to v. 2301.

4262   *Between two fingers*: see note to vv. 2779–81.

4270   *when Prophet Moses came . . . heart aflame*: see note to v. 16.

4271   Heading   *O hills and birds, repeat his praise!*: Qur'an 34: 10.

4290   *I am God's Speech, subsisting through His Essence*: this is the orthodox Sunni understanding of the theological status of the content of the Qur'an as God's Speech, although its actual wording is considered inherently temporal and created.

4329   Heading   *And use your horses . . . against them!*: Qur'an 17: 64, where it forms part of God's instructions to Satan.

4347   *None of the sweet sea joins the salty sea*: an allusion to the famous statement about this being a sign of God's creation in Qur'an 25: 53.

4391   *Its root is firm, its branches in the sky*: Qur'an 14: 24, in the course of a comparison of healthy and unhealthy trees for the purpose of an analogy.

4443   *He loves and they love*: Qur'an 5: 54, a verse frequently cited in discussions of the possibility of a relationship of love between God and Man.

4470   *Paradise is surrounded*: part of a saying of the Prophet Mohammad.

4475   *'Against your will come!' speaks to just the former. 'Come willingly!'*: Qur'an 41: 11, where, in the process of creating the heavens and the earth, God tells them to come into being willingly or unwillingly.

4489   Heading   *If you ask for a decision, the decision has come*: Qur'an 8: 19, where God is understood to be addressing the members of the Prophet Mohammad's Qoraysh (see Glossary) tribe, who have rejected and declared war against him. The 'decision' would then refer to God's support of Mohammad and his followers, enabling them to be victorious in their conflicts with the Qoraysh.

4491   *Lat and fellow idols Ozza and Manat*: these are three of the idols worshipped by the contemporaries of Mohammad at the Kaaba (see Glossary) in Mecca. See, further, note to v. 3233.

4505   *We gave you victory!*: Qur'an 48: 1, the start of the chapter called 'Victory', which has been interpreted traditionally as referring to 'the Hodaybiyya events'. At Hodaybiyya the Muslims made a truce with the Qoraysh (see Glossary) of Mecca, thereby confirming their newly acquired position of strength.

4506   Heading   *We have opened to you a victory*: Qur'an 48: 1.

4508   *What happened with Qurayza and Nadir*: Qurayza and Nadir refer to two Jewish tribes in Medina who opposed the Prophet Mohammad and were consequently expelled and eliminated from the city.

4532   *To Joseph's keeper his shirt . . . from afar and knew*: an allusion to Qur'an 12: 93–6, which describes the restoration of Jacob's sight by the placing of his son Joseph's shirt over his face as a sign (presumably through its smell) that he was still alive.

4540   *I who can make the moon split suddenly*: an allusion to the miraculous splitting of the moon by the Prophet Mohammad.

4576   *If there were no believers*: Qur'an 48: 25, where God explains to Mohammad why He did not ordain for him to enter Mecca at the time of the Hodaybiyya pact—lest any believers be harmed by the conflict.

4578   *He restrained your hands*: Qur'an 48: 24. See preceding note.

4593 '*Against your will come!*' . . . '*Come willingly!*': Qur'an 41: 11, where, in the process of creating the heavens and the earth, God tells them to come into being willingly or unwillingly.

4598 *The notebook of religious men's taqlid*: *taqlid* refers to the scholastic principle of following the established tradition of one's religious school out of loyalty and convention.

4618 *a palm-fibre cord*: see note to vv. 1665–6.

4642 *Be! And it was*: see note to v. 3400.

4664 *everything will perish but His face*: Qur'an 28: 88, where it is emphasized that there is no deity except Him.

4689 *God does what He should will*: Qur'an 3: 40, where it is stated to explain to Zechariah how it is possible for him to father John the Baptist.

4693 *Be!*: see note to v. 3400.

4694 *He's not less than . . . That bore a camel that then bore another*: this refers to the Qur'anic (e.g. 91: 13) story about the Prophet Saleh, who caused a pregnant camel to come out of a mountain as his miracle to the Thamud (see Glossary) community.

4697–8 *Phoenix of God . . . From Qaf*: in medieval Islamic cosmology, Qaf refers to a range of mountains that surrounds the world and marks the border with the spiritual realm. This is where the phoenix-like mythical Anqa bird is believed to reside.

4725 *sama*ʿ: the Arabic term for the practice of meditative listening to music, which is a characteristic form of worship for Sufis. This often includes dance (e.g. the Whirling Dervishes), and is designed to induce ecstasy in the participants. The same term can also be used to mean simply 'a concert'.

4744 *The Arabs have named wine 'continual'*: one of the Arabic words for wine, *modam*, also means continual.

4781 *through its scent, make Jacob see*: see note to v. 4532.

4783 Heading *Whoever does an atom's weight of good work will see it*: Qur'an 99: 7, where it refers to Judgment Day at the end of time, which is signalled by a huge earthquake.

GLOSSARY

Aad one of the vanquished nations referred to in the Qur'an (e.g. 7: 69). They lived just after Noah's time and became proud because of their prosperity, which led them to reject the prophet Hud who had been sent to them. They were destroyed in the end by a roaring wind.

Abdal in popular hierarchies of the Friends of God, the Abdals are members of one of the highest ranks below the Pole, or *axis mundi*. Their name, which means 'substitutes', has been explained as an allusion to their fixed number (usually 40) being constantly maintained, by means of immediate substitution whenever one of them passes away.

Abu Lahab *see* BU LAHAB.

Alast the Qur'anic 'Covenant of Alast' (7: 172) is when mankind testified that God is the Lord by saying 'Yes!' in response to His question 'Am I not (*alasto*) your Lord?' This is understood to have taken place when mankind was pure spirit in the presence of God, before entering the world, and it is this event which the Sufi practice of SAMA' is intended to re-enact.

Anas ben Malek a young follower of the Prophet Mohammad in Medina, who is believed to have survived him by approximately eighty years.

Azrael the Angel of Death, who appears in many stories to signal to individuals the imminence of their death. This is represented memorably in one of the shorter stories in Book One of the *Masnavi* (see vv. 960–74).

Bal'am son of Ba'ur Bil'am ben Be'or of the Old Testament (Num. 22–4), who is the archetypal sage led astray by pride and lust. He is believed by exegetes to be referred to in Qur'an 7: 175.

Bayazid Abu Yazid al-Bestami (d. 874), an eminent Sufi from what is now north central Iran. He is a highly popular figure in Persian Sufi literature, in particular because of the many bold and controversial statements he is reported to have made, such as 'There is nothing under my cloak but God.'

Bohlul an ascetic living during the reign of the Abbasid caliph Harun al-Rashid (r. 786–809) of *The Thousand and One Nights*. Bohlul was renowned for appearing and sounding mad because of spiritual intoxication.

Bu Lahab (lit. 'Father of Flame') an uncle of the Prophet who was his mortal enemy. He and his wife are condemned in the 111th chapter of the Qur'an, which has also been named *lahab*.

Emran the Arabicized rendering of 'Amram', the biblical name of the father of Moses and his brother Aaron. The story of Moses' birth presented by Rumi here has antecedents in the Islamic 'Stories of the Prophets' genre.

Esrafil the angel who, according to Muslim eschatology, signals Judgment Day at the end of time with a blast of a trumpet.

hadith a report that conveys the words and/or deeds of the Prophet Mohammad. These reports are the literary expression of the normative example of the Prophet, his *sonna*, and as such are considered by most Muslims to be second in authority only to the Qur'an as a source of knowledge. Originally transmitted orally, they have been examined for authenticity, classified, and compiled into numerous collections for ease of reference. Their importance in Rumi's *Masnavi* is therefore representative of the Islamic tradition in general.

Hakim Ghaznavi Sana'i a twelfth-century Persian mystical poet from Ghazni, which is located between Kabul and Kandahar in contemporary Afghanistan. He spent most of his adult life in Khurasan, including in Rumi's native Balkh. Rumi frequently acknowledges the influence of Sana'i (d. 1131) on his own work, in particular that of his *The Garden of Truth*, which is the oldest work of the mystical masnavi genre.

Hallaj Mansur ebn Hosayn al-Hallaj (d. 922), a controversial Arabic-speaking Sufi of Persian origin whose death on the gallows is believed to have been a major turning point in the history of Sufism. He is famous for his alleged utterance 'I am the Truth', the most notorious of the theopathic utterances made by Sufis. Rumi's predecessor Faridoddin 'Attar, in whose eyes Hallaj was the most important Sufi of the past, writes that this utterance was the reason for his execution, but this is not supported by the sources stemming from the time of the events (see further 'Hallaj' in the *Encyclopaedia Iranica*). Rumi on a number of occasions justifies Hallaj's utterance, arguing that it expresses greater humility than saying 'I am the slave of God', as one's own existence is not even acknowledged (the 'I' in 'I am the Truth' is God).

Hamza the subject of a popular biographical tradition exemplifying bravery which is traditionally understood to have stemmed from the biography of the Prophet Mohammad's paternal uncle Hamza ebn Abd al-Mottaleb.

Hareth Hareth ebn Hesham was one of the leaders of the QORAYSH during the battle of Badr against Mohammad and his followers in Medina. The traditional biography of Mohammad includes an antecedent to Rumi's story about his encounter with Satan (see SORAQA).

Harut and Marut a pair of fallen angels referred to in the Qur'an (2: 102). According to the exegetical tradition, they looked down on Man for his sinful nature, but when put to the test on earth themselves, they became prone to lust and tried to seduce a beautiful woman; that woman became Venus, while Harut and Marut were imprisoned forever in a well in Babylon as punishment.

Homa a mythical bird comparable with the phoenix, but particularly associated with soaring at the highest levels of the heavens and bestowing kingship, which are both alluded to in instances where the Homa is mentioned in this book.

Jonayd Abu'l-Qasem al-Jonayd (d. 910), a Sufi who was widely recognized as the supreme authority of his generation. He lived in Baghdad, although he was born and brought up in Persia. In later tradition, his teachings are often described as representing a more circumspect 'sober' Sufism as distinct from the 'drunken' Sufism associated with BAYAZID.

Kaaba the approximately cube-shaped building in Mecca towards which Muslims pray and around which they circumambulate during the pilgrimage. According to Muslim tradition, it was constructed by Abraham and Ishmael for the worship of God, but was later turned into an idol temple. Mohammad's mission to establish Abrahamic monotheism is symbolized by his destruction of the idols at the Kaaba after the Muslim conquest of Mecca.

Kalim the traditional Islamic epithet for Moses, because he was 'the one spoken to by God' according to Qur'an 4: 167.

Kerbala a city 60 miles south-west of Baghdad in Iraq where the Prophet Mohammad's grandson Hosayn and his followers were gruesomely massacred in 680 on the order of the Umayyad caliph Yazid.

Khezr a figure usually identified with Enoch (Elias), and described in the Qur'an (18: 65) as someone who has been taught knowledge from God's presence. He is the archetypal spiritual guide in the Sufi tradition. The Qur'anic story about Khezr (18: 65–82) describes Moses as seeking to become his disciple in order to learn some of his special knowledge. Moses is warned that he does not have the patience required, but is finally accepted on the condition that he should not question Khezr about anything. Moses fails to refrain from questioning Khezr, and on the third such occasion Khezr dismisses him. Khezr appears to Sufis in eras beyond his own lifetime and is believed to possess the water that gives eternal life.

Korah a biblical figure (Num. 16) who is also mentioned in the Qur'an (28: 76–82, 29: 39, and 40: 24). As a punishment for behaving arrogantly towards Moses and hoarding his wealth, he gets swallowed up by the earth.

Loqman a sage and ascetic, after whom Qur'an 31 is named. He is attributed in particular with various proverbs and fables and has often been identified with Aesop.

Ozayr Ozayr is usually identified with the biblical Ezra. However, the Qur'anic reference to him (Qur'an 9: 30) makes the irreconcilable claim that he was worshipped by Jews as 'a son of God'. Muslim accounts of his life include stories about his doubting predestination and physical resurrection, which Rumi's story probably draws upon. Most significantly, Qur'an 2: 259, which contains a similar reference to the revival of a donkey, had already been associated with Ozayr in the exegetical tradition.

Qoraysh Qoraysh is the name of the tribe into which the Prophet Mohammad was born in Mecca in about 570. The leaders of the tribe rejected Mohammad and forced him out of Mecca, after which they waged war against him and his followers in Medina.

Resurrection this refers to the end of time when the dead are resurrected and the truth is revealed. Rumi uses this Qur'anic image frequently to represent the experience of mystical enlightenment, through which reality can be witnessed in this life.

Rostam the heroic Persian king whose feats are recounted in Ferdowsi's *Shahnama* (Book of Kings).

sadr, sadr-e jahan the title used in the twelfth and thirteenth centuries for the rulers of Bukhara, which is today located in Uzbekistan close to the border with Turkmenistan.

Saleh Arab prophet mentioned several times in the Qur'an (e.g. 7: 73–9), who was sent to the THAMUD.

sama' the technical term for the practice of meditative listening to music, which is a characteristic form of worship for Sufis. This often includes dance (e.g. the Whirling Dervishes), and is designed to induce ecstasy in the participants. The same term can also be used to mean simply 'a concert'. See further ALAST.

saqi the cup-bearer. In Sufi poetry the *saqi* can also represent the Sufi master or God.

Seven Sleepers in the Cave seven companions who, together with their dog, are described in the Qur'an (18: 9–26) as hiding in a cave during the reign of the tyrant Decius, and praying to God for protection. They slept there for some 309 years before waking up and returning to the outside world, though it seemed to them like a single night. Their experience is referred to in the Qur'an as a demonstration to sceptics of God's power both to protect his faithful servants and to resurrect men on Judgment Day. In the earlier Christian version of this Qur'anic story, they are known as the Seven Sleepers of Ephesus.

Sheba a nation ruled by a queen mentioned several times in the Bible as well as the Qur'an (27: 22–44). In the Islamic exegetical tradition, their queen is known as Belqis. A hoopoe reports to SOLOMON about having seen a people ruled by a very rich queen, who worship the sun. Solomon gives the bird a letter of invitation to take back to her. Eventually, the queen visits Solomon and is so amazed at his knowledge and miracles that she follows him in surrender to God.

Solomon the prophet and king who is described in the Qur'an as possessing deep wisdom and having been granted power over nature, including knowledge of the language of the birds (e.g. 27: 15–44).

Soraqa in accounts of the battle of Badr found in the traditional biography of the Prophet Mohammad, Soraqa ebn Malek was the leader of the QORAYSH whose form Satan took in order to persuade them to persevere and wage war against Mohammad and his followers (see HARETH).

Thamud an ancient nation referred to on several occasions in the Qur'an (e.g. 7: 73–9, 4: 23–31, 11: 61–8). They hamstrung the she-camel of the Prophet SALEH, which had been sent miraculously by God out of a mountain to test their willingness to share water and pasture. They were destroyed as a result by either an earthquake (7: 78) or a mighty blast of noise (4: 31, 11: 67), or perhaps a combination of the two. More elaborate versions of this story describe Saleh as suggesting that they might be forgiven if they catch her foal, but it escapes and disappears into the mountain.

vakil the *vakil* was a senior administrator at the court of the *sadr* in twelfth- to thirteenth-century Bukhara, and therefore part of his inner circle.

Water of Life the Water of Life is a miraculous stream or fountain which grants eternal life. It is found usually in darkness and with the help of KHEZR.

*The
Oxford
World's
Classics
Website*

www.worldsclassics.co.uk

- Browse the full range of Oxford World's Classics online

- Sign up for our monthly e-alert to receive information on new titles

- Read extracts from the Introductions

- Listen to our editors and translators talk about the world's greatest literature with our Oxford World's Classics audio guides

- Join the conversation, follow us on Twitter at OWC_Oxford

- Teachers and lecturers can order inspection copies quickly and simply via our website

www.worldsclassics.co.uk

American Literature

British and Irish Literature

Children's Literature

Classics and Ancient Literature

Colonial Literature

Eastern Literature

European Literature

Gothic Literature

History

Medieval Literature

Oxford English Drama

Philosophy

Poetry

Politics

Religion

The Oxford Shakespeare

A complete list of Oxford World's Classics, including Authors in Context, Oxford English Drama, and the Oxford Shakespeare, is available in the UK from the Marketing Services Department, Oxford University Press, Great Clarendon Street, Oxford OX2 6DP, or visit the website at www.oup.com/uk/worldsclassics.

In the USA, visit www.oup.com/us/owc for a complete title list.

Oxford World's Classics are available from all good bookshops. In case of difficulty, customers in the UK should contact Oxford University Press Bookshop, 116 High Street, Oxford OX1 4BR.

A SELECTION OF OXFORD WORLD'S CLASSICS

THOMAS PAINE   **Rights of Man, Common Sense, and Other Political Writings**

JEAN-JACQUES ROUSSEAU   **The Social Contract**
Discourse on the Origin of Inequality

ADAM SMITH   **An Inquiry into the Nature and Causes of the Wealth of Nations**

MARY WOLLSTONECRAFT   **A Vindication of the Rights of Woman**